Contents

PSYCHOLOGY

ARTIFICIAL INTELLIGENCE

Dedication

As a young man, I stumbled upon a book I still find inspiring. It began this way:

'I am a human being, whatever that may be. I speak for all of us who move and think and feel and whom time consumes. I speak as an individual unique in a universe beyond my understanding, and I speak for man. I am hemmed in by limitations of sense and mind and body, of place and time and circumstance, some of which I know but most of which I do not. I am like a man journeying through a forest, aware of occasional glints of light overhead, with recollections of the long trail I have already travelled, and conscious of wider spaces ahead. I want to see more clearly where I have been and where I am going, and above all, I want to know why I am where I am and why I am travelling at all . . . '

N. J. Berrill Man's Emerging Mind

Berrill characterizes his book as one man's contribution to developing a scientific concept of man. This book is my imperfect contribution to that same end: it is in a tradition, begun by Norbert Wiener and Warren McCulloch, which rises directly to Berrill's challenge. The central goal of that tradition is the explanation of intelligence, both artificial and natural.

' . . . a stick thrust in the water felt straight and looked bent to a Greek. The sun moved for the inquisition, the earth for Galileo. Light is a wave for Schroedinger and a particle for Heisenberg. But even the last have had their Dirac. The seeming contradictions vanish in the grace of greater knowledge. We have learned that the answer depends upon how we ask the question. And we have learned to ask the question so as to get answers of a kind we can use . . .'

Warren S. McCulloch Through the Den of the Metaphysician

What I do began with the questions of Berrill and proceeds with the vision and hope of McCulloch. This work is dedicated . . .

with gratitude and affection
to those friends
from whom I have learned so much
with the hope that others
may learn a little from me

Robert W. Lawler, January, 1997

Introduction

COMPUTERS AND PEOPLE[1]

Is playing with computers good for children? Couldn't it be bad? Might they not begin to think of themselves and others as machines? Here is a story about how my daughter, Miriam, pretended to be a machine — the Logo turtle — and what she made of that.

This night is the last night of summer, so defined by the children's having to be in school on the morrow. Over the summer they have gradually become accustomed to going to bed late, and now, in order to rise early, they should go to bed early. No one found this argument convincing. We negotiated a compromise that the children get into pyjamas, return for dessert (delayed by conversation with dinner guests, Jose and Fernando), and then go off to bed. Robby lived up to the agreement; Miriam would not.

When given a direct order to go to bed, she went to my bed instead of hers. I had mentioned during dinner the children's inclination to play turtle. Fernando tried to help. Miriam, FORWARD.' She did nothing. I advised him that he had omitted the carriage return. Upon his 'carriage return' Miriam complained, 'You haven't told me how far to go', chuckled, and popped back onto my bed. Gretchen attempted 'FORWARD 100, carriage return.' With the gripe 'You haven't told me how to 'FD100' still in the air, I described this bug as the well known space omission between command and input. Fernando was then precise: 'Miriam: FORWARD, space, 100, carriage return.' Miriam played fair and proceeded stepwise (counting each step) down the length of the loft. At first, we expected 100 steps to be too few. Miriam counted '70' in the kitchen and at '88' gleefully announced 'Out of bounds' as she walked into the wall in the hallway. While so close to her bed room, she picked up her 'security blanket' (the air was chilly) and came skipping back into the living area.

The game wore on (hide turtle under the blanket, and so forth), after a while became wearing, and I directed her to bed with the threat of physical force. Miriam replied, as she has for some months now, with the counter-threat 'I'm quitting your research, Daddy, I really am.' Having thus preserved her dignity, she acquiesced to the demand that she go to bed.

In this incident and many others, Miriam showed that this robot-role which she was willing to adopt was one she subjected utterly to her ends as a person. Playing turtle was an enrichment of her repertoire, not a constraint upon it. As we paraphrase William Blake:

Tools were made; born were hands.
Every child understands.

---

1. 1981. Published in MIT AI Memo 652 & Logo Memo 60, 'Some Powerful Ideas'
    1982, April. Published as a series 'Logo Ideas,' Creative Computing

ADVICE TO A TEACHER [2]

I write out of my own experience and about that experience, but my situation has been different from yours. You've had to worry about instructing twenty or thirty children. I have merely had to play with two children — and those children were my own and I knew them well. I write here also with the conviction that your work in the future will be more like my experiences than it has been. Computers will permit the construction of intellectual worlds where children will be able to spend much time learning effectively on their own. This will give you more time to know the individual children and to intervene in their learning as the advisor you, their parents, and the children themselves hope you will be.

Geometry was an important central theme of instruction in our laboratory at the MIT Logo project because its founder invented a kind of geometry called 'turtle geometry.' It is distinguished from others by being a geometry of action. The leading actor is 'the turtle.' Either a mechanical robot or a triangular cursor on a video display screen, the turtle goes forward some distance or turns through some angle on command. If its pen is down, the turtle draws a line. When my children were six and eight, I introduced them to SHOOT, a simple turtle geometry game. A setup procedure drew a target and placed the turtle at some random screen location. To score, the children had to turn the turtle right or left some angle to point it at the target, then SHOOT forward some distance into the target. The game was easy for them to play and they enjoyed it. (They even played the game without the computer; setting a hula hoop on the floor for a target, the children took turns playing turtle and keyboard commander.)

Robby, the older child, came to want a more complicated game. He was fascinated by the air battles of World War II and asked me to make a game where the targets would be airplanes. READY-AIM-FIRE (we called it R.A.F.) satisfied him; even more, it engaged him. Robby spent the better part of an entire day trying to score more kills than von Richthofen, the famous Red Baron of World War I. This game permitted him to do what he wanted — play in his own fantasy world. It permitted me to introduce him to Cartesian coordinates.

The style of instruction presented in this story is opportunistic in the extreme. It depends on three things: the initiative of the child to connect his computer activities with what he knows about other things that concern him; the flexibility of computer systems to enable the building of simple models; the knowledge and values of a teacher in shaping particular procedures through which the child's objectives are achieved in such a way that the child is introduced to important ways of looking at and describing the world.

---

2.   1981. Published in MIT AI Memo 652 & Logo Memo 60, 'Some Powerful Ideas'
     1982, April. Published as a series 'Logo Ideas,' Creative Computing

VARIABLES AND ABSTRACTION [3]

The Logo turtle can't deal with abstractions. It must go forward some specific amount or turn through some specific number of degrees. When you key 'FD :some-distance', the LOGO interpreter evaluates the symbolic name 'some-distance' (looks in the box or storage cell to determine its contents and substitutes that contents for the expression ':some-distance').

People apparently can deal with abstractions, but find problem solving easier when they don't have to do so. Most often when a new procedure is being written, people use specific operand values, e.g. FD 100, which they later change to variable form, such as FD :some-distance. The nature of the abstraction involved is common to some other examples of mathematics as well. The famous mathematician **Bourbaki** describes the creation of an axiomatic system as proceding from the mathematician's working out a series of theorems with very concrete examples in mind and subsquently examining the inferences of his theorems to define precisely which characteristics of his examples were used by the theorems. In a third step, he redefines the set of objects to which his axioms apply as that most general class of objects having all those characteristics used in the theorems. That is, he *bases* his *generalization on the operations* he performed and *not on a list of the characteristics of the example* he began with. We stress that the process through which a child generalizes a procedure after creating a concrete product with a concrete precursor, *this child's play, is a particular kind of abstraction of value in the most intellectual endeavors as well.*

This mathematical form of abstraction is called *reflexive abstraction* by **Piaget**, where he sees the child creating his own mind through processes of thought that are like those of Bourbaki's mathematician. This points to the most significant potential impact of computer experience on children developing their minds. Reflexive abstraction may become more 'natural' to them than what Piaget calls 'Aristotelian abstraction' (abstraction by feature selection and classification) with which Piaget contrasts it. That is, more children of the future may more often think like mathematicians than do children of today.

---

4. 1981. Published in MIT AI Memo 652 & Logo Memo 60, 'Some Powerful Ideas'
   1982, April. Published as a series 'Logo Ideas,' Creative Computing

Education

WORKING ON THE AMERICAN DREAM[1]

A paradox lies at the heart of problems in American education. We hear on every hand that the system is in crisis. This is surely true. Yet our major universities are the envy of the world. America has long made a more profound commitment to democratic education than any other nation in history. Both the land grant colleges and the private universities testify to this. Especially in areas of science and technology, American researchers are unequaled for productivity and creativity. There are authentic virtues in the American system that are unparalleled. But our school children perform on tests no better than do those in the third world and uniformly less well than do the students of the other developed nations. We need to understand better what makes for powerful minds. We need to do better for more of our young people what we do very well for a few.

A Framework with a Few Suggestions

With the availability of new technologies that promise to change the everyday world, it is tempting to ask how we can exploit that technology to its fullest extent. This leads all too easily to expertise oriented proposals for Federal support. It is not appropriate, in a time of financial uncertainty and educational crisis, to let a technology dominated view apportion limited resources for intervention. We need to focus on nationally important issues, asking what ends will be advanced by research. Still, it is wise to work from strength, applying our best ideas to our most profound and pressing problems. Given the open borders of western nations to the flow of people, ideas, and products, we need to consider both domestic and transnational dimensions of any initiatives, as well as what is needed and what may be possible. Going beyond exploiting technology, let me suggest three arenas in which the Federal government might fulfill its purpose of promoting the common good.

Competing with Other Producers

As a nation, we compete for various market shares with others in the world. Our children do not perform so well on tests as those of schools in other developed nations. Our technical graduate schools, university faculty, and laboratories have a high number of immigrant engineers and scientists. Will more trained, skilled workers flock to these shores when today's debts become tomorrow's taxes? While grateful to these American

---

1. 1987. Unpublished commentary prepared for the Federal Congress' Office of Technology Assessment.

latecomers who help us compete on a global scale, we still must ask how it could be that our society and educational system render so many of our native born children uninterested in technical mastery of the intellectual world or unfit to achieve it. Such fears, questions, and the need to compete have long supported federal investment in science and math education. Federal support — whether from civilian or military sources - has led to much of the work that is best in cognitive science and educational engineering. Theoretical issues, such as the context dependency of knowledge or the organization and reorganization of knowledge in individual minds, are central to addressing economics related issues of training for future jobs. The cognitive sciences offer promise here. The challenge is one which they better address than can any other discipline. Such work should be continued and exploited as we begin to confront the employment crises of tomorrow.

Social Needs
Polyglot Education
The School systems of California and Florida are staggering under the influx of Spanish language students. Some cities of these states are becoming dominated by what many Americans would consider an alien culture, falling prey, as it were, to uncontrollable immigration and the revenge of the cradle. It is clear that the assimilation of these Spanish speaking children, these future citizens, into the American system is an inescapable challenge. This suggests policy focus on ways in which technology can influence bi-lingual and multi-cultural education. There is promise for bilingual use of computer-based microworlds with young children. The social objective of such computer experiences would be to give children native to either language the opportunity to learn reading and writing in the native tongues then to contrast their native language with that used by their playmates in comparable activities. Providing funding to develop, explore, and exploit such educational resources with Headstart and primary school children would be a way immediately to address a significant social problem. Such research would have both significant practical and theoretical dimensions. These experiences surely would not harm the children and could be of considerable value to them and the society as a whole.

Minority Teachers for Tomorrow
The pool of young minority teachers is evaporating. In the state of Michigan there are only 11 certified black male teachers age 26 or younger. There are four times as many black females of that age. There are sixty or so young black teachers among a total educator population of more than 100,000 in the state. While black males comprise 2.5% of that total, and blacks of both gender comprise 8-9% of the total, most of the black teachers are aged 40 to 50 years. The large numbers of talented blacks being admitted to Michigan University (both male and female) are now choosing to enter careers in business and engineering instead of teaching and nursing — traditional paths of opportunity in the past. Today's enhanced opportunity for individuals may be creating a catastrophe for tomorrow's education system. Should these observations prove representative of national trends, alternative inducements will be needed to attract talented minority teachers back into schools. Financial incentives could be important in a

time of increasing higher education costs. Graduate assistants in education schools make very little. When both their small income and tuition remission are taxed, very few are making a living wage. When they become teachers, they will not make very much either. An expansion of education loans specifically for teacher preparation — with later loan forgiveness based on later service in minority schools — might be a significant attractor. Trying to enhance the status of the job by providing both training with and access to state of the art educational technology is a second obvious possibility.

Mother Hens for Headstart

Project research reports suggest that Headstart helpers (adults who help the centre director in care of the children) get at least as much out of new experiences with computer technology as do the children. These helpers typically have minimal job skills and minimal education. They are employed at minimum wages. Whenever they develop enough skill and a record of regular employment, they leave Headstart centres for other jobs (the next step in their 'Career path' is typically a trainee position at McDonalds). If these people are good for the children they work with, could we not provide a real 'Career path' for them of a suitable sort? Headstart works; it provides cognitive gains for disadvantaged children. However, when the children enter the regular school system, their relative advantage dissipates as they pass through later grades. Imagine the Headstart helpers as mother hens with a brood and consider this idealized scenario. Let's suppose the children have Headstart programs extended and augmented as they move into primary grades. As the mother hen moves through the grades with her brood, they are all promoted (but she gets a raise). The mother hen is not only is a helper to teachers, she provides a kind of personal continuity rare in education. She becomes a student again herself, better able to learn the second time while helping her brood.

Such a program, if well worked out, might help preserve into later years the gains typical of Headstart experience. They would help some marginally employable people work their way out of the underclass and would also provide a small cushion against the impending crash in the population of young minority teachers. I believe currently available, older computers, with currently producible software, could help make such a program work.

Partnerships

Experimental Future Schools

Regular institutional structures are necessary for enduring change. The country needs experimental schools, and more than a handful. As the primary agents responsible for education, state governments are in the position to make meaningful, practical experiments for future schooling. Several already do so and seek the best direction they can get. Each state should be encouraged, and even supported, in attempts to articulate its unique vision of the education appropriate for its people and to implement that vision in a model school. Each could, nonetheless profit from contrasting and comparing its best future vision with the others of the union. One Federal role in planning for the future of education could be essentially hortatory and facilitative, urging all the states to develop plans for model schools and using the Federal structure and contacts to make relevant connection between different projects and advisors who might be of some particular use.

Moving from studies to action is essential. It is also the point where a judicious use of Federal matching grants could make a difference between plans being forgotten or experiments undertaken. Some states might not have sufficient resources, especially in hard times. But the experiments done in any state would be of value to the others for comparison and contrast, especially when one considers the mix of urban, suburban, and rural schools found in all states.

Problems and Opportunities

Can we look through our problems to see new opportunities? If we are developing a need for more extensive bilingual and bicultural education, and if we have an existing national infrastructure for education, can we not proceed with our development of new material for learners which will:

- highlight the most effective and useful ideas of modern society
- segregate the intellectual core of ideas from culture and language specific materials
- embody the ideas in computer-based microworlds:
    - whose appearance or graphical interface can be altered for different cultural contexts
    - whose surface language can be modified by an experience teacher-user for use by pupils of different natural languages.

We can. I hold out the prospect of a global curriculum, based on the best abstract ideas of our modern civilization, but embodied in concrete forms adapted for the different and various cultures of the world. If we can better understand how to help build powerful minds, the American educational system as a whole may better approach the standard of excellence its outstanding members achieve. Our existing educational infrastructure can help us develop an intellectual core for a global curriculum. This could lead to software and instructional products, embodying our best understanding of the world but designed for cultural adaptation. More importantly, as we improve the education of our society's children, we can help educate the world's children as well as our own. This may be one way where America can both earn a leadership role and enhance international understanding without undercutting cultural diversity.

RESEARCH FOR EDUCATION [2]

A dialogue between R. W. Lawler and Oliver G. Selfridge

Bob   American society has been undergoing major transformations from the electronic revolution, from nuclear family fragmentation, from the disappearance of minority role models in the education system, and even from changes in social perceptions of the value and necessity of labor. It is very clear that America's public education system is in trouble. I have committed a large part of my life to work in the area, and I wonder whether the educational technology community can develop innovations of real value as opposed to projects whose primary outcome is career advancement. What are the problems?

Oliver   There's no clear answer. We need to ask fundamental questions about issues relevant to education. We need to ask what learning consists of in kids and in grownups. Is teaching a foreign language different from teaching arithmetic? I think it probably is, in all the important details. Is there anything at all conceivably general about instruction? I think not, but if somebody wants to look at that, let him look. What kinds of games can we play which will make it attractive for kids or grownups to learn something? How do we understand and measure motivations? How do we put together a vocabulary that will permit us to talk consistently about motivations and motivation structures?

Finally, we have to ask organizational questions. How do we fit all those questions together in a way that can be thought about and that can be a base for research? Without a generally accepted base, we won't get any kind of durable change. You've mentioned a lack of role models. Well, teachers need them too, and they need to see research being done by great people. Even if it doesn't apply directly, such research will surely make teaching easier and more effective.

Didactic and Constructive Views

Bob   Educators generally view knowledge as something to be transmitted from one person to another. My sense is quite different, that self-construction by the student of his own knowledge is central. We need to develop constructive alternatives to students 'getting taught.' Years ago in a BYTE magazine article, I claimed that 'the central question of education is how one can instruct while respecting the self-constructive character of mind.' I still think that's true, but I need to develop some more explicit and better articulated description of my answer. There are of course many proponents of this viewpoint.

Oliver   None of us has a competent expression of what education's about. And if we had, it still wouldn't face up to problems of others' views because it won't face up to their values, depending on whom you're talking to. Education is not like a problem in physics with something to be solved. It's about how to make things better. It's a control process that we're worrying about. Being precise is difficult because we're aiming at the high level issues, like respect for learning and the applicability of learning outside the schools.

---

2. 1989. Chapter 12 of *AI&Ed*, Vol. 2 (1992).

Just to take issue with what you said, an important question is the extent to which knowledge is stuff that is transmittable by a teacher at all. Clearly some is, some isn't, and some can go either way. Telling someone, however accurately, how to ride a bicycle is no help; a teacher, or better yet a parent, can help a child learn, but not by transmitting knowledge. That Sofia is the capital of Bulgaria is most easily transmitted from a teacher or, equivalently, a book or an atlas; and there is no way that a child can derive it just by thinking about it, the way he can discover arithmetic facts. I think that probably educators know all this too. But your point is well taken.

'Should' Questions

Bob   Let me raise one possible kind of education problem with an example. As a child my son seemed to have some natural talent for singing—which could have been developed for his own lifelong satisfaction. In such a situation, what would be the right thing to do?

Oliver   That's a 'should' question. It has to do with what is worthwhile.

Bob   For me, that's a reasonable question: what are the worthwhile things?

Oliver   Well, in some sense it isn't a reasonable question, in that there isn't an answer. I mean it's not a question that can be argued about; it's an expression of your own values, a different kind of question. Is it worthwhile to make money? Surely, for many reasons. Is it worthwhile that making money is the over-riding justification for everything? Not for me, and, I am sure, not for you. *My* primary should is different: to find out the truth about the world.
Here's another example of how not to think about education.

Education is not Physics

Oliver   At a conference recently someone said we need 'a physics of software.' Such a program is not feasible, because in software there aren't any physical truths with which you can get as accurate as you want by trying hard enough; and not only accurate but precise, with physical laws which are real laws instead of tendencies. I'm sure education is very much more like software than physics, even if there is some precision to be had. With respect to any vision of educational innovation, we must realize that the physical sciences are very special and limited, and thus provide generally a poor archetype. In physics, things work because you can narrow down consequences and bound them, and look down into detail. The accidents of context do not have much affect on the outcome of lawful relations.
In education, we can't do that; to discuss a vision of education means we have to look upwards to purposes and values at least as much as downward to detail. We must ask what kind of society do we want and do other people want, and even what will other people want after they've been well educated. To present a dream about education is to ask what culture is about; and to ask what cultures will be about or be wanting; and to ask what the distribution of human goals is going to be. This isn't to say such questions are not answerable. It's essential to ask such questions, but the process of creating answers is going to be rather difficult and quite different from doing a hard science.

Bob   Your friend Von Foerster said it very well, 'The hard sciences appear hard because they tackle soft problems. The soft sciences face the harder problems.'

Is a Common Curriculum Possible?

Oliver   And because of the difficulty of education research, too often the content falls by the wayside. I recently met a fellow who studies instruction. Not instruction with respect to any domain. Not instruction with respect to any age or pupil set. He doesn't want to instruct anything particularly, just instruct in general. My own conviction is that nothing much will come of this.

Bob   I share his interest. There's a profound question, in fact, of how much domain independence there can be in education. Is it possible to imagine creating a general curriculum for a wide diversity of people; one focused less on specific context than ideas of proven power? Consider it as a thought experiment designing education for colonies in space. For those strange new artificial worlds, which have to be completely designed, what sorts of minds and educations should people have in such an environment?

Oliver   We don't need the space station as context to discuss the issue. Let's look at the question directly. What have you in mind?

Bob   If then we think about the content fields of knowledge, we need to ask what are they? How stable are they? Are they independent of what we want to do? What is the nature of knowledge? And how can we imagine a way of people relating to one another in respect of the different fields of knowledge which will focus on the most important ideas, and how can we think about what people should know, what their minds should contain?

Oliver   You used 'should' several times. Exactly where does that should come from?

Bob   Right at the heart of education is the question of freedom and individual choice; how do the goals of a teacher relate to those of a student? As we look at our own children, do we want our children to grow up to be the kinds of people we are— and the answer may very well be yes— or to be people who will most effectively adapt to the circumstances they find themselves in? Or do we want them to grow up to be people who have visions of their own to which they will try to make the world adapt? There probably is no single answer to any one of those.

Oliver   There can't be, of course. I'd say that any vision of ours has to be with respect to those values and just those. At some level those values and decisions aren't right or wrong, at some level those are the way we are. It's not education to enforce values—because values will change with knowledge—it's education to support them. It is not just a farcical idea to teach values, but it can also be extraordinarily destructive— look at Hitler. I always say a pox on ideologies, but I have an ideology of my own which is very like yours, with your notions about freedom and so forth. Maybe we've spent enough time talking about this level of generality, but I think it always should be borne in mind that values are held with respect to a society and a culture, and, for me at least, without regard to any binary notion of good and evil.

Cantor's Theorem

Bob   Let's get specific then. Suppose we made a catalog of terrific ideas. My common curriculum would be such a collection, whether in music or athletics, or in language or mathematics. The issues are what should such a catalog contain and how do the contents relate to what a person knows. Let me give you an example. I think that Cantor's proof—

Oliver   His Diagonal Theorem—

Bob   If you will, his proof of the non-countability of the reals is one of the simplest and most elegant arguments I know. I would like students to run into that, see it with the same intensity I have to its power and beauty. So I would propose that proof as one straightforward enough to be accessible and exotic enough to be engaging, as an example of what might go into a common constructive curriculum. (See Box below.)

Oliver   I am not arguing that Cantor's proof is not beautiful and compelling. Indeed, the intensity of feeling that a mathematical fact may offer is as great as any. On viewing for the first time certain infinite series of Ramanujan, G. N. Watson says:

'[I felt] a thrill which is indistinguishable from the thrill which I feel when I enter the Sagrestia Nuovo of the Capella Medici and see before the austere beauty of the four statues . . . which Michelangelo has set over the tomb of Giuliano de'Medici and Lorenzo de'Medici.'

But there could never be more than one citizen in a thousand who could appreciate that. I don't know that there are any ideas that should be part of everybody's education. I don't know whether that's a should, or a should not, or a never mind. Let's face it, Bobby Fischer, as a world-class chess master, probably related most of his life to playing chess. That's where his beauty was. He wouldn't give a damn about infinite sets—why should he? But I do think most kids are a little broader than that.

Bob   That's the question I'm raising: can one in principle imagine the existence of such a thing as a student-centred curriculum? ... or do we have to look at education as a process of individual and personal negotiation between individuals who know each other? Can there be in principle such a thing as a common student centred curriculum?

Cantor's Proof of the Non-Countability of Real Numbers

Are the real numbers countable? We start by assuming the opposite: that the real numbers, both rational and irrational, can be all put in one to one correspondence with the natural numbers, and are thereby countable. Let us consider only those numbers between zero and one, each one represented symbolically as a decimal. Write them in an array; by assumption, this array contains all the real numbers between 0 and 1. If there is inevitably some decimal number not in this collection, then the numbers between zero and one are not countable. Here is an example of the array:

.	2	6	0	1	1	...
.	6	3	4	2	5	...
.	1	9	7	0	3	...
.	1	4	4	8	6	...
.	7	9	5	5	4	...

Let us construct the decimal number represented by the diagonal, that is, by the bold-faced digits, .23784 ... . Now let us construct another number that differs from that one in every digit; it might be .12673 ... . This new number will be different from every number in the collection in at least one digit and is therefore not in it. Consequently, the real numbers between zero and one are not countable.

IN THE LAP OF THE MACHINE [3]

Microcomputers are just beginning to enter American homes and schools. They are an everyday fact of life for a few children and they will soon become commonplace for many more. So it is hardly too soon to wonder what effects computers are likely to have on our children. Will computers change the way children learn? Will computers change the sorts of people our children become? I believe the answers may well be yes, and although it is too early for conclusive proof, I can offer here a story that supports my belief.

I have worked in the computer industry for over fifteen years, and when my children were born I became interested in the potential impact of early computer experience on children's learning. Several years ago, in collaboration with the LOGO project at MIT, I began an intensive study of how daily access to a computer influenced the way my two older children—then aged six and eight—learned the basics of arithmetic. By the time their younger sister Peggy turned three, a microcomputer had become standard equipment in our household, and I began to develop several programs to give Peggy access to the machine.

Playing with these programs in her own way and on her own initiative, Peggy has begun to do something that looks very much like the beginnings of reading and writing. All this has happened in the last seven months, but the way it has happened is at least as interesting as the claim itself or the extent of its truth.

What is it like to put a microcomputer in your living room and let your three year old play with it? The answer depends on who you are, on your knowledge and values. The computer entered my living room and my family life because it is part of my culture and not—in case anyone wonders—because I am prepping my toddler to enter medical school. My interests in children and computers led me to gather a great deal of detailed information about what Peggy knew before her first encounter with the computer and how her knowledge changed over the time she has been interacting with it. The following sketch is based on my observation of only one child's learning, but I believe it will be of general interest because microcomputers are penetrating our society now and Peggy's story provides some advance information about how that fact may affect our children.

Children typically learn to read at school around the age of six. A few teach themselves to read earlier. Rarely, one hears of children as young as three reading the New York Times to their parents and so forth. Peggy, at the age of three, even living in a bookish family, did not know how to read in any substantial sense before her computer experience. Her knowledge of letters at three years and three months of age was quite

---

3. 1981. First published in the Boston Review (1982, June), in an issue dedicated to Computing, under the editorship of Eric Wanner. See also the next text 'Beach.' Some parts of this article are subsumed in 'Computers and Literacy in Traditional Languages,' appearing later in this text.

specific and limited. She recognized only a few letters as distinct symbols with any meaning. For example, she knew that 'P' was the first letter of her name. She also recognized 'G' as the 'mommy letter' because her mother's name is Gretchen.

What was Peggy's understanding of spelling? One incident gave me some inkling. My oldest daughter was learning a bit of French; one day Peggy claimed that she knew how to 'spell French' and continued, 'un, deux, trois, quatre, cinq.' At another time her spelling of 'French' was 'woof boogle jig.' (Some of you may recognize this as the Klopstockian love song from a W.C. Fields movie.) Peggy seemed to have the general idea of spelling as decomposing a meaningful whole into a string of essentially meaningless symbols, but she had not yet learned any of the culture-standard assignments of letters to words.

Peggy's ability and willingness to identify a string of symbols as a particular word came from a very specific beginning. After receiving a book as a gift from her older sister (who then wrote PEGGY LAWLER on the fly-leaf, Peggy interpreted all small clusters of alphabetic symbols as 'Peggy Lawler.' Later, as a consequence of being often read to, she became able to recognize the word 'by,' which appeared on the title page of every book we read to her. There is no reason to believe she had any idea of what 'by' might mean in that context. She did recognize that same word 'by' in quite a different context, spontaneously pointing out the word in the line 'These Romans are crazy, by Jupiter!' from an Asterix cartoon book. Her knowledge of reading as a process for interpreting graphic material is best seen in her observation when we read a book together, that she read pictures and I read words. From her remark, we can infer she would 'read' by inventing a story based on her best speculation about the pictures' meaning. She assumed that I was doing the same with the words. Not a bad assumption, but completely empty of any information about how written words signify as they do.

Contrast the foregoing sketch of Peggy's knowledge at three years and three months with what she now knows seven months later. Her knowledge of letters is essentially complete, in that she discriminates the 26 letters of the alphabet and can name them. Her knowledge of words, in the sense of interpreting them one at a time, is significantly greater. She reads more than 20 words, most with complete dependability. But unlike children who have learned to read and write by conventional means, she sees the spelling of words as step-by-step directions for typing a name into the computer. Although her general idea of what book reading is may not have changed, she has a different and powerful idea of what reading single words means that derives directly from her experience with computer programs I wrote. (I call the computer environments created by the programs I have written 'microworlds,' following the terminology of Seymour Papert [Mindstorms, 1980.])

Peggy's introduction to computers did not have much to do with 'reading' in terms of content. But her desire to control the machine led her into typing on the computer her first 'written' word. Having helped load programs by pushing buttons on a cassette tape recorder, one day on her own Peggy typed 'LO' on the keyboard of the computer terminal and then came seeking direction as to what letter came next. A few days later, she typed the 'LOAD' command while the rest of the family was at lunch in a different room.

The initial microworlds were one for moving coloured blocks around on the computer's video display screen and another (made for her older sister but taken over by Peggy) which created designs by moving a coloured cursor about on the screen. Her older sister used this drawing program to make designs, but Peggy's first design was a large box—which she immediately converted into a letter 'P' by adding the stem. Letters intrigued Peggy. They were a source of power she didn't understand.

A few days later, Peggy keyed the letter 'A' and explained to me that 'A is for apple.' Her comment suggested a way we could—on the computer— make a new kind of pre-readers' ABC book. A child's conventional book of ABCs typically offers a collection of engaging pictures displayed in alphabetic order with a large, printed letter associated with each picture. The child looks at the pictures and is informed 'A is for apple.' The relationship of letters to pictures is exactly the opposite in the ABC microworld we invented. The letter is the 'key' for accessing the picture. That is, typing the key for the letter 'D' on the computer's keyboard produces a picture of a dog on the computer screen. Instead of responding to a statement such as 'See the doggie. D is for dog,' Peggy was able to try any letter on the keyboard, first, to see what it got her, and later, if the picture interested her, to inquire what was the letter's name. She was in control of her own learning. She could learn what she wanted, when she wanted to, and could ask for advice or information when she decided she wanted it. The ABC microworld was tailor-made for Peggy. The shapes were selected and created on the computer by Peggy's older sister and brother, aged ten and twelve. As a consequence of playing with the ABC microworld, Peggy developed a stable and congenial familiarity with the letters of the alphabet.

More complex and interesting than the ABC microworld, the BEACH microworld provides a backdrop for action that can be controlled by the child. Waves and a beach in the fore-ground, with grass above, rise to a road, more grass, and clouds at the top of the display. Against that backdrop, Peggy could create a small picture of an object by specifying a name, then manipulate the picture with commands typed on the computer keyboard. Peggy typically began constructing a scene by typing the word SUN. A yellow circle would appear in the waves. She would raise it to the sky by keying the word UP repeatedly, change its colour or set it in motion with another word, and go on to other objects. She could, for example, make a CAR image appear by keying that word, change its location with commands UP, DOWN, MOVE, and specify its heading and velocity with TURN, SLOW, FAST, FASTER, and HALT.

These microworlds were created using LOGO, an easily comprehensible computer language which permits the programmer to assign meaning to any string of letters by writing a simple procedure that is activated whenever that string of letters is typed. LOGO's procedure definition was especially valuable in customizing the BEACH world. When Peggy first used BEACH, she was unhappy with the speed of the objects and asked, 'How can I make them zoom, Daddy?' Nothing was easier than to create a new word, ZOOM, the procedure for which would set the velocity of the object with a single

LOGO primitive command. In another instance, Peggy's older sister made a horse-and-rider design and wrote a PONY procedure to create that object and set it in motion. After watching her sister edit that shape design, Peggy imitated the specific commands to create her own new shape. (She could not well control the design and ended with a collection of perpendicular lines. Asked what it was, she first replied, 'A pony,' then later, 'Something important.') It is very likely that primary-grade children could create their own designs and would copy and alter procedures to expand or personalize the vocabulary of BEACH-like microworlds.

As a direct consequence of playing with the BEACH world, Peggy learned to 'read' approximately twenty words. Initially, she keyed names and commands, copying them letter by letter, from a set of 4 x 6 cards that I made up for her. Soon, her favourite words were keyed from memory. Less familiar words she would locate by searching through the pile of cards. When her mood was exploratory, she would try unfamiliar words if she encountered them by chance. Now, when shown those words—on the original 4 x 6 cards or printed elsewhere—she recognizes the pattern of letters and associates it with the appropriate vocal expression. Further, the words are meaningful to her. She knows what they represent, either objects or actions in the BEACH microworld. In the past, children have always learned to read words as alphabetic symbols for ideas to be evoked in the mind. For Peggy, words are that, but they are something else as well—a set of directions for specifying how to key a computer command. What is strikingly different in this new word-concept is that the child and computer together decode a letter string from a printed word to a procedure which the computer executes and whose significance the child can appreciate. Because the computer can interpret specific words the child does not yet know, she can learn from the computer through her self-directed exploration and experiment.

The basic lesson I draw from this story is NOT merely about 'motivation'—although Peggy did enjoy playing with these microworlds and learned from doing so. There is a more revolutionary aspect, one that is paradoxical as well. This new technology, although it may seem highly artificial, can make possible a more 'natural' absorption of knowledge than learning to read from the printed page. The character of words experienced as executable procedure names brought Peggy into a new relationship with language, one different from what has been characteristic of learning to read in the past.

Learning to read from print is necessarily a passive process for the child. Words on the page stand for other people's meanings. Until children start to write they can't use written words for their own purposes. Microcomputers put reading and writing together from the start. A word that Peggy can read is also one she can use to produce on the computer effects that interest her. For Peggy, reading the alphabetic language has become more like what every infant's learning of the vocal language is like. Speaking is powerful for the infant, even for one who commands but a few words, when a responsive person listens and reacts. Likewise, the production of alphabetic symbols—even one letter and one word at a time—can become powerful for the young child when computer microworlds provide a patient, responsive intelligence to interpret them.

The change wrought by microcomputers may not be profound for Peggy. She would have learned to read anyway at six or five instead of three; but for many other children in the world— those with less responsive families and teachers, for example—the chance to use language symbols in microcomputers may give them a new access to the power of written words which can truly be called revolutionary. The computer revolution is worthwhile only if it liberates people. It has the potential to do so if those who care about individuals' freedom and development join in shaping this plastic medium more to the service of mankind than narrow technical or commercial interests might be inclined to do.

PARTICIPATORY SOFTWARE [4]

Abstract

I begin this discussion reporting some legitimate fears people have about the potential impact of technology on their children and conclude that the practical problems of humanizing technology are addressable if people can and do cooperate and participate in the construction of computer experiences which will shape the lives of their children. Our world is becoming progressively artificial. For a humane democracy to survive, the technology of intelligent machines must be controlled by the people for their own best development.

Personal computers have seized America's imagination, but many thoughtful people are worried, worried especially about their use in education. There are the practical and economic fears, that schools will invest in this technology beyond their means and then be saddled with equipment which no one knows how to use and which may not be what is really best suited for their needs. Such are legitimate concerns. Some people wonder how expenditures for this new technology can be justified at all when there are experienced preschool teachers making minimum wage, and when there are national preschool programs that spend less than 15 dollars a year per child for supplies.

Even more profound worries trouble those who fear that technology will dehumanize education or those who are committed to supporting subdominant cultures within American society. Such fears are also legitimate, and they are shared by people from other nations around the world. It was my privilege, while I worked in Paris at the World Centre for Computers and Human Development, to meet representatives from several of the smaller countries of Europe. These people expect children to be changed by their experiences with intelligent machines. They told me of their fear of solid state software, their fear that languages and intelligent facilities built into computers in foreign factories would simultaneously engage their children with a dehumanizing technology and alienate them from the languages and cultures of their homelands.

At the end of these notes, I propose that in education, instead of solid state software, we should prefer something different, a sort of 'do it yourself' software that I call participatory software. Along the path to that conclusion, I want to consider some specific ideas about learning, to notice some computer facilities that can be especially significant (sprite graphics and the Logo language), and to focus, for discussion's sake,

---

4. 1984. This is the text of a presentation made to the regional directors of Headstart at a meeting at the University of Maryland. A modified version of this text was subsumed in 'Shared Models: the Cognitive Equivalent of a Lingua Franca,' in *Artificial Intelligence and Society* (Elsevier, 1989). Republished as Chapter 1 of *AI&Ed*, Vol.2 (1992).

on a particular purpose, something one might want to achieve with computers: I will explore how computers can help young children develop pre-reading and reading skills. The following discussion goes forward in two stages. First, I'll draw upon material from my book, Computer Experience and Cognitive Development (distributed in the USA by John Wiley, 1985) to exemplify how a reasonably mature performance can be traced down to the concrete details of everyday behaviour. Then I will go on to suggest how you might use such a point of view about cognitive development in thinking of good things for your children to do.

Anchoring with Variation

In Computer Experience and Cognitive Development, I analyze case study material about a six year old child, my daughter Miriam, who was under intense observation for six months. She came over to the laboratory to work with me, and I made tape recordings of all our experiments. Beyond transcribing these recorded experiments, I made exceptionally detailed naturalistic observations of her behaviour. This was possible because I was the primary caretaker in her life then; we spent all our time together.

A Math World Example

I will use one incident from that study to illustrate the idea of anchoring with variation in arithmetic problem solving. Miriam at six years had not been to school other than a non-didactic kindergarten. She was sitting in our kitchen one day with her eight year old brother, Rob, a second grader. The children were making a kind of play-dough by mixing flour, salt, and water, kneading it all together, and folding it over in plies, rolling it thin, then folding again. My son counted the plies as he folded them over ' . . .ninety three, [then he rolled it thin], ninety four, ninety five, ninety six.' Since the lump was getting very unwieldy, he took a knife and cut the stack of 96 plies in half, put the second piece on top of the first, and said, 'Now we've got 96 plus 96.' Miriam said immediately, ' That's a hundred and ninety two.' This was a surprising mental calculation for an unschooled six year old. My son turned to his mother and asked, ' Could that possibly be right?'

Before I tell you what happened next, let me go back a little bit in the history of Miriam's developing mind to describe what her knowledge of number was like, so we can understand in detail how she came to this surprising result.

Well Known Results as Anchors

Like many children her age, Miriam remembered some simple sums and counted on her fingers. She had even developed a slightly more sophisticated counting procedure, where she could sum seventeen plus six, for example, by beginning 'seventeen, [then counting with her fingers] eighteen, nineteen, twenty, twenty one, twenty two, twenty three.' That summarizes Miriam's counting when we started our research.

At the MIT Logo project, Miriam came to do a lot of addition with big numbers, numbers like twenty, and forty, and thirty five. We played with a very simple computer game, called SHOOT. A circle was drawn on the video display screen, and the child commanded an object, which we called the screen turtle — a little triangle — and tried to turn that turtle so it would point to the circular target. In making such turns, sometimes Miriam would confuse right and left. She might turn left 35, for example, instead of right 35. To achieve her goal after such an error, she had to do either a right turn 35 and then a second right turn 35 or a single right turn 70. In such a fashion, this world of homely computer play led her into calculations with big numbers. She was able to add numbers like 35 plus 35, this way: '30 plus 30, that's like 3 plus 3 [counting on her fingers], 60, and 5 plus 5 is 10 more, seventy.'

The number 90 is a very important number when you're working with geometry, and you have to know right 90 means a specific thing — turn right through 90 degrees. As we began our experiments, my daughter didn't know that. During one game, Miriam pretended she was the turtle and Rob directed her 'right 90'. Miriam didn't know what to do, so she turned some (about 30 degrees), counted one, and continued turning and counting. After a few complete turns, she realized that although her action made sense one step at a time, it couldn't be what right 90 meant. Rob provided a little instruction. 'You do it this way,' he said. 'You stand still and you look straight ahead. Hold out an arm, the right arm — now keep your arm right there, don't move it. Then you jump your body around under your arm. That's what right 90 is.' From further experiences with this little world, she learned that 90 plus 90 amounts to 180 degrees. Back to our story about those plies of clay-like material. When Rob asked his mother if this answer of '192' could possibly be right, Miriam spoke up and said, 'We know that 90 plus 90 is 180, and 6 is 186 . . . [then counting on her fingers] 187, 188, 189, 190, 191, 192.' She gave him a proof for a calculation that seemed extra-ordinary, but the roots of her ability were based very directly on the particulars of her concrete experience. (My research focuses on such detail in order to make it possible to understand the processes of learning.)

Let me now characterize this process of my daughter's mental calculation in the terms of two psychologists from Stanford, Amos Tversky and David Kahnemann. They asked how people make estimates for calculation problems that are too hard to solve. Their characterization, which describes my daughter's mental calculation, is that she 'anchored' her thinking at a particular result, 90 plus 90 is 180, and then she performed variations on that well known result with other procedures, concatenation and finger counting in this case. To me, her working of this problem represents the basic situation which people learn through solving problems at the frontier of their knowledge.

If we take seriously such a vision of the role of very concrete and specific knowledge as the roots of competence in performing mental calculation, we might ask 'What could possibly be the specific elements of knowledge which underlie a much more complicated mental performance, such as reading.' Let's address that question now.

Anchoring with Variation and Reading: a word world example

I'm lucky to have not merely one daughter, but three. I've been performing a detailed study of my second daughter's cognitive development during the period in which she's been learning to read. We've had computers in the house all the time, and I have made things for Peggy to play with, because I play with the computers myself, because I like her, and we like to play together. As background, let me review some of the kinds of knowledge about words Peggy had and then go on to discuss how her computer experiences have affected her developing language skills.

The reading study began when she was about three years old. There were many books in our house, but the word knowledge she got from them was quite limited. For example, one of the few words Peggy recognized early was 'by,' because it was on the title page of all those stories that my wife and I read to her. She saw again and recognized 'by' in other contexts. In reading an Asterix cartoon book, an import from France, one of the characters would frequently say things like 'By Jupiter.' Peg would recognize that word without having the faintest idea what it meant. A second kind of word knowledge she had was the names of members in our family. I am fortunate to have received many love notes from her, which begin 'To Dad' or 'Bob', present a picture, and conclude 'Love, Peggy'. The sound of 'Bob' was clearly associated with its well known spelling. The real novelty in her experience was using the computer and learning a number of specific words with the computer.

Introducing Microworlds

Scenes

I made for Peggy on a sprite graphics microcomputer a picture of a little scene to represent the beach where she and I often went to play, collect shells, and so forth. In this little world of experience, one can use single words to perform either of two functions. The first function is to create an object. The second is to manipulate the object. The word SUN creates a little yellow ball on the display screen. The word UP moves the object up from its initial location. Other words can change the object's location, direction, or colour, and set it in motion. This collection of programs provided Peggy a little world of experience which she could populate and manipulate through the use of individual words. I call such a scene and collection of active objects a computer microworld.

Activities

It's possible to populate the scene with a realistic collection of objects. Peggy's scenes were more fanciful. She would often have multiple suns of different colours in the sky. It was her privilege to make the world be what she wanted. Typically, she would go through a prepared collection of 4 x 6 cards and select one for use at the keyboard. She might or might not know what the word meant. For a word she knew, its use satisfied her objective. A word she did not know became the source of a discovery. An error or a guess became, often enough, the occasion of a pleasant surprise. The objects, once their recognizable shapes appeared, became the focus for manipulative activities, often as members of a representational scene, equally often as agents for extreme action (making the SUN ZOOM across the sky) or absurd juxtapositions (a HOUSE in the road or under water). Such programs within the computer embody a little bit of knowledge which a child can call upon when she wants it, if she wants it. She can perform little experiments on things which will increase her knowledge directly in a straightforward and comprehensible way.

Adapting the Microworld For the Child

Images of Objects

Some people may be a little concerned, thinking perhaps that very young children may not be ready to begin typing words. Peggy began with a very simple microworld whose objective was the following: when the child pressed any key, there was displayed on the screen of the computer a shape which she could recognize and might have some significance in her life. The shapes were made specifically for her by her older brother and sister (aged 10 and 8 then). The most unusual one goes with the letter N. Peggy has a red nightgown, her favorite article of clothing. My older daughter knew that and proposed we make N the nightgown letter so it would be special for Peggy. Years later, Peggy still distinguishes between N and M as the 'nightgown' and 'moon' letters. The central point here is personalization of computer facilities to reflect something of significance to the particular experience of a little child. The value of such personalization is clear. How hard is it? Not very. A five year old can make sprite design with a graphics shape editor. Miriam at age 8 made most of the 26 shapes used by the program.

Procedures as Names of Objects and Actions

Even more important for children than modifiable screen images is the ability to create new words. For example, when first introduced to the BEACH microworld, Peggy created a SUN image and moved it up to the sky. Informed she wanted to set it in motion, I proposed the word SLOW and found it for her. She wanted the sun to move faster. When I produced the card with the word FAST, its effect was still not satisfactory. 'I want it to ZOOM,' she told me. Nothing easier. Using the Logo programming language, I wrote for her the following procedure:

```
TO ZOOM
SETSPEED 25
END
```

The microworld was then more to her liking. ZOOM became one of the first words she could read and key with full comprehension.

Some days later, Miriam played with Peggy while I was away from the house. Together they decided the BEACH world should have a PONY. They made a pony design with the graphics editor, and Miriam wrote a procedure to create it (by copying and changing the SUN procedure). This is her procedure:

```
TO PONY
NEXT PLACE
SETSHAPE 14
SETCOLOUR WHITE
SETSPEED 5
END
```

Adapting Microworlds to Other Languages
When I joined the World Centre for Computers and Human Development in Paris, my family moved to France. Miriam, then 10 years old, translated the BEACH microworld for use with French words, as she proudly noted 'in only five hours.' That's true, but it is not something I want to make any claims about. What I consider significant are two characteristics of the computer language she was using which permitted her to do so. Logo is a high level language. This means you have a lot of power available to you through a series of reasonably simple language commands. No less important is that Logo is a procedural, interpretive language. This means you can make new words whenever you need to do so. Since those words can be any string of letters entered at the keyboard, the words can be those of any alphabetic language.

Adapting Microworlds to Other Cultures
While in Paris, I worked as a consultant and instructor to colleagues from other countries. My most interesting work was with Senegalese, some government computer scientists and primary instructors from a laboratory school of the Ecole Normale Superieure at Dakar. When we met in Paris, they asked me how they could adapt this computer technology and these programming ideas for use with children in Senegal. Literacy is an issue that is central for their nation.

The Senegalese hope to develop materials in their traditional language which will permit their children to view Wolof as a language of the modern age as well as the home. They can make the attempt because the computer language they have adopted permits them to define new words whenever they want to — and those letter strings can be words in Wolof.

If a microworld such as BEACH, the French version PLAGE, or a much different Wolof variant XEW were seen as a reading program, it would clearly embody a limited, a pre-syntactic kind of language use. Yet such materials could be precisely what PRE-readers need — if we take seriously the Piagetian idea that mature performances emerge from the interaction of different but compatible precursors. If children begin to know very well the meaning of many words, such as they could learn from a large number of microworlds, something very special may begin to happen.

Anchoring with Variation in Reading

An Anecdote

There has been a long-standing debate among educators as to the relative importance of a child's ability to recognize individual words and the child's ability to analyze words she could not recognize at first encounter. (This is the 'whole word' versus 'decoding' controversy.) Cast your mind back to that earlier example of my daughter's calculation. It was very important in adding 96 plus 96 that Miriam knew a result that she could hold on to, like 90 plus 90 is 180, to get her close the solution of her current problem. Think about reading in the same terms, and consider this example. My second daughter Peggy sat at the kitchen table the other night, poring over the pictures in a cartoon book, and she asked 'How do you say the word 's-o-b'?' And then she continued, 'It must be /sob.' The child encountered a word she didn't recognize, then figured out how to pronounce it. This is one problem solved in the much longer effort to comprehend the alphabetic code through which the sounds are represented as letter strings.

How did Peggy solve this problem? I asked her, 'Why do you say that?'. Peggy replied, 'Well, it's like 's' with Bob.' My name is one she knows very well, as a sound and an associated string of written symbols. Anchoring her analysis of 's-o-b' at the letter configuration 'b-o-b' and its spoken association, Peggy varied her interpretation to make a good hypothesis about how that word should be pronounced; from that partial result, she could speculate about the meaning of the word in the context.

The Engineering Challenge

Let's suppose that problem solving through 'anchoring with variation' is an important precursor activity through which a child typically learns those elements of knowledge and those skills which permit her to comprehend how English phonemes are encoded as letter strings. The educator's challenge — it is a knowledge engineering task — is to ask 'how would you go about making facilities to help children learn an optimal set of anchors?' I approach the task this way. First, I would analyze the monosyllabic words of the language to choose those which best represent the phonetic/orthographic correspondences. [5] From these I would try to select those words for which little pictures could represent objects and words that understandably represent actions which change the state of such objects. Finally, I would develop a collection of microworlds — which could be augmented and tailored to the specific experiences of individual children — whose vocabulary would cover the largest possible collection of potential word-anchors for use in later reading activities.

Participatory Software

Who is able to create this kind of educational software? Different people can make different parts. For example, my interest is in how ideas develop. I focus on problem

---

5.   See the later abstract in this book of 'Computer Microworlds and Reading,' in the AI section.

solving processes and on content analysis, as a curriculum specialist would. As an experienced programmer interested in making programming accessible to other people, I make models of microworlds. High level languages, such as Logo, provide a tool for other people to make their own versions of microworlds tailored for use by individual children. Who can participate in this process of tailoring microworlds? Shapes can be made easily with a graphics editor. Even some little children of five years can make their own. Parents can make them for their young children or toddlers. Older kids, parents, teachers, and helpers can make new words for playing with. Kindergarten children can do so for themselves. Background scenes can be made by more technically inclined people, adults or adolescents (some younger children can do so), but if scene-making seems beyond the reach of young children, please observe that even little kids can say what they want the scenes to be. Developing new microworlds requires both ideas about content and technical skill; people can cooperate with one another. That is the main point: many people with different skills can participate in developing computer based materials which will help make the whole world more comprehensible to children. This is what I mean by participatory software.

If you're thinking of introducing technology into a preschool program, the technology should be one that parents, teachers, and their helpers can master and control.

In the close social situations of early childhood education, where adults and children can work as a group on providing a good learning environment for the little children, it must be clear to the children that the technology they have available is not something created by and only supportable by remote experts who shape their lives but care nothing for them.

I began this discussion noticing some legitimate fears people have about the potential impact of technology on their children. I conclude with the conviction that the practical problems of humanizing technology are addressable if people can and do cooperate and participate in the construction of computer experiences which will shape the lives of their children. Our world is becoming progressively artificial. I have set forth some ideas about technology here as a psychologist and information systems engineer. I hope that I have also spoken to you as a father of children and as a fellow citizen. For a humane democracy to survive, the technology of intelligent machines must be controlled by the people for their own best development.

BEACH MICROWORLD [6]

The BEACH microworld is a collection of procedures. BEACH creates a scene on the video display. Other words (procedures) create objects (sprite-carried shapes) and manipulate them. The purpose is to create and control objects using one word at a time.

To begin, type BEACH and hit return; a scene will appear on the display. Select a name from the word list which follows. When you key the name, a picture of that object will appear on the screen. This newly created object is the CURRENT OBJECT.

Peggy Lawler using the Beach Word World

Select any desired word from the ACTION word list; keying that word will change the state of the current object. For example, keying FAST will make the object move in the direction of its heading at a FAST speed. To change colours, type PAINT followed by a space and colour name, such as RED.

To get some previously created object to respond to commands after you have created another object, type the following: TELL :name (for example, TELL :SUN). If there is more than one such object, only the last one will respond.

BEACH is a microworld for pre-readers. A young child can USE alphabetic words to create and control objects, and from their use can learn what they mean in this limited context. If there are older people around, they can make designs to represent new objects (with the shape editor) and write procedures to create and manipulate those objects. Pre-readers will have a novel experience of words, one where the alphabetic 'written' word is a set of directions for keying a computer command. They will be using words to control the computer. This use of words contrasts with words in text, whose meanings are interpersonal communication puzzles, to be decoded and then associated with private memories (as in reading).

Young children will learn to read these words as they type them on the computer for controlling the BEACH microworld. They will be learning to read and write at the same time. This experience with words working to do their bidding will help children understand by contrast the less obvious and more complex use of words in printed materials.

Words of the BEACH Microworld

To see a typical BEACH scene, type SCENE.

---

6. 1989. This short text is a set of instructions for introducing and using the programs with young children at Headstart in Lafayette, Indiana.

Names	Actions	Colours
BIRD	PAINT :colourname	(BLACK, for example)
BOAT	DOWN	BLUE
BOY	DRIVE	GREEN
CAR	FAST	GRAY
DOG	FASTER	ORANGE
FISH	FLY	RED
GIRL	GALLOP	WHITE
HOUSE	HALT	YELLOW
MAN	JOG	PURPLE
MOON	TURN	
PINE	SAIL	Other Words
PLANE	SLOWER	WIPE, NEXT,
PONY	SWIM	PLACE, LINE,
SUN	WALK	WATER, SAND,
TREE	UP	SKY, FIELD,
TRUCK	ZOOM	ROAD

HEADSTART PROGRESS REPORT [7]

Mary Hopper and Robert W. Lawler

Introduction

The goal of the Headstart Apple Logo Project is to explore novel ideas about the potential impact of computer experience with language based microworlds on pre-readers. An initial pilot study demonstrated the feasibility of implementing microcomputer technology in preschool settings, and the potential of Word Worlds to be a refreshingly motivating and effective method for introducing young children to reading. Further investigations are now being carried out to gain further insight into how the success with Word Worlds is best achieved, and to explore to what degree products can be developed to achieve the same effects using software and hardware technology currently available on the market.

Word Worlds

Word Worlds are computer-based learning environments, or microworlds, for inductive learning of language. Word Worlds encompass objects and processes that children can get to know and understand using the power of typed words. Word Worlds do not focus on ' problems ' to be done, but on 'neat phenomena' that are inherently interesting to observe and interact with. Children learn from such experience because they are personally engaged in tasks which will make the specific knowledge worth learning as an aid in achieving some of their personal objectives.

The educational value of a Word World is in building the simplest model of language which a reader needs as an acceptable entry point to beginning knowledge of reading. Word Worlds are designed for children, little kids who are no longer infants. Whether they go to school or not, they are prereaders. They may not recognize all the letters of the alphabet and probably cannot specify the letters' names or phonemes which they typically represent. They can take turns with considerable sensitivity and are quite able to use speech to specify for others what they want them to do for them (see Logo and Videodisk Applications, Lawler & Papert, 1985).

The Pilot Study

This pilot study set out with two basic goals. The first goal was to explore the feasibility of implementing microcomputer technology in preschool settings. The second goal was to determine if Word Worlds had the potential to be a motivating and effective method for introducing young children to reading.

---

7. 1992. Unpublished. Over a period of several years, Mary Hopper was the organizer and primary agent of the research done with my graduate students at the Lafayette Headstart Centre.

This study was carried out for a period totaling six months. There were three classrooms involved in the project, with from 12 to 15 children and two teachers in each room. However, due to limiting circumstances, only one class's data was sufficiently complete to be reported in this summary.

Pretest Results

The main experimental materials used during the pretest were the ABC Sprite Logo program, the Beach Sprite Logo program, 3 X 5 flash cards with printed capital letters, 3 X 5 cards with the Beach words and 3 X 5 flash cards with a few common words. Typically, researchers asked the children if they recognized specific letters (such as the first one of their names) or words on a card, and then had the child type what was on the card and observe the computer screen. In addition, the Karpova Word Counting Task and interview were used to evaluate the children's conceptual knowledge of words.

Of the 15 children who were in the experimental class for the duration of the study, 6 children knew no letters and no words at first. Another 8 children knew less than 12 letters and no words. Among these 8 children, the letters which were recognized on sight tended to be the letters in the child's name or one of their family member's names. When the children were asked if they recognized 'stop' or 'mom', the answer was commonly 'no'. Only one child did know 24 letters and recognized the word MOM. No one recognized any of the words from the BEACH microworld.

Thus, the preliminary finding is that in this population most children do not recognize individual letters of the alphabet. Some recognize letters as a kind of thing and refer to any letter or number as 'ABC'. A few children can identify letters or numbers, but do not discriminate between or exhibit a sense of sequence or purpose to them. Most of the children know no words at all. The Karpova task is definitely beyond the reach of these children. They apparently have no explicit notion whatsoever of what 'words' are, and what is meant by the term when it is used.

Post Test Results

Children showed definite growth in letter and word knowledge. Five students knew all of their letters and three or more words, which they could both identify on three by five cards and type into the computer in order to control it in some desired fashion. Nine (9) students recognized from 1 to 6 letters, while also demonstrating some knowledge of how to use from one to three of a group of words which were used frequently in the Word Worlds (UP, ZOOM, FLY, DOWN, GO, WALK, CAR, TRUCK, RED). Only one student did not demonstrate evidence of either letter or word knowledge. However, over the course of the project, this child showed tremendous growth in fine motor control of the keyboard and attribute matching of letters on cards to letters on the keyboard.

Sign Posts to New Directions from the Pilot Study:

Word and Letter Knowledge

A conservative interpretation of the pilot study results show definite evidence of growth due to use of Word Worlds, yet researchers involved in the project did not believe these results accurately reflected the degree of actual positive outcomes achieved on one hand, while they also reflected evidence of lower outcomes than might have been expected on the other.

One hypothesis about why the level of expected outcomes did not occur is that an overemphasis on instruction in letters as prerequisite to word knowledge contributed as a limiting factor. There was no way to tell from the data whether greater word knowledge and letter knowledge was due to prerequisite knowledge of letters or whether the children who knew their letters constructed their knowledge as a consequence of their experience with the words. For this reason, detailed video taped sessions of the complete introductory and practice process are now being gathered to determine the answer to this question.

Sign Posts to New Directions from the Pilot Study:

Structure of Implementation

Limiting circumstances which occurred during the pilot study did provide important information about the relative merits and disadvantages associated with the different approaches used for implementing and studying technology and instructional software in pre-school classroom environments.

In one room, the Word Worlds were implemented in a structured fashion, with a research assistant present at all times who provided the children with one on one instruction on a regular basis. All data collection for this room also took place in a structured setting. Evidence of growth was present in the data from this room, but the overall approach did not appear productive. One of the limiting factors in this room's results may have been an overemphasis on letter instruction over word experience on a day to day basis, and little opportunity for social interaction between children during learning.

In a second classroom, an unstructured instructional setting was implemented by the teachers themselves, with only periodic research assistant support after the initial introduction of the worlds. This also was not a productive approach, due to teacher inhibition about their own computer use in the absence of the research assistant, and reluctance to let the children play with the computer without direct adult guidance at all times. This occurred even though the teachers would often let the children do many other equally challenging activities independently.

Experiences in both of these classrooms demonstrated that, if computers are to become integrated components of the classroom environment, extensive in-service training and flexible support for teachers must be an intricate part of implementation. These programs should be structured around not only helping the teachers become more

Type of Skill	Average Pretest Score	Average Posttest Score	Average Growth
Programming	1.13	3.40	2.26
Computer Use	2.00	3.80	1.80
Word Skills	0.66	3.26	2.60
Letter Skills	1.86	3.40	1.53

Room1 / Morning Session / Fall 89 - Spring 90

confident in their own computer use, but also helping them to become comfortable with a much more relaxed approach to their student's independent and frequent use of the technology available in the classroom, once initial introductions to materials are complete.

The most powerful support for this argument can be found by examining the success of the approach used in the third room at Headstart. In this room, a relatively unstructured and relaxed independent learning environment was created, where the children could use their imagination and curiosity to freely explore the Word Worlds with a brief period of adult supervision at first, then relatively independent use alone and with peers later on. This approach occurred because the research assistant support and involvement in this room was flexible. While the research assistant was available much of the time, the teachers were also encouraged to experiment and implement the worlds in the research assistant's absence, which the teachers did successfully by modeling the relaxed approach to letting the children use the technology with only minimal adult supervision and intervention.

In order to gain broader success in all rooms, this year we have implemented more extensive workshop and training activities for the teachers at Headstart. We now provide an initial in service workshop with the following agenda:

Let's Talk Computers
1. Staff fears
2. How to set up the computers

3. Getting reacquainted. How to enter and exit.
4. How to work with children. What to do.
5. New ideas and Programs

A second training session is designed to introduce the teachers to how to begin to make simple microworlds of their own. This session covers the topic of drawing backgrounds and objects with different colours. A third training session covers the formation and control of sprite objects. The initial reactions to the expanded training opportunities have been positive. We are also providing a low level of research assistant present in all rooms, where assistants are trained to model a relaxed and unobtrusive approach to allowing the children to work alone and in groups.

Sign Posts to New Directions from the Pilot Study:

Data Collection

In the third room, there was also a more effectively structured situation used for data collection. More positive evaluation results during the post-test situation were obtained on video tape for this room because the data collection was done within the same classroom where instruction took place. During data collection efforts with the other two rooms, strong evidence was collected to support that while video tapes recorded in structured and artificial situations yield videos of higher technical quality, which can be easily viewed and understood after the fact, the much more optimal performance of the children is captured in the loosely structured and chaotic environment of the classroom. While some of the quality of the video tapes made in the actual classroom situation of the third room often had to be sacrificed, the quality of the information that remained was more valuable.

It is because of this that the results from the third room during the pilot study were both more complete and interesting, and the children from the third room are the focus of this summary of results, even though the technical quality of the video records was fairly poor. At the present time, one room has been selected to be the focus of detailed data collection with a video camera. In this room it has been possible to set up the camera in an unobtrusive, yet effective position to collect all interactions made at the computers in that room. Most of the data collected in this situation will prove to be very valuable in the analysis and explanation of how letter and word knowledge develop during interactions over the course of months.

COMPUTERS AND LITERACY IN TRADITIONAL LANGUAGES[8]

Reference
Peggy

Robert W. Lawler in collaboration with Mamadou Niang and Moussa Gning

Microcomputers are pouring into homes and schools in the industrialized countries and will soon be flooding the world. It is hardly too soon to wonder what effects computers are likely to have on our children. Will computers change the way children learn? Will computers change the sorts of people children become? I believe the answers may well be yes, and although it is too early for conclusive proof, I can offer here a story that supports my belief.

I have worked in the computer industry for sixteen years, and when my children were born I became interested in the potential impact of early computer experiences on children's learning. Several years ago, in collaboration with a computer language project at the Massachusetts Institute of Technology, I began an intensive study of how daily access to a computer influenced the way my two older children—then aged six and eight—learned the basics of arithmetic. By the time their younger sister Peggy turned three, a microcomputer had become standard equipment in our household, and I began to develop several programs to give Peggy access to the machine. Playing with these programs in her own way and on her own initiative over the following months, Peggy began to do something that looks very much like the beginnings of reading and writing.

What is it really like to bring a microcomputer in your home and let your three-year-old play with it? The answer depends on who you are, your knowledge and values. The computer entered my home and my family life because it is a part of my work. It was my pleasure to write some simple programs for my daughter's entertainment and edification. My interests in children and computers led me to gather a great deal of information about what Peggy knew before her first encounter with the computer and afterwards. Between her ages of three years three months and three years ten months, Peggy began to read and write. The following sketch of how this happened is based on my own observation of only one child's learning; it is fair to say, however, that I have an enormous amount of detailed information about what this particular child knew and how that knowledge changed over a long period of time. I believe this sketch will be of

---

8. 1983. UNESCO Courier, (1983, march). This article was written at the request of the English Language editor of the UNESCO Courier, with his agreement that the 1981 article from the Boston Review could be used as a concrete example to illustrate a more general hope of ways that computing could aid in education and development around the world. Published in 27 languages around the world.

general interest because Peggy's story provides some advance information about how computer experience may affect our children.

In the USA children typically learn to read around the age of six. Most learn to read at school. A few teach themselves to read earlier. Peggy, at the age of three, even living in a bookish family, did not know how to read in any substantial sense before her computer experience. Her knowledge of letters at three years, three months was quite specific and limited. She recognized only a few letters as distinct symbols with any meaning. For example, she knew that 'P' was the first letter of her name. She also recognized 'G' as the 'mummy letter' because her mother's name is Gretchen.

What was Peggy's knowledge of spelling like? One incident gave me some inkling. My oldest daughter was learning a bit of French: one day Peggy claimed that she knew how to 'spell French' and continued, 'un, deux, trois, quatre, cinq. ' Another time her spelling of 'French' was 'woof boogle jig. ' Peggy saw 'spelling' as decomposing a meaningful word into a string of essentially meaningless symbols and had not yet learned the standard spellings of words.

Peggy's ability and willingness to identify a string of symbols as a particular word came from a very specific beginning. After receiving a gift book from her older sister (who then wrote Peggy Lawler on the flyleaf), Peggy interpreted all small clusters of alphabetic symbols as 'Peggy Lawler. ' At a later point in time, as a consequence of being often read to, she became able to recognize a single, two letter word, 'by', which appeared on the title page of every book we read to her. There is no reason to believe she had any idea of what 'by' might mean in that context. Her knowledge of reading as a process for interpreting graphic material is best seen in her common observation that she read Pictures and I read Words. From her remark. we can infer she would the same with words. Not a bad assumption, but completely empty of any information about how written words signify as they do.

Contrast now her knowledge seven months later. Her knowledge of letters is essentially complete, in that she discriminates the 26 letters of the alphabet and can name them. Her knowledge of words, in the sense of interpreting them one at a time, is significantly greater. She reads more than 20 words, most with complete dependability. But unlike children who have learned to read and write by conventional means, she sees the spelling of words as stepwise directions for keying a name into the computer. Although her general idea of what book reading is may not have changed, she has a different and powerful idea of what reading single words means that derives directly from her experience with my computer programs. Peggy's introduction to computers did not relate directly to 'reading' in terms of content, but her desire to control the machine led her into keying on the computer her first 'written' word. Having helped load programs by pushing buttons on a cassette tape recorder, one day on her own Peggy typed 'LO' on the terminal then came seeking direction as to what letter came next. A few days later, she typed the 'load' command while the rest of the family was busy elsewhere.

I call the computer environments created by the programs I have written 'microworlds.'[10] The initial microworlds were one for moving coloured blocks around on the video display screen and another (made for her older sister but taken over by Peggy) which created designs by moving a coloured cursor. While her sister used this drawing program to make designs, Peggy's first drawing was a large box—which she immediately converted into a letter 'P' by adding the stem. Letters intrigued Peggy. They were a source of power she didn't understand.

A few days later, Peggy keyed the letter 'A' and explained to me that 'A is for apple.' Her comment suggested away we could—on the computer—make a new kind of prereaders' ABC book. A child's book of ABC's typically offers a collection of engaging pictures displayed in alphabetic order with a large, printed letter associated with each picture. The child looks at the pictures and is informed 'A is for apple.' The relationship of letters to pictures is exactly the opposite in the ABC microworld. The letter is the 'key' for accessing the picture. That is, keying the letter 'D' produces a picture of a dog. Instead of responding to a statement such as 'See the doggie. D is for dog,' Peggy was able to try any letter on the keyboard, first, to see what it got her, and later, if the picture interested her, to inquire what was the letter's name. She was in control of her own learning. She could learn WHAT she wanted, WHEN she wanted to, and could ask for advice or information when SHE decided she WANTED it. The ABC microworld was tailor-made for Peggy. The shapes were selected and created on the computer by Peggy's older sister and brother, aged ten and twelve. As a consequence of playing with the ABC microworld—and with another to which we now turn—Peggy developed a stable and congenial familiarity with the letters of the alphabet.

More complex and interesting than the ABC microworld, the BEACH microworld provides a backdrop for action. Waves and a beach in the foreground, with grass above, rise to a road, more grass, and clouds at the top. Against that backdrop, Peggy could create a small picture of an object by specifying a procedure name, then manipulate the picture with commanding procedures. Peggy typically began constructing a scene with the word SUN. A yellow circle would appear in the waves. She would raise it to the sky by keying the word UP repeatedly, change its colour or set it in motion with another word, and go on to other objects. She could, for example, make a CAR image appear by keying that word, change its location with commands UP, DOWN, MOVE, and specify its heading and velocity with TURN, SLOW, FAST, FASTER, and HALT.

These microworlds were created using Logo, an easily comprehensible computer language which permits you to assign meaning to any string of letters by writing simple procedures. Logo's procedure definition was especially valuable in customizing the BEACH world. When Peggy first used BEACH, she was unhappy with the speed of the objects and asked, 'How can I make them zoom, Daddy?' Nothing was easier than to create a new Logo word, ZOOM, which set the velocity of the object with a single primitive command. In a further instance, Peggy's older sister made a horse-and-rider design and wrote a PONY procedure to create an object with a horse-and-rider design and set it in motion. After watching her sister edit that shape design, Peggy imitated the

9. Following the terminology of my colleague Seymour Papertin his book *Mindstorms*.

specific commands to create her own new shape. (She could not well control the design and ended with a collection of perpendicular lines. Asked what it was, she first replied 'A pony, 'then later, 'Something important. ') It is very likely that primary grade children could create their own designs and would copy and alter procedures to expand or personalize the vocabulary of BEACH-like microworlds.

As a direct consequence of playing with the BEACH world, Peggy learned to 'read' approximately twenty words. Initially, she keyed names and commands, copying them letter by letter from a set of cards. Soon, her favourite words were keyed from memory. Less familiar words she could locate by searching through the pile of cards. When her mood was exploratory, she would try unfamiliar words if she encountered them by chance. Now, when shown those words—on the original cards or printed otherwheres— she recognizes the pattern of letters and associates it with the appropriate vocal expression. Further, the words are meaningful to her. She knows what they represent, either objects or actions.

In the past, words for reading have always been an alphabetic symbol for an idea to be evoked in the mind. For Peggy, words are that but something else as well—a set of directions for specifying how to key a computer command. What is strikingly different in this new word-concept, as contrasted with quasi-phonetic decoding, is that the child and computer together decode a letter string from a printed word to a procedure which the computer executes and whose significance the child can appreciate. Finally, because the computer can interpret specific words the child does not yet know, she can learn from the computer through her self directed explorations and experiments.

The basic lesson I draw from this story is NOT merely about 'motivation'—although Peggy did enjoy playing with these microworlds and learned from doing so. There is a more revolutionary aspect, one paradoxical as well. This new technology can make possible a more 'natural' absorption of knowledge. The character of words experienced as executable procedure names brought Peggy into a new relationship with language, one different from what has been characteristic of learning to read in the past.

Learning to read from print is necessarily a passive process for the child. Words on the page stand for other people's meanings. Until children start to write, they can't use written words for their own purposes. Microcomputers put reading and writing together from the start. A word that Peggy can read is also one she can use to produce on the computer effects that interest her. For Peggy, learning the alphabetic language has become more like every infant's learning of the vocal language. Speaking is powerful for the infant, even for one who commands but a few words, when a responsive person listens. Likewise, the production of alphabetic symbols—even one letter and one word at a time—can become powerful for the young child when computer microworlds provide a patient, responsive intelligence to interpret them.

Since speech is natural to man in all the various cultures of our world, it is reasonable to ask whether the most general and powerful elements in Peggy's experience with writing can be adapted for use in cultures other than the one to which she is native. If computer technology could make learning to read and write more like learning to speak and understand, it would be capable of changing profoundly the intellectual character of the world in which we all live.

The essential power available through the Logo computer language is that a word, any string of symbols, can be given a function. For example, the word 'SUN' can cause the execution of a computer procedure which produces a graphic image representing the sun. Because both the spelling of a word and the meaning given to it are assigned through writing a procedure, the words of computer microworlds are independent of the 'natural' language of the programmer. For example, the same procedure which creates the 'SUN' could be given the name 'SOLEIL' (French) or 'JANT'(Wolof). Although computer words may be language independent, anything made for use by people is culturally bound. Only people who share the same cultural experience scan know which objects and actions within a culture will be congenial to the children and will relate to the kind of homely experience which is close to their hearts and will continue to engage them in learning and loving learning.

The people who should determine what computer experiences are offered to children should be the children themselves, their parents or their teachers—or others who are close to the children and share their experiences—hopefully, sensitive, caring instructors with a progressive commitment to what is best for the children they love. Computers and their languages should be accessible to such people, easy for them to use as a casual, creative medium. If they are not so, the children of the world will not be properly served.

One lucky day, Peggy and I showed her BEACH microworld to two such men, Mamadou Niang and Moussa Gning. These gentlemen, Senegalese teachers who had come to the New York Logo Centre for an introduction to computers and the Logo programming language, were engaged by these microworlds I had made for my daughter. They told me that the Senegalese people are much concerned with the issue of literacy and hoped that computers could make learning the written word more congenial to the children of their nation. Their colleague and technical adviser, Mme Sylla Fatimata, later explained the importance computers could have to their children in this way.

The children of Senegal typically live in a personal, warm family setting until they are of school age. At home, they live and grow in the culture of their traditional languages, such as Wolof. At school age, they go off to a cold and impersonal place where all the language and all the lessons are French. Some children survive and thrive there, but many are terrified and refuse to learn. For them, learning in school means alienation from the people they love, and they reject that alienation even though they are encouraged to adopt it.

French is the dominant language through which the Senegalese deal with the exterior world. It is the language of opportunity within the government and commerce. Further, it is the language which has dominated the schools and continues to do so. The Senegalese intend to protect and advance their traditional languages by turning the tide of modern technology to their own use, specifically by developing literacy in Wolof among their children. Although Wolof has been written—in an extended Roman alphabet—for more than a hundred years, only during the last decade has the transcription of the language become standardized throughout the country. Consequently, and ironically, many learned people of their land, literate in French and even Arabic, are illiterate in their traditional language, the language they use in their homes and in conversation with their African colleagues at work.

Wanting to change this situation, the Senegalese believe they might better create programs for computer use in Wolof than in French or in the language of whoever makes the machines, and they have good reasons. Because there exists now no rigid 'curriculum' for computer education in French, and because they have not invested years in teacher training in French language computer instruction, they imagine correctly that this new technology has a revolutionary potential which can be used to support their traditional language and culture if they but seize the opportunity.

With others of the Senegal Microcomputer Project, Mamadou Niang and Moussa Gning came to extend their introduction to Logo in Paris—at the World Centre for Computation and Human Development. Because there is no better way to learn how to use a computer language than to use it for some significant purpose, I offered Mamadou this challenge, 'You imagine some such microworld for the children of Senegal, and I will help you make it; let's work together to make something your young students will love.' Mamadou noted that, of course, there are beaches in Senegal and the great city of Dakar, but that since an objective of their work was to appeal to all the children of Senegal, it would be more appropriate to think of images of the countryside. He proposed a village backdrop, with some small buildings and a well. To enliven such a scene, one would need people and the animals of the country life, perhaps a cat, horses, cows and so on. We agreed to make only a few objects, and thereby leave for the children the pleasure of creation; we would let them decide what they wanted in their world—and provide the tools for them to make it.

Since we come from cultures so much apart, it is appropriate to comment on our way of working together. We laboured to share ideas. Our working tongue, our *lingua franca*, was French; after all, in Paris *tout le monde parle français*. Mamadou and Moussa spoke French much better than I did. I was grateful that they would tolerate my poor French so that we could work together. The computer we used was an English language Logo computer. When they succeeded in helping me understand their objectives, I would propose and demonstrate programming capabilities and techniques to embody what Mamadou wanted in the microworld. In a kind of 'pidgin' language, French, English, computerese, they began to program with my guidance a little scene, some designs of objects to fit in that scene, and some computer procedures to control their appearance and actions.

When we had created a scene with a number of French language procedure names— when we had the conceptual objects of this world more or less under control—we began to discuss using Wolof. This is where Moussa played a most significant role. As the leading primary-grade pedagogue for Wolof instruction in Senegal, he was able with confidence to assign definitive spellings to the procedure names we used to create and manipulate the objects of our village microworld. (Sometimes this involved consultation with the others of the Senegalese delegation, including the linguist, Pathe Diagne.)

Because the Logo language permits any string of 'keyable' symbols to be the name of a procedure, we were able to convert French-named procedures such as 'SOLEIL' and 'MARCHE' to their Wolof equivalents, 'JANT' and 'DOXAL' (the 'X' is pronounced as in Spanish). Thus we arrived at the assembly of procedures and designs capable of producing the village microworld, 'XEW'. (The sound of the name 'XEW', meaning 'scene', begins with the Spanish 'X' and rhymes with the English 'HOW'.)

If the village microworld seems bare and crude, there is good reason. It was not made to impress programmers or civil servants. It is less a product than a project with a few examples of what is possible. This world is one to be created by the children of Senegal. Why should I tell them what they want? Why should even their teachers tell them what creatures and people to put in the worlds of their imaginations?

It was Mamadou who best expressed the right way of viewing the village microworld. When I said that the design of 'FAS' was incredible, looked ever so little like a horse, he replied 'I'm sure the children will make a better one. '

After their introduction to Logo — through the adaptation of ideas for their country—my colleagues have returned to Senegal to begin a pilot project with children in the experimental classes of the Ecole Normale Superieure. The first of the ideas that have been important in progress to this point was the adoption of Logo as their preferred computer language. Choosing Logo was important because Logo permits the definition of new computer procedures and because the language is both powerful and accessible. The second is the commitment to congeniality, to adapting ideas to maximize their applicability in terms of their own culture. This is the dimension where accessibility of the programming language to amateurs is important. Parents, teachers, and older children may know best what children will accept and understanding and extending studies now underway at the Ecole Normale Superieure in Dakar. It also depends on the availability of suitable computer equipment. Their brave experiment could be one of the most important in the world; it deserves watching and support.

COMPUTERS AND THE WORLD CULTURES (UNESCO proposal)[10]

Computer technology is bursting out of the industrially advanced nations and beginning to cover the entire globe. Japan, the United States, and European countries are entering now a major competition to make computers that will capture the world market in the coming decades. Will these computers serve the needs of people or will they undermine what we hold most dear? Thoughtful men, in the smaller countries of Europe as well as elsewhere, fear the computer revolution as a carrier of intellectual and cultural colonialism. If the world is more than a marketplace, we need to think deeply and act vigorously to advance the adaptation of intelligent technologies to forms which will be culturally congenial.

The richness of humanity is the diversity of its cultures, but now as never before the destructive power of modern technology requires we recognize we are many peoples of one world. Complementing the rich cultural diversity of our traditions, the growth of a common, scientific knowledge inspires the hope that we may achieve and share a secondary culture of ideas. Computers, which can help represent explicitly the best ideas of modern science, can aid in the diffusion of such powerful ideas to create a popular, secondary, scientific culture.

Central Representations for a Popular Scientific Culture

The central representations of modern science are 'ways of looking at the world.' They are equally useful to children and adults. Simplified computer models of the everyday world, computer microworlds, can help people understand and learn; they provide a toy to tinker with, from which to learn a scientific view of 'what's what' and 'how it all fits together.' More advanced computer facilities provide tools for more advanced work. Computer microworlds are popular in a specific sense: they do not train anybody to do any job, even though playing with them provides a sufficient orientation for a more purposeful training to follow. In this specific sense, they are suitable for the introduction of inexperienced people to the possibilities of modern technology.

Here follow succinct descriptions of important ideas which, embodied in computer microworlds, could comprise a basic 'curriculum' for the age of intelligent machines. This is a curriculum without schools, without credentials, in which the most important element is the communication of powerful ideas. Experience of computer based microworlds could supplement the schooling many children now receive and could

10. 1983. Unpublished. The text was prepared to create and win a position as director of education and computing at UNESCO. Once my appointment was approved by the American Embassy to UNESCO and by Director General M'Bow, I accepted the offer. Immediately thereafter, the decision was made by the US administration to withdraw from UNESCO. The offer to me was withdrawn; the position was given to a Russian interested in using expert systems in education.

compensate a little for those of any age who have not had the opportunity to learn as much as they would have liked.

Computers permit general and powerful ideas to be made clear through concrete examples. Computers will be especially useful in the following areas:

- Language
- Space
- Mathematics
- Process and Result
- Physics
- Logic

Language:
Computer languages use words or other sequences of written/typed symbols to stand for actions they can perform. The essential novelty computers introduce for literacy is creating a new function for single words and simple phrases; that is, controlling the computer itself. This new utility for simple, keyed phrases provides a new path for learning words, their meanings, and the rules of correspondence between spoken sounds and written words. It is very important that the computer used permits people to define new procedures of their own and to give them names that are meaningful to them; it is also important that the symbols used for individual keys can be changed to suit various language requirements.

Space:
Cartesian space descriptions are fundamental to much modern mathematics. Such space descriptions can be introduced through computer-based activities which use them without mathematical complexities. Body-centred geometries describe objects and designs in space by listing the actions followed in tracing the outlines. Such geometries are easier for people to understand than Cartesian descriptions of space; they can be introduced even to very young children and unschooled adults because the actions are similar to people's movements, and outlines are like the path a person follows moving from one place to another.

Mathematics:
Variables are names associated with changeable values. Understanding how the behaviour of processes change as values vary is a central part of computer experience. Once the idea of a variable has been introduced, mathematical functions can be seen as a special class of processes, that is, those which create 'output values' for each set of input values. This idea reduces the mystery of large areas of mathematics.

Process and Result:
Computers make possible the construction of little worlds of experience which are capable of being completely described. A description which names every element of a system and which specifies how every transformation of a system affects the values of the elements is called a formal state description. To know that such descriptions are possible and to have clear examples of them is very important because the achievement

of such descriptions is a primary goal of scientific theory. Emergent phenomena are those which appear from the interactions of the various elements of a system without any specific direction that they do so. Repetitive procedures which draw designs provide clear examples of emergent phenomena. Creating and analyzing emergent phenomena provides a powerful model for understanding any sort of complex process.

Physics:

Computer-based microworlds are 'ideal' worlds. Objects move without friction, for example. Thus computer microworlds can sometimes better represent the general and powerful ideal laws of science than can everyday experiences. Contrasting the formal description of a static object with that of a dynamic object presents in clearest possible form the central idea of Newtonian physics: force is a velocity changer. The capability of creating multiple and various models of the same domain of phenomena can bring thought experiments, so powerful in the development of physics knowledge, within the reach of a much broader spectrum of people than has ever been possible before.

Logic:

To the extent that logic is one way of representing the states, relations, and transformations of things and processes, in a practical sense logic is a subset of the study of representations; this study is the central theme of the discipline which has become known as artificial intelligence. Introduction to the ideas and computer languages of artificial intelligence will play an increasingly central role in tomorrow's world of ubiquitous computation. Representing objects or organizations as named lists of properties permits the development of procedures to perform the fundamental operations of hierarchical classification. Since sets can be represented as lists without ordering, the logic of set theory can be explored by writing procedures for the manipulation of 'dis-ordered' lists. Although not a domain of traditional logic, constructing and contrasting unstructured and hierarchically structured systems of procedures develops what will surely be essential logical skills in the future.

Computing

WHAT'S A POWERFUL IDEA? [1]

Everybody knows what a grapefruit is and how to cut one in half. When you cut a grapefruit 'properly,' perpendicularly to the core, the cut face shows a pattern like a wheel. A little energy and perseverance are all you need to dig out and enjoy the juicy meat from between the spokes. But there must have been a time when you didn't know which way to cut a grapefruit. Did you find out how the hard way? What happens if you divide the grapefruit the other way, along the core? It is nearly impossible to eat the still buried meat, for the tough skin of the sections is an intact obstacle. The grapefruit looks pretty much uniform on the outside of its skin, but when you look inside you can see there is a very specific and important organization that you must understand if you want to get at the meat.

This very simple, very concrete situation provides a useful way to look at many other very troublesome problems. It points up the issue that how you analyze a problem, whether your analysis goes 'with the grain' or 'against the grain,' can make a world of difference in how hard the problem is to solve. The intrinsic character that gives such an example power in thought is its simplicity, in the sense that given the perspective of the idea (embodied in the concrete example), the primary conclusions that can be drawn are obvious without long chains of arguments. Such ideas are elegant in the mathematician's sense. The extrinsic root of power is the example's fruitfulness, how well it can serve in helping you understand other problem situations by analogy.

The more powerful ideas you have the better. If you have only one way of looking at a situation, you are a prisoner of a limited point of view. If you can interpret a situation in terms of several possible models or representations, you can compare the fit of each to judge which is the most appropriate. As a situation changes, some alternative model may come to fit the situation better than the one originally best. Could it be that the flexibility of mind we ascribe to 'smart' people derives directly from their having a well developed stock of such powerful ideas?

The computer-based microworlds described in the following notes present different representations embedded in activities that some children will enjoy. From playing with such microworlds, those children will better understand 'what's what' later, whether they face problems in a more formal environment or solve problems of their own posing.

---

1. 1981. Published in MIT *AI Memo* 652 & *Logo Memo* 60, 'Some Powerful Ideas'
   1982, April. Published as a series 'Logo Ideas,' *Creative Computing*

MICROWORLDS AND LEARNING[2]

The central problem of humane education is how to instruct while respecting the self-constructive character of mind. Teachers face a dilemma in motivating children to do schoolwork that is not intrinsically interesting. Either the child must be induced to undertake the work by promise of some reward or he must be compelled to do the work under threat of punishment. In neither case does the child focus his attention on the material to be learned. The problems are someone else's problems. The work is seen as a bad thing because it is either an obstacle blocking the way to a reward or a cause of the threatened punishment.

Psychologists know that – however much insights do occur – learning is often a gradual process, one of familiarization, of stumbling into puzzles and resolving them by proposing simple hypotheses in which a new problem is seen as like others already understood and performing experiments to test the latest 'theory.'

Computer-based microworlds can be seen as sets of programs designed to provide virtual, streamlined experiences, play-worlds with agents and processes one can get to know and understand. Properly designed microworlds embody a lucid representation of the major objects and relations of some domain of experience as understood by experts in the area. This is where the knowledge of the culture is made available, in the very terms in which the microworld is defined.

Children can absorb that knowledge because the microworld is focused not on problems to be done, but on 'neat phenomena' - these show the power made available by knowledge about the domain. If there are neat phenomena, then the challenge to the knowledgeable expert is to formulate so crisp a presentation of the elements of the domain that even a child can grasp its essence. The value of the computer is in building the simplest model which an expert can imagine as an acceptable entry point to his own richer knowledge.

If there are no neat phenomena that a child can appreciate, he can make no use of knowledge of the domain. He should not be expected to learn about it until he is personally engaged with other tasks which will make the specific knowledge worth learning as an aid in achieving some other personal objective.

---

2. 1981. Published in MIT *AI Memo* 652 & *Logo Memo* 60, 'Some Powerful Ideas'
    1982, April. Published as a series 'Logo Ideas', *Creative Computing*

RESOLVING PROBLEMS[3]

Some problems you want to put behind you — like having to do what you don't want to do, and not being able to do what you do want. Such problems should be resolved. Other kinds of problems have a friendlier face, and certain of them are worth solving and re-solving. Think about making a circle. Doing so is a classic Logo problem for beginners. Novice learners are typically asked to 'do-it-yourself', to walk through the problem by simulating the turtle. Their typical explanation of what they are doing as they walk In a circle is that they go forward a little and turn a little and do it again. This explanation translates directly into the Logo circle:

    TO CIRCLE
    FORWARD 1 RIGHT 1
    CIRCLE
    END

The Logo circle is very easy to make with a Logo capable computer, but it would be difficult to make such a circle by drawing on a piece of paper. The Logo circle is very perimeter-focused because the turtle knows nothing at all about 'centres'. (This leads to interesting bugs and problems in turtle geometry procedures.) The Logo circle is natural in the sense that it is no more than the path of an activity as familiar as walking.

In plane geometry if you ask, 'What's a circle?' the object, 'the locus of all points in a plane equidistant from another point', is easy to construct with a compass, and not even hard to construct without one. The Euclidean circle is as 'natural' as the Logo circle in the following sense: imagine a person sitting; the figure traced by the farthest reach of his arms is as circular as the path followed by any person imitating the Logo turtle. The Euclidean circle is centre-focused, and the circle is the boundary of the centre's territory. Can you get a computer to draw a Euclidean circle? There are several ways. If your computer speaks 'polar', you can specify the definition of a circle with the simplest of equations, radius = constant. Descriptions of circles in polar coordinates are simple, but they get complicated quickly if located away from the coordinate system origin.

While the description of a circle in polar coordinates still keeps in mind the relation of the circle to its centre, and to a process a person could use unaided to make a circle, the description of a circle in a system of Cartesian coordinates becomes remote from the process of generating a circle:

    X2 + Y2 = C2

This algebraic equation for an origin centred circle (of radius 'C') specifies that the circle is the set of all point pairs (X,Y) in a Cartesian coordinates system which satisfies the equation. The primary relationship between the circle and 'something else' is here between the circle and the Cartesian reference frame. This contrasts with the Logo circle (where the primary relation was between the circle and its process of creation) and the Euclidean circle (where the primary relation was between the circle and its centre). The

---

3. 1981. Published in MIT *AI Memo* 652 & *Logo Memo* 60, 'Some Powerful Ideas'
    1982, April. Published as a series 'Logo Ideas,' *Creative Computing*

Cartesian description of the circle and other curved lines, although central to the development of modern mathematics and science, seems relatively un-natural as compared to the Logo and Euclidean circles, because of the extent to which the person is removed from the description of the circle.

Summary

Scientists have recommended re-solving problems through the ages. Descartes recommends that whenever you encounter a new idea, you bring it into comparison with all the other ideas you hold as valuable and try to appreciate their interrelations. Feynman, a famous physicist of our time, relates that his practice as a student was typically one of solving a problem whatever way he could, then, with a worked out solution to guide him, to re-solve that same problem in as many different other formalisms or frames of reference as he could. As you use Logo, you might think about how you might try to achieve your projects using other geometries as well.

ZOOM [4]

ZOOM is a Logo language program written to introduce novices to both turtle geometry and the experience of programming. It is a Logo language and turtle geometry interface whose purpose is to provide a rich experience of the domain (turtle geometry) while permitting a gradual development of programming knowledge.

By a rich experience of the geometry I mean one where each action has an immediate result, usually perceptible immediately (pen-up and pen-down are not so); where experiment is very easy and mistakes are not forbidding. Within ZOOM, keyed entries are single characters, (the exceptions are program names and operand values). The capabilities of ZOOM are two: basic operation of the turtle (forward, right turn etc.) and program generation from a list of previously executed operations. Programming knowledge will develop in four phases.

Introductory Phase

There are two simple steps. First is use of the letter C to clear the display. This is a command to the computer and not an erasure-like action ascribed to the turtle. The second step is introducing the four operations of the geometry: forward, back, right turn, and left turn. No operands are used for the four operations. The turtle zooms ahead or back a fixed distance; he turns right or left through a fixed rotation. These operations, executed in whatever orders the novice chooses, will give him a rudimentary feeling for the primitives. The clearing operation makes any mistake correctable by re-executing the preceding operations. The conclusion of this phase is with familiarity of the four operations and the clearing command to the computer.

Remembering Things Phase

The first class of items the novice instructs the turtle to remember are the operations penup and pendown, viewed as remembering to keep the pen up and remembering to keep the pen down. The second class of items for the turtle to remember are resettings of the default operands for the geometry operations. Specifically, the character T produces a statement that the turtle turns so many degrees and a request for a new value for the operand. The character Z produces a statement that the turtle zooms so far and a request for a new value. The purpose served here is the introduction of an intermediate unit (of variable size) with a perceptible value. In contrasting this unit, which can be perceived by and is thus meaningful to the novice, with the degrees and turtle steps, the latter units, of no apparent meaning, can be rendered meaningful and the numbers required as operands for the basic operations can be explained as required by the turtle's different sense of 'how much of a thing' matters.

---

4.   1976 Unpublished. Subsumed in Chapter 2 of *C&C* (1986).

Remembering How to Phase

Programming, within ZOOM means 'the turtle's learning a name to call all the things he has done since the last clearing command'. Programs are useful to the turtle (and the novice) so that he can remember what he has done and do it again any time the novice wants him to. Once someone has pushed the keys 48 times to make a 24 sided 'circle ', he will want to save himself that trouble in the future. Fascination with the ability to create a figure by giving a name, as contrasted with additions of keying, leads to proliferation of that figure and directly to super-proceduralization.

Reflective/Analytical Phase

Once a session with ZOOM has ended, an examination of the programs generated will show the following:

1. the relative simplicity of super-procedures (the ROSE made from the CIRCLE will have many fewer statements than the procedure for the CIRCLE).
2. the repetitive operations generated by key-pushing can be simply reformulated in two ways:

a. if a box has been made 60 units on a side by a sequence of 6 FD 10 operations, the meaning of FD 60 can be rendered very clear. The justification is that it's easier. One may think of this editing procedure as correcting the mistakes of another (the ZOOM program) or as a kind of definition of what a programming operation is: doing or repeating some small unit of action until you've done it as much as you want to. This is condensing a string of identical operations through summing the operand values.

b. the generalization is from condensing a string of identical operations to condensing couples of operations, e.g. FD 10, RT 15, as units of programming. It is through this generalization that the power of subproceduralization is revealed.

When the novice has progressed this far, he is no longer a novice but a neophyte and well on his way to becoming a computer cuckoo. He can explore turtle geometry with a triple foundation to his understanding:

1. the distinction between operations and operands.
2. a translation from units meaningful to him to units meaningful to the turtle.
3. an understanding developed through concrete experience of the power of hierarchical proceduralization.

ZOOMing with Robby [5]

After I had written the preceding text, my son Bobby, aged six years four months, spent four days with me at Logo. The Children' s Learning Lab served as a home base whence we made excursions in the Boston area. Bobby spent a half day or more at Logo each day and during those times played with whatever available toys his will directed him to: sometimes the tinker-toys or the multi-way rollaway, sometimes drawing with crayon on the back of abandoned terminal printouts and, of course, with the Logo computer system.

---

5.   1976 Unpublished. Subsumed in Chapter 2 of *C&C* (1986).

The examples at the end of this paper show some of my preconceptions of how one might get into explaining the ideas of the preceding text. And we did step through that exercise eventually (Bobby was that generous with me), but not until several days had passed . . . for Bobby had his own ideas .

When we first entered the Learning Lab, late of a Sunday afternoon, Bobby saw Henry Minsky, a Logo person about twice Bobby's age, executing his Lunar Lander programs. The visually striking aspects of the program execution are the drawing of a moonscape (with cliffs, a building, a canyon, etc.) and the use of the display turtle to represent the landing vehicle. Bobby decided he wanted to make one of those.

After logging in, I explained that we could run a program I knew, called ZOOM, that would make it easy for him to draw pictures; that the way to run the program was to tell the computer the program's name, and that we spoke of this as 'invoking' a program. (Here I was trying to give Bobby the conventional name for the new procedure he was learning so that he could refer to the procedure and talk about it. Bobby typed in ZOOM and carriage return).

When we printed out the instructions, he said I would have to read them to him (a half page printout is imposing to someone who is working on reading one sentence at a time), but he didn't listen when I read them. We kept the list by the terminal for later reference. Forward (F [FD 20]) and right (R [RT 9O]) and clearscreen (C [CS]) is where we started. But there was a problem right away; Bobby's plan called for starting at the upper left edge of the display with a clear screen. The turtle started at the centre of the screen and drew a line whenever he was moved. This is where the fundamental difference in our objectives became clear to me, Bobby wanted to solve that particular problem; I wanted him to develop a way of thinking about Logo operations and programming. It is in trying to bridge this gap that anthropomorphization is so useful. One can think of learning the Logo operations and their programming as like learning what kind of creature the turtle is. This is useful because what the child knows about himself can be points of connection about which questions can be raised. For example, in solving Bobby's problem, after looking at the pen mechanism on the floor turtle and explaining how it could be up or down and explaining how you can tell the turtle where it should be, I was able to raise the issue of whether the turtle would forget to keep his pen up if he got busy doing the other things we wanted him to do. Bobby and I forget, but the turtle doesn't; he remembers very well. The process this example represents is this: a frustrated objective becomes a particular problem; solving that particular problem involves looking at the mechanism of the system; the language in which you discuss the particular problem, to the extent it makes contact with what the child knows, permits his formulating the solution (and reformulating the particular problem) within a developing framework that has systematic properties, e.g. turtles remember very well what you tell them, . . . even if people don't.

When Bobby got the display turtle to the edge of the screen, he began to draw quite happily. He made a cliff, a landing site, a building . . . and developed a problem: the width of his building (20) was the smallest unit of distance he could command the turtle to move so he was unable to make any windows. (Henry's building had windows.) He let the problem slip by and went on to draw another cliff going down into a canyon. His dissatisfaction became very clear. He wanted to make some tiny rocks at the bottom of the canyon and asked me how to do it. I warned him that it would be a very long explanation and asked if he really wanted to know. He did.

I was pleased, for one of my subordinate objectives was raising the issue of the units of things and how they relate to number. He played turtle. 'Forward', I said. Bobby took a step Forward; another step. 'Forward', I said, 'Two steps.' 'Do you have to tell the turtle how many steps to take?' We went to a different terminal, not using ZOOM, but connected to the floor turtle . I keyed [FD l] and the turtle twitched. 'Did he move?' 'Yes, Dad, but he didn't go anywhere.' [FD 100] I next keyed in. Bobby came back and took a look at the terminal printout. He said that 100 steps didn't take the turtle very far. The conclusion was clear that turtle-steps were tiny. I introduced that specific name at that time. Back at the display running under Zoom, a single character [F] left a 20 unit line. I admitted that and I told the turtle to remember to go 20 turtle-steps every time we said forward. 'How far can you go in 20 steps, Bobby?' Bobby paced off twenty steps and from the hallway noted that turtle steps are tiny. At this point I told Bobby the program was called Zoom because when you say [F], the speedy display turtle zooms forward however many turtle-steps you told him to remember.

We went back to zooming, and I showed Bobby how to change the number of turtle steps the turtle should zoom. After making a few rocks, Bobby went over to look at Henry's moonscape and came back puzzled. He wanted to make a 'slope-y' line but the turtle always made Square corners. How can you explain to a child what 90 degrees means? Bobby had seen the display turtle turn through 90 degrees when he commanded a single right [R]. Playing turtle, he and I made 90 degree turns . I said when I turn, right or left, that's how much of a turn that matters to me. How much of a turn matters to a turtle is different. Much as the turtle makes tiny turtle steps too small for us to see, he makes little turns, called degrees, much smaller than our turns. When we want the turtle to turn, we have to tell him how many little turns we want him to make. The number 90 meant very little to Bobby. He could say the name but he had no idea what to make of it. He asked what was a good number to use for making slope-y lines. I told him 15, which he remembers well. Knowing that 90 degrees make square corners and 15 degrees make good slopes, he is bound to ask himself about the numbers in between. I was more lucky than well organized in finding the question of units arising first in the linear rather than in the rotational dimension. I was lucky because it seems easy to connect the idea of tiny turtle-steps to a child's experience. Inducing the idea of a small turn might be harder for a child. But, having done the first, the extension of the explanation to the rotational case was easy.

The next problem we encountered was a big one. Bobby started making his slope-y line and got carried away with it; the line carried the drawing to the far edge of the screen in an uninteresting way. He wanted to get rid of the part of the line he didn't like. The display system doesn't let you do that. 'Oh Brother!' Bobby cleared the screen and replicated his earlier work to his own satisfaction. I stopped and asked, 'Suppose you make another line you want to get rid of?' Bobby maintained he would be exceptionally careful. I told him I knew a good trick we could use so he wouldn't have to be so careful - making a program. 'What's a program?' It's telling the turtle how to do something (that's the programmer's view of it) . We had made the turtle remember things: to keep his pen up; how many turtle-steps and degrees he should zoom or turn. A program is remembering how to do something. (That's the turtle's view of it) . How do you make a program in zoom? You key the letter 'P' . Bobby did that. The turtle asked the cryptic question ' Program how to what?' Bobby read the question but was puzzled. I explained that when the turtle remembered how to do things, he needed to know what name you gave to doing that - so you could tell him later when you wanted him to do it. Bobby declared his work was named 'big building' and asked how to spell it. ''b-i-g-b-u-i-l-d-i-n-g'. He asked if we could call it something else. I answered that if he could remember what he called it, the turtle could remember too, so any name was good. 'BB' was chosen. The program was created and the turtle claimed he would remember how to 'BB'.

The next step (and the immediate one for which the program generation was a preparation) was a tricky one . Tricky, because it depended on Bobby's trust in what I told him would happen and because his work, the display drawing on which he spent the past hour and a half, was at risk. I told him to clear the screen. He did it. 'Do you think the turtle will remember how to draw your big building?'

We returned to the new word in his vocabulary, invoke. I explained that if you tell the turtle the name of a program, he will execute it. Bobby invoked 'BB' . He was surprised and utterly delighted when it worked. From this point on, his work was considerably less at risk. He could make a checkpoint anywhere and continue from there with only the newly keyed commands needing re-entry if he changed his mind about his intentions. Bobby continued from that point to create a moonscape of which he's very proud.

There were other developments over the next few days . Dissatisfied that his building had no windows, Bobby decided to make a separate building and put windows in it . His separation of the entities 'window' and 'building' seemed a good opportunity to introduce the idea of subproceduralization. I suggested he draw a window first, then he could tell how big he should make the building. He followed that direction and we worked together on getting the windows into the building. Bobby has had an experience of using subproceduralization, but I do not believe he has seen the power of the idea. (One direct reason is that the cumbersomeness of commanding the turtle to move to the locus for the window overwhelmed the sense of simplicity in creating a window with a name.

We played with the floor turtle several times, and Bobby decided to draw a building there. Well and good. We spent some time figuring out the change of scale, what would be the best number of steps for the floor turtle. When Bobby was all set, I asked him where the building was going to go. For the first time in my life, I saw him construct beforehand a very specific plan. By specific, I mean detailed to the point of writing down on the paper: 'floor here' three times with arrows pointing to the target location; 'roof' three times at the far edge of the paper; a line of arrows showing where he wanted one of the walls; and an 'S' to mark the beginning point for the building. Having discovered how to make a building in the Logo language on the display system lead him to planning in a domain superficially different but with the same operations. We might consider further exploiting the functional isomorphism of the floor and display turtles.

The final development was my attempting to wean Robby from using zoom (its intended use is purely introductory) . With the previous discussion of 'how much of a thing matters' to the turtle, I tried to explain the operation/operand structure of commands. 'We also spent time examining programs Bobby had caused zoom to generate. I tried to relate for him how [FD 20 FD 20 FD 20] is the same as [FD 60] ' . . . and use this to explain what addition is. (Bobby can add some of the low numbers [and two digit numbers ending in zero]). I believe he understood.

Conducted in two or three long sessions and a few short ones this experience with zoom was a productive mini-course for both my son and I.

CONCRETE ACTION IN A NON-SQUARE WORLD[6]

Two of Robby's current interests have come together in a productive way. Following my buying him a new tool box, he elected to take up wood working in an after school program. His delight in building ship models led him to declare he was going to build a 9 foot long wooden aircraft carrier. I voiced absolute objection but, content to let the fantasy grow, said he could plan the ship and scale down the model later to some reasonable size. Later he asked advice:

Robby: Dad, how much is 9 feet take away four?
Bob: 5 feet.
Robby: No, I mean take away 4 inches.
Bob: Come here and I'll show you.

Robby came to my desk and worked out this exercise:

9'	—>	8' 12"
-4"	—>	-0' 4"
??	—>	8' 8"

This dimension, 8' 8", is for the sub-structure of the carrier. The 9' flight deck will overhang 2 inches at each end.

In response to this and other expressions of the need to draw plans, I introduced Robby to orthographic projection (front, side, and top views). Thus, when last week I entrained him in my task of building a run for our dog (of 2 x 3's and hardware cloth), it seemed appropriate to ask him to draw plans. This was even more the case because I had formerly asked Robby to compute dimensions on the sizing drawing to determine how long should be the 2 by 3's we needed to make the frame. We were to enclose the two ends of an area 11' 3" wide. Because I knew the available lengths of 2 X 3's are 12', 14', and 16', I set up the three sums underneath the drawing and had Robby compute the board residues we would have after cutting out our lengths. We selected the 14' length as what we wanted because each board would yield a length and an end piece (we did not expect to need a 5' high fence for our Scotch terrier).

In the process of explaining that sizing drawing and my objective for the project to Robby, I drew on the reverse of the 3 x 5 card with drawing A, the drawing B (see Figure: Four Drawings). The purpose was to locate our additional fence in a picture Robby would recognize (the fence behind the back of the house we lived in). As I gathered my tools and set up saw horses for working on, Robby drew his 'plan', drawing C. Contrasting drawing C with drawing B, you will notice it has vertical lacing similar to my earlier drawing (the hardware cloth, with its square mesh, was rolled up beside where Robby was sat drawing his plan), and his drawing is more detailed in showing

6. 1977, Unpublished. Subsumed in Chapter 3 of *C&C* (1986).

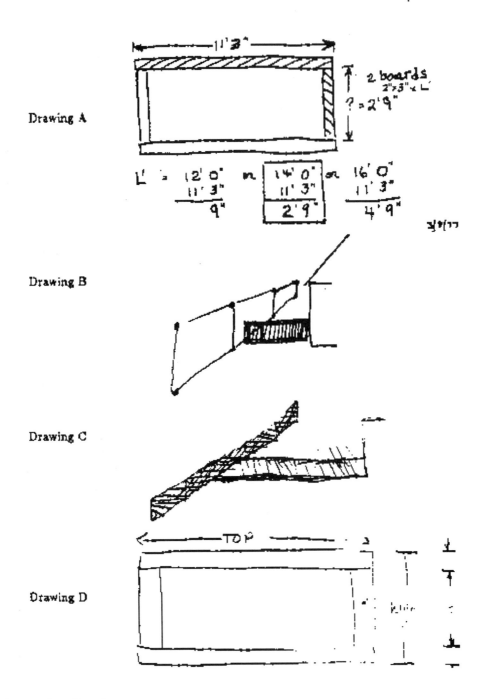

Figure: Four Drawings

the diagonal mesh of the chain link fence. Robby's drawing placed our planned construct in its setting, its context, but was useless for keeping track of the various dimensions one might want to use in calculations. I showed Robby, in drawing D, the kind of plan I had in mind and tried to indicate its purpose. I was surprised that his new idea of a planning drawing leaned so to verisimilitude.

Since Robby did not seem interested in my abstract drawing, we proceeded to the morning's rough carpentry. If you can't compute precisely the sizes of the parts you need, you can fall back on the handy-man's technique of transferring dimensions, i.e. you lay a board next to the place it is to go and mark off the size it need be to fit. We proceeded in this simple, traditional way.

Transferring dimensions is frequently the procedure of choice in the repertoire of both the craftsman and the handy-man; one reason is that the rustic carpenter is thus less vulnerable to the failings of his calculation skills; a second is that few things in this world, either natural or manufactured, are square; a third reason, decidedly relevant in this case of force fitting a wooden frame between a chain link fence and a masonry wall, is that you must sometimes worry about how your new manufacture relates to other things it is used with. Thus one lesson Robby could find in this project is that if you can't make an abstract plan, the concrete constraints may be enough, may even be your best bet, to finish the work at hand. Similarly in calculations, if you don't remember or can't understand some perfect algorithm, your commonsense knowledge helps you muddle through and may even be adequate to your needs. Though on the surface this may seem a negative lesson, it may be among the most important notions he can come to appreciate. Indeed, if particular solutions to problems are messy and inelegant, general solutions to really hard problems are usually impossible. As the characterization of his learning shows, such a conclusion is quite congenial to Robby's own problem-solving practice.[7]

---

7. See 'The Character of Natural Learning', p. 51 ff in *C&C*.

EXTENDING A POWERFUL IDEA[8]

The Argument

Mathematics is much more than the manipulation of numbers. At its best, it involves simple, clear examples of thought so apt to the world we live in that those examples provide guidance for our thinking about problems we meet subsequently. We call such examples, capable of heuristic use, POWERFUL IDEAS. This chapter documents a child's introduction to a specific powerful idea in a computer environment. We trace his extensions of that idea to other problem areas, one similar to his initial experience and one more remote. [9]

Introduction

The new availability of computer power to children in schools poses forcefully the question of the computer's role in education. Here we present a case study of computer-based learning that goes beyond drill-and-practice and game playing to show how particular experiences carried a specific idea of general applicability into a child's mind and how this idea was effective subsequently in his freely-chosen and self-directed problem solving. The stepping of variables — by which we mean the development of and the decision to apply a systematic mental procedure for isolating and incrementally changing one of several variables — is an idea of general applicability. Genevan psychologists have noted this idea as a very important one in that configuration which leads to the systematic thought of the adolescent (Inhelder and Piaget, 1958). The stepping of variables is the idea whose history we will trace in one child's mind.

The subject of this case was Robby, my son, just turning eight years old at the time of the study. With his sister, Miriam, two years younger, he participated in an intensive six-month study at the Logo project of the MIT Artificial Intelligence Laboratory (see *OCL* and *CECD*.). Robby had visited the lab many times in the preceding years and had frequently participated in earlier studies. He brought to this work two mental predispositions which are relevant to what follows. First, he was inclined to call upon symmetry as a generative idea (this observation will be clarified subsequently). Secondly, his approach to problems was surprisingly systematic for one his age. [10] Such

---

8. An earlier version of this chapter appeared in 'The Journal of Mathematical Behaviour', Volume 3, No. 2 (1982, Summer).

9. Acknowledgement: A discussion of this material with Gary Drescher helped to clarify some issues touched upon in this chapter.

10. (2) For example, at age 7;8;8 on Piaget's 'bead families' task (Piaget and Inhelder, 1975), after attempting to arrange combinations of five things taken two at a time by an empirical procedure, Robby spontaneously started the task a second time, grouping his bead couples in five groups by the colour of one bead and joining with each base-colour bead another one of a different colour.

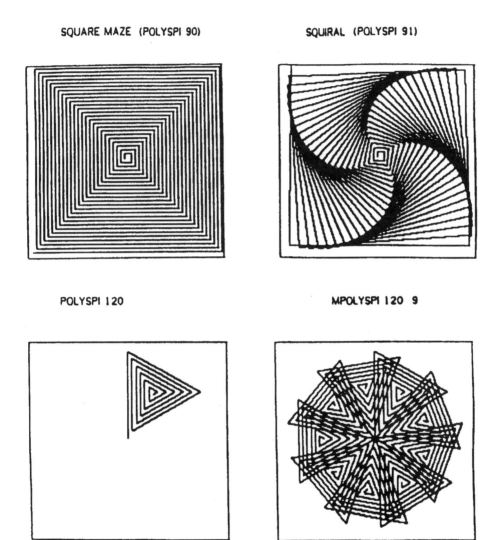

Figure 1. Basic Mazes and Squirals

systematicity is not usually met until the age of ten or twelve years. Before we turn to the case material wherein systematicity plays its role, we must first present some folk-history on the procedures Robby encountered.

Polyspirals and Variables

Imagine that one day a child invented the 'squiral' while trying to draw a square maze. The Logo turtle moves forward, turns a right angle, then repeats these actions, increasing the distance of the forward move with each repetition. In getting the angle 'wrong' while attempting a square maze, the child discovered that if the turtle turns through an angle near but not equal to 90 degrees a four-armed spiral emerges from the drawn shape (see Figure 1).

Emergent effects such as this appear regularly in turtle geometry, and are very striking. The nature of the Logo language and the spirit in which students use Logo make it easy and natural for students to change programs in various ways. The 'square maze' and 'squiral' programs were modified, by students, to produce the 'polyspi' (short for polygonal spiral). The actual Logo program that produces these figures is as follows:[11]

```
TO POLYSPI
FORWARD :distance
RIGHT :angle
MAKE 'distance (:distance + :delta)
POLYSPI
END
```

The general meaning of these Logo commands can be inferred from the example. Details are not important for the purposes of the present chapter, except to note that 'distance, 'angle, and 'delta are variables, and must be initialized. This means that the computer must somehow be told what number to associate with the named variables 'distance, 'angle, and 'delta.

The fifth line in the POLYSPI listing is of special importance. The procedure POLYSPI calls on itself! A feature of the Logo language makes this possible. Notice, however, that before calling on itself, the procedure has changed the value of one of the variables; this is done in the line:

```
MAKE 'distance (:distance + :delta)
```

Consequently, the result of POLYSPI calling itself is to execute the procedure another time with the value of the distance variable incremented; the procedure stops when the turtle goes off the edge of the display screen. A number of the designs produced by the POLYSPI procedure from the near- regular polygonal angles are very pretty. The emergent effect of such designs can be compounded, as by a procedure I composed, MPOLYSPI (short for multiple polyspi), to make even more complex and attractive designs (see the triangular POLYSPI and its nine-fold compounding in Figure 1B).

---

11. We signify references to variables by preceding them with quotes; executed procedures are referenced in capitals, and definitions of terms are enclosed in double quotes. ':' is an operator in Logo which means 'give me the current value stored for this variable name'.

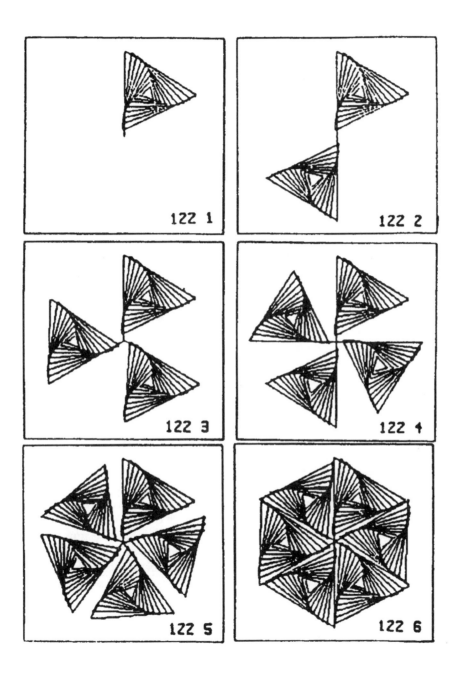

Figure 2. Multiple Polyspirals: a Shape Family

Emergent effects in turtle geometry cover a range which permits mutual engagement and learning by both children and adults — and thus they became a topic of exploration in many of the research sessions Robby and I spent at the Logo lab.

Robby's introduction to variables went forward in several small steps. Initially we played games with a set of labelled match-boxes and card- written commands for changing or examining the contents of the boxes. We presented the image that global variables were functionally like little boxes with contents that one could examine and change by commands of the Logo language. Consequently, Robby's first use of polyspi procedure involved a 'set- up' procedure whose functions were to clear the display screen of the previous design and to permit his keying of initial values for 'distance, 'angle, and 'delta. Subsequently, we explained 'input variables' as a keying convenience which permit an integrated set-up procedure. The form of the 'polyspi with input variables' is this:

```
TO POLYSPI :distance :angle :delta
FORWARD :distance
RIGHT :angle
POLYSPI (:distance + :delta) :angle :delta
END
```
(Here the incrementing of distance is implicit in the polyspi self-invocation.)

Ideas and Families of Shapes

A primary intellectual challenge in exploring polyspi designs is how to impose some comprehensible order on their considerable variety. Notice, now, that the polyspi procedure with a zero value for delta will draw polygons. For such polygons drawn with angle values dividing evenly into 360, the polygons are regular and closed; after turning through 360 degrees, the turtle retraces its original path. In second grade, Robby had learned the names of some geometric figures and the number of their sides. For example, he knew that a regular hexagon has six sides. When the input angle is that of some closed polygon, e.g. 60, the polyspi procedure with small positive values for delta draws figures we called 'mazes'. We distinguished between such mazes and other shapes. Robby and I together produced a 'family of mazes', i.e. a collection of the regular polygonal spirals with three through eight sides. We printed these designs and displayed them on the wall. My intention was that individual members of this series of figures could serve as 'anchors' for further exploration, both connecting to Robby's previous knowledge of geometric forms and serving as reference bases from which other shapes could be seen as variations.

Figure 3. A Hexagon Based Shape Family.

A Didactic Introduction to Shape Families

In the next Logo session on this theme I presented explicitly the objective of developing 'families of shapes' and showed Robby several examples of such shape families. The first, reproduced in Figure 2, shows six shapes made by incremental change of the MPOLYSPI 122 'folding factor' from one to six. Thus the single sub-figure, a POLYSPI 122, is repeated an additional time in each of the five successive designs. Similarly, a second example of a shape family (not shown) displayed changes in the six-fold MPOLYSPI 122 as the value of delta was reduced from seven to one. The 'lesson' I professed with these examples was that focussing on the systematic changes of a single variable was a fecund method for understanding the results from the complex interaction of several variables. Whether or not Robby accepted my 'lesson' or used what I showed him in another way is an issue we will discuss subsequently.

The Child Exploring the Space

Robby had the opportunity to construct his own shape family. (I had been careful to leave him the most interesting variable for his changing.) I proposed building a shape family around one of the mazes as an anchoring value. Robby selected the hexagonal anchor and enthusiastically created and printed the designs of Figure 3, then hung them in order above his desk. In subsequent sessions, he constructed a shape family anchored at ninety degrees, first increasing the angle value and later (beginning at eighty-five degrees) approaching the anchor from below. This concluded the didactic phase of Robby's introduction to shape families.

A Polyspiral Variation

The increment input to the POLYSPI procedure (the variable called delta) is applied to the first of the two other variables, 'distance and 'angle. What happens if delta is applied to augment angle instead of distance? Few people have any intuitive answer for such a question and most become easily confused in trying to imagine what design would be created. With small values of delta (and with an initial angle of zero), the turtle will move off in one direction and gradually spiral into a node. (For this reason, the procedure was named 'inspi' by its originator, Marvin Minsky):

```
TO INSPI :distance :angle :delta
FORWARD :distance
RIGHT :angle
INSPI :distance (:angle + :delta) :delta
END
```

(See several examples of basic Inspi designs in Figure 4.)

The Subject's Initial Inclination

When he was first introduced to inspi designs, Robby's inclination was to vary 'angle. After trying INSPI (10 0 2) at my direction, he executed INSPI (10 90 2). (The effect of

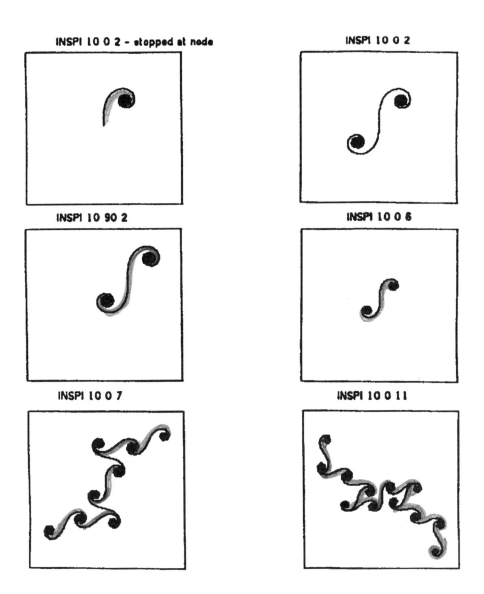

Figure 4. Six Drawings Made by the INSPI Procedure

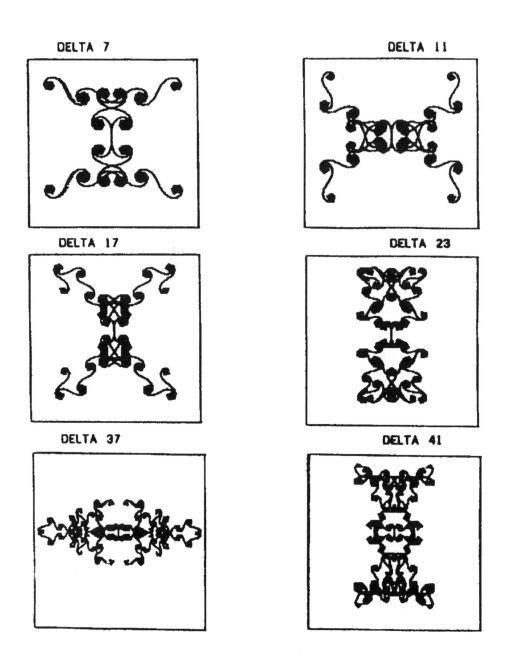

Figure 5. A Selection of Robby's Symmetrical INSPI Designs

these input values, shown in Figure 4, is to alter the centre location and orientation of the design.) When I tried to discuss changing other variables, Robby's personal agenda came forward in comments such as these: 'Hold it, Dad, all I want to make it do is go the other way'; 'I want it in the exact same direction, but opposite.' After a few false starts, I followed his lead:

Robby: How do you get it to go the other way? . . . It goes right. I want to make it go left.
Bob: We'd have to change the A procedure (we had renamed inspi A because it changed angle values).
Robby: Why don't you make a B procedure, to make it go the other way?
Bob: Why don't you?
Robby: [a complaint] I don't know how!
Bob: You copy the A procedure, but where it says 'right' you change it to 'left'.

After creating the symmetrical procedure, Robby still inclined to vary 'angle. I intervened to focus his attention on delta as a possibly potent variable, but he could not be interested at all. When he refused to follow my forceful suggestion to execute INSPI (10 0 7), I did it myself with those inputs and had the satisfaction of hearing him admit, 'I wish I had done that.'

Symmetrical Inspi Designs

Robby now began to make the symmetrical inspi designs of Figure 5, using his B inspi procedure with inspi procedure A. As the complex symmetries of the two-fold INSPI (10 0 7) developed, he exclaimed, 'Isn't that wild!' I offered 11 as the next delta candidate. After printing out the second symmetrical design, I proposed (would that I had bit my tongue) this speculation:

Bob: Why don't you try the next prime number? It turns out — and I never would have guessed it — that prime numbers —
Robby: [interrupting] Do this? [referring to the symmetrical INSPI (10 0 11)]
Bob: Why don't you give 13 a try? . . . I'm not quite sure, but that's my speculation, anyway. I'm sorry I told you that. Maybe I should have let you have the chance to figure that out.
Robby: Yeah . . . but I don't know the prime numbers very well.

Understanding and Delight as Motives

After executing the symmetrical INSPI 13's, Robby concluded, 'Every time we do it, they're getting super-er.' We conclude that Robby's strong confidence in the heuristics of pursuing symmetries in design was amply confirmed. This use of a heuristic is one clearly focussed on the objective of generating interesting designs. If there were any motive to understand better these inspi designs through symmetry it must have been relatively insignificant compared to his delight in creating them.

Self-direction and Taking guidance

My uncertain speculation that primes had something to do with creating interesting designs inspired Robby to produce a complete set of symmetrical inspi designs for all the primes between seven and fifty.[12]One might imagine he took my advice because he is a suggestible boy and easily led. The opposite is more nearly true. Two examples stand out. At my direction, he tried some large-value deltas. When I called his attention to the puzzle of the minimal design (a small straight line) made with the initial angle zero and delta 180, Robby continued from there with elegant symmetrical designs, based on delta values of 187 and 206, then decided, 'I think I'll go back to using primes.' After producing designs for delta values of twenty-nine and thirty-one, he decided that thirty-three was not a prime and rejected it as a candidate value.

Knowing that thirty three would produce an interesting design, I pushed him to try it, but he refused. 'No, I'm going to use only primes.' He then figured out the values of primes thirty-seven, forty-one, forty-three, and forty-seven and completed his own creation — the family of symmetrical, prime-based inspi designs.

What do we make of this material?

Most obvious is that the world of experience confirmed the value of Robby's heuristic, 'try symmetry,' as a generator of pretty designs. Second is that even though the inspi procedures led to results less intuitively accessible than those produced by the polyspi procedures, Robby explored this world of inspi designs in a systematic way that amounted to a first extension of the idea of variable stepping. That is, Robby settled on delta as the most potent variable for these designs and followed my 'prime hypothesis' to generate the next candidate delta value for creating a design. I believe we can infer that his experience of this inspi world confirmed the value of stepping variables as a heuristic.

Learning a Heuristic

The symmetry heuristic is good for generating designs; what is stepping variables good for? Did Robby appreciate this as a second heuristic for generating pretty pictures or did he see it as a way of organizing the world to understand it better? This distinction is one that we make, one that we might call upon in judging a possible claim that Robby learned a heuristic that is good for some specific purpose. I believe rather that Robby learned a heuristic that was specific with respect to activity but vague with respect to purpose. Although he may have begun to apply the heuristic to generate interesting results, his ability to select and order them through the 'prime hypothesis' helped define what was interesting about them. The final outcome for him was the better

---

12. The apparent complexity of an inspi design is determined by the sequence of values of the angle variable. Most significant is the remainder left when the increment value is divided into 180 and 360. As the simplest example, consider the case where the initial value of 'angle is zero and 'delta is ten. After some iterations, the turtle will turn right through this sequence of degrees [170 180 190]. RIGHT 180 turns the turtle around completely. RIGHT 190 is equivalent to LEFT 170. Thus, at the first node, the turtle begins executing steps which invert, in reverse order, each preceding step. Since ten divides into 360 with no remainder, we can see that there will be another node at an 'angle value of (180 + 360) degrees, after which the turtle will once more retrace its path. The primes are merely a subset of the numbers which don't cause the turtle to retrace its path after the second node.

comprehension of something worthwhile understanding (in terms of his judgment of what was worthwhile). This point is illustrated in the final incident reported here.

Beyond the Laboratory

Because Robby lives with me, it has been my privilege to observe how these experiences at Logo were reflected in his later problem solving. Some six months after our study at the Logo project, a parent visiting his third grade class introduced to Robby the 'paper-rings puzzle.' This bit of topological magic leads to the 'squaring' of two circles. (It is a puzzle in the sense of creating a surprising result.) I recommend you try it. Here's how it's done:

1. Cut two paper strips of equal length (eight inches will do).
2. Draw a line down the middle of each.
3. Bend each strip of paper into a circle and tape the juncture.
4. Join the circles at tangents perpendicularly and tape the juncture.
5. Cut around the middle line drawn on each circle.

When two strips of equal length are so connected and cut, the surprising result is that the strip-halves end up taped together as a square.

Re-play

Robby enjoyed this activity when shown it. Several days later, I removed a pattern of strips he had made from a paper on my clip-board. When I interrupted his reading to give him the sheet of paper, Robby recalled the game and quietly took it up on his own. He was very happy when the procedure produced a square and showed it to his mother and me. We neither paid much attention. Going on to three circles, Robby cut two of the three along their mid-lines. He judged (in error) that he had finished by finding a square with a bar (a double-width strip) across the centre. It lay flat. Still no one paid attention.

He went on to four circles. When he cut all the mid-lines, what he got was a confusion of flopping paper strips. I advised him to try getting it to lie flat. He was delighted when he achieved this goal and subsequently taped the paper strips to a large piece of cardboard. The resulting shape is Figure 6.

Elaboration

But why stop at four? Robby went on to cut and connect five circles. When cut, the five circles separated into two identical non-planar shapes. He taped these to another piece of cardboard. On trying to tape the floppy figures made from cutting six rings, Robby succeeded with great

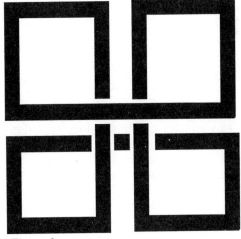

Figure 6.

effort. He decided the problem was getting too complicated to be fun and quit.

When I recalled his attention to the figure made by cutting two of the three circles and pointed out that the middle bar of his figure was double-thick, Robby agreed he had cut only two circles. He saw immediately that this square would divide into two rectangles. 'The five's made two too. Hey! I've got a new theory: the odd-numbered circles make two and the evens all stay together.' Robby could not prove his conjecture, but in the course of one discussion when I asked how he had gotten the idea of this exploration, he explained, 'Dad, it's just like what we did at Logo with the shape families. I changed one thing, a little at a time.'

Mixed Purposes

Robby's explanation witnesses that he conceived of his exploration in terms of that past Logo experience. This does not imply that the Logo shape families marked his first encounter with or use of the idea of controlled changing of a single variable. We may infer, nonetheless, that he owned an example of this idea crisply applied to a complex but comprehensible range of interesting phenomena, and further, that it did provide him guidance for thinking about a problem met subsequently. He appreciated his Logo shape families experience as embodying a powerful idea.

Did he apply the heuristic because it might generate new results or because it might help him understand a range of puzzling phenomena? We can not profitably make such a distinction if his purposes were mixed. The two aspects of purpose we might choose to distinguish appear to have been inextricable for him. He used this powerful idea as a heuristic for orderly exploration to generate interesting results in a comprehensible way.

What Follows?

We have come to the end of this story, but the question remains 'where does this powerful idea of variable stepping go from here?' We find a hint in the discussion of Robby's new theory. His conjecture, that the odd-numbered chains make two separate figures, was based on the regularity he observed in five cases (with two through six rings).

When I asked him to prove this new theory, his method of choice was empirical — he constructed a seven-ring puzzle and cut each of the rings. (I did not suggest his doing so. I wanted him to reflect more.) He clearly expected the seven rings to separate into two figures and took their doing so as proof of his theory. What is significant in this observation is the way hypothesis testing emerged as a minor variation from a preceding activity which was a theory-free but orderly exploration of an interesting domain. Variable stepping had become for Robby a way of approaching the world, of seeing 'what's what.' The power of the idea — as witnessed by Robby's quick invention of his new theory — is that from 'what's what' 'what follows' is 'intuitively obvious.'

DESIGNING COMPUTER-BASED MICROWORLDS[13]

Designing computer applications for education might be called cognitive engineering, for its objective is to shape children's minds. Such a goal must carry with it a commitment to cognitive science, the study of how knowledge functions and changes in the mind. In light of the profound influence of computers in the schools, designing educational applications without such a commitment would be irresponsible.

I believe that Jean Piaget, the Swiss student of knowledge, formulated the general solution to the problem of how intelligence develops. Although the field of cognitive science has advanced beyond Piaget's innovative theories by revising and extending them, his insights into the nature of learning continue to influence teaching methods. The union of computer microworlds and Piagetian theory is the subject of this article.

Piaget and Education

Central to the work of Piaget is constructivism, the view that the mind incorporates a natural growth of knowledge and that the mind's structure and organization are shaped by interactions among the mind's parts. In *The Science of Education* and the *Psychology of the Child* , Piaget challenges educators to answer two questions: How does instruction affect what is in the mind? and What remains in the mind from the process of instruction long after the time of instruction has passed? In the same work, Piaget disputes both the effectiveness and the ethical correctness of many of the practices of modern education:

'If we desire to form individuals capable of inventive thought and of helping the society of tomorrow to achieve progress, then it is clear that an education which is an active discovery of reality is superior to one that consists merely in providing the young with ready-made wills to will with and ready-made truths to know with.'

The Dilemma of Instruction

Given Piaget's view that learning is a primary, natural function of the healthy mind, we might consider instruction in any narrow sense unnecessary. Children (and older students of life as well) learn the lessons of the world, effectively if not cheerfully, because reality is the medium through which important objectives are reached. Nevertheless, in certain situations children often rebel against the lessons society says they must learn. Thus the educator's ideal of inspiring and nurturing the love of learning frequently is reduced to motivating indifferent or reluctant students to learn what full functioning in our society requires.

---

13. 1982. Published in *BYTE* Magazine's Logo special issue (1982, August).

Teachers face a dilemma when they try to move children to do school-work that is not intrinsically interesting. Children must be induced to undertake the work either by promise of reward or threat of punishment, and in neither case do they focus on the material to be learned. In this sense the work is construed as a bad thing, an obstacle blocking the way to reward or a reason for punishment. Kurt Lewin explores this dilemma in 'The Psychological Situations of Reward and Punishment.' The ideas of Piaget and Lewin have led me to state the central problem of education thus: 'How can we instruct while respecting the self-constructive character of mind?'

Computer-Based Microworlds

In Mindstorms: Children, Computers, and Powerful Ideas, Seymour Papert proposes computer-based microworlds as a general solution to the problem of motivation. One argument for Papert's proposal runs as follows: learning is often a gradual process of familiarization, of stumbling into puzzlements, and resolving them by proposing and testing simple hypotheses in which new problems resemble others already understood. Microworlds are in essence 'task domains' or 'problem spaces' designed for virtual, streamlined experience. These worlds encompass objects and processes that we can get to know and understand. The appropriation of the knowledge embodied in those experiences is made possible because the microworld does not focus on 'problems' to be done but on 'neat phenomena'—phenomena that are inherently interesting to observe and interact with.

With neat phenomena, the challenge to the educator is to formulate so clear a presentation of their elements that even a child can grasp their essence. A well-designed computer microworld embodies the simplest model that an expert can imagine as an acceptable entry point to richer knowledge. If a microworld lacks neat phenomena, it provides no accessible power to justify the child's involvement. We can hardly expect children to learn from such experiences until they are personally engaged in other tasks that make the specific knowledge worthwhile as a tool for achieving some objective. This amounts to an appropriate shifting of accountability from students (who have always been criticized for not liking what they must learn) to teachers, those who believe that their values and ideas are worth perpetuating.

LEARNING ENVIRONMENTS: NOW, THEN, AND SOMEDAY [14]

Complaints about 'Computers in Education'

Microcomputers inexpensive enough for widespread use in education became available in the late 70s in the USA — even some with enough capacity to support conversational programming languages. Such micros seemed a significant change from existing time-shared systems. Many educators saw the promise of micros, and parents, in their eagerness to do what they imagined best for their children, with personal contributions and political pressure led school systems to invest heavily in that technology. Have those computers produced results which justify the hope placed in them? I think not. The disappointment expresses itself in four common complaints:

About computers in education, generally:

THEME	SPECIFIC COMPLAINT
Effect:	Computers have not improved education.
Value:	Computer experiences are inferior to real ones.

About learning environments:

THEME	SPECIFIC COMPLAINT
Clarity:	The notion is not clear and distinct.
Design:	Nobody knows how to make them.

The specific complaints we will pursue here are those focussed on the themes of effect, clarity and design. I conclude with some suggestions for future work.

The Limited Impact of Computers in Education

The introduction of microcomputers into the education system has disappointed many people who had hoped their presence would engender reforms leading to education both more congenial to children and more effective than the norm of past generations. There has been no widespread recognition of any such dramatic impact. Why? In a review of *Computer Experience and Cognitive Development*, Erik DeCorte noted:

> 'I point to the immediate connection between the book and the current inquiries about using computers with children. Some have claimed that computer experience, and the ability to program in particular, would influence in a positive way the learning and thinking capacities of children. In contradiction to the image produced by the rest of the available research literature (See DeCorte & Verschaffel, 1985), Lawler's study produces positive results concerning the cognitive-effects hypothesis . . .'

---

14. 1986. Published as Chapter 1 of *AI&Ed*. Vol. 1 (1987)

Such negative outcomes as others report, when the result of thoughtful experiments which are executed with care, have the proper function of constraining the enthusiastic claims of the overly optimistic. On the other hand, I am convinced that one reason for the difference of outcomes noted by DeCorte is a consequence of different levels of detail of the studies. Too much evaluative research has the flavor of I/O models: some INPUT should produce some OUTPUT; some INSTRUCTION should produce some OUTCOME. If the true orderliness of human behaviour becomes evident only when one looks very carefully at extremely tiny details, most experimental efforts to assess computing's impact will show negative results, unless they examine the PROCESS between input and output, the PERSON between instruction and outcome. Studying the knowledge and functioning of one mind in detail permits a depth of understanding of the student's mind and development normally beyond the reach of research with a broader focus. We need to go beyond evaluative studies of broad claims in order to advance our understanding of human cognition, specifically in respect of the issues of the malleability of the natural mind and of the long-term effects of specific experiences on the lives of individuals: both, for me, are central issues for the science of education.

Comments such as the preceding, though true and valuable, evade rather than answer the question raised by DeCorte's observation. It is the case that early Logo claims looked to widespread results so obvious and striking that corroborating or disambiguating experiments would not be required. No such strong outcome has occurred. Computers, as introduced in schools, have not had so beneficial an impact as their early proponents suggested they might. Let's reflect on this problem.

The Worst Case: The Problem is Not Solvable

Despite widespread research in several paradigms directed to improving children's mathematical competence through using computers, there is a general impression, based on test results, that arithmetic skills have been deteriorating over the past 25 years. One suggestion for reacting to this situation comes from a parody, 'The Uses of Education to Enhance Technology' (author unknown).

'It's time to face the facts: all previous efforts at educational reform have been failures. The harder we try, the more innovations we make, the dumber the students get. This is eloquently pointed out by proponents of the 'Back to Basics' movement in numerous riots and book burnings across the country.

'The solution is clear. It is simply not possible to educate children. If repeated attempts to improve the quality of education only make matters worse, then the obvious way to make matters better is to try to degrade the quality of education. In fact, carrying this argument to its logical conclusion proves that the best educational reform would be to abolish efforts at education altogether. This conclusion is hardly new and has been previously argued by such thinkers as Holt and Illich. But they also foresaw the serious impediments to this scheme. It would abolish the major value of the school system, which is to supply employment and positions of power. . . . But now, with modern technology, we see a way out of this dilemma. The solution is absurdly simple: by placing computers in the schools, we can let the teachers teach the computers and send the children home . . . Specifically, we envision an educational system in which each child is assigned a personal computer, which goes to school in place of the child. (Incidentally, it should be noted that the cost of such a personal computer is not large. Even at today's prices it is probably not much more than the average family would spend on a catastrophic medical emergency). . .'

Those of us who are laughing through our tears cannot escape the need for a different way of dealing with the issue. Try to take a broad view. It is possible to believe that the problem has not been a 'local' failure, ascribable in some simple way to faulty research, slow technology transfer, or intractable institutions.

An Explanation: Social Changes are Dominant

The problem may be profound and even could involve deterioration in the learnability of common sense knowledge. Changes in the everyday world can completely overwhelm our hopes to teach children skills we know they will need later. Consider these observations (from Lawler, 1985) as an example of ways in which social forces can radically alter the cognitive impact of domains of common sense knowledge.

Vignette 55

'Since the beginning of the High School Studies Program, the children and I have come to Logo to use the system from 8 to 10 a.m. The children have become accustomed to mid-morning snacks. The favourite: apple pie and milk. At their young age, Robby and Miriam get money from me, and we talk about how they spend it. A piece of pie costs 59 cents. A half pint of milk is 32 cents. So Miriam told me this morning, and these figures are familiar. As we got her snack, I asked Miriam how much we would have to pay the cashier. After a few miscalculations, she came to a sum of 91 cents and seemed confident it was correct. I congratulated her on a correct sum and asked the cashier to ring up our tab: "92 cents".

'"92 cents?" I asked the cashier to explain. She said the pie is 55 cents and milk 30 cents, thus 85 cents and the tax, 7 cents. "See. Look at the table."

'I am at a complete loss as to how to explain this to Miriam. Not only is the 8 percent food tax dreadful in itself, but it is rendering incomprehensible a primary domain of arithmetic that children regularly confront — paying small amounts of money for junk food. Otherwheres, Miriam used "the tax" as a label for the difference between what is a reasonable computation and what you actually have to pay somebody to buy something . . .'

The observation suggests that a specific governmental policy has, as a side effect, been making the world less sensible and harder to learn about. If, to get accurate results, a child must learn to multiply and round (for computing a percentage tax) before learning to add, he is in BIG trouble. If it does no good to calculate correctly, because results will be adjusted by some authoritatively asserted incomprehensible rule, why

bother to be over-committed to precision? If addition no longer adds up,
.d is arithmetic? If you can't count on number, what can you can you count on?
.edge is not useful, why bother with it?

.nplex technology may also be making the world less comprehensible, but the
effec.s are not uniform. Calculators and modern cash registers which compute change
obviate the need for much mental calculation. Contrariwise, it is possible to argue that
technology is making access to reading knowledge easier. These observations leave us
with more questions than answers, but the questions are addressable and significant
ones: to what extent is it possible to learn what one needs to know through everyday
experience? How do side effects of decisions by adults constrain or enhance children's
ability to learn about the world in natural ways?

An Excuse: The Political Climate has been Adverse

After such observations, it is reasonable to ask how political decisions — such as support
for research — have influenced the use of computers in education. For many years the
federal government, through various agencies, was a major supporter of research into
technology for education. The impact of the first Reagan budget — which proposed to
reduce funding for research in science education from $80M to $10M in one year — led
to significant demoralization of that community and deterioration of function within its
organizations. The decimation of this community was decidedly unhelpful and may
have engendered some of the chaos and superficiality of work evidenced as
microcomputers were sold by the private sector to the education community throughout
the United States. On the other hand, one must note that the more generous support
provided by the French Government's founding of *Le Centre Mondial pour l'Informatique et
Ressource Humaine* had no happier outcome, as noted by Paul Tate in Datamation.

The Centre intended to use microcomputers to take computing to the people
through educational workshops in both the developed and the developing world.
Field projects were set up in France and Senegal, and research schemes were
introduced covering interactive media, systems architecture, AI, user interfaces, and
medical applications. It was to be an international research centre independent of all
commercial, political, and national interests. Naturally, it failed. Nothing is that
independent, especially an organization backed by a socialist government and staffed
by highly individualistic industry visionaries from around the world. Besides,
altruism has a credibility problem in an industry that thrives on intense commercial
competition. By the end of the Centre's first year, Papert had quit, so had American
experts Nicholas Negroponte and Bob Lawler. It had become a battlefield, scarred by
clashes of management style, personality, and political conviction. It never really
recovered. The new French government has done the Centre a favour in closing it
down. But somewhere in that mess was an admirable attempt to take high
technology, quickly and effectively, along the inevitable path into the hands of the
public. The Centre had hoped to do that in different countries. . . The Centre is
unlikely to be missed by many. Yet, for all its problems, it made a brave attempt to

prepare for some of the technical and market realities of the next few years. We regret that such a noble venture met with such an ignoble end.

An Excuse: Available Hardware has been Inadequate

There is no question that the introduction of computers in education was a financial success — for some few companies — but the record with respect to product engineering and the advancement of social goals is one of nearly consistent failure. Consider, as an example, this brief review of the development of Logo-capable microcomputers for education:

- The GTI 3500 (a DEC LSI-11 with a Minsky-designed front end, the '2500') was an interesting product that came to market too early. The 2500 implemented a special video-turtle primitive, spin (proposed by D. Hillis), which set the object rotating at a constant angular velocity. This machine would have been very useful to physics and engineering students had it survived.
- Texas Instruments supported the development of Logo for the TI-99 at the MIT Logo Project. The turtle geometry component of the system was quite inadequate. The sprite graphics system, which originally had been an uninteresting feature of the hardware, proved in the end to be a liberating addition to the repertoire of tools which could be used for educating children with computers. The TI-99 captured a significant portion of the education market, and the company made good money with their product. Nonetheless, TI withdrew the product, even though their president wanted the corporation to remain active in that market. This decision had a radical, negative impact on the production of software for education. I have been told that many small educational software development efforts collapsed after this decision was taken.
- The Apple II offered the best early versions of turtle geometry and list processing with Logo. Both it and the IBM PC were technically adequate systems for the time but were really more suited for use by junior high and older students. For use with younger children, the systems were, in fact, regressions from the graphics capabilities available in the TI-99.
- Atari Logo offered two advances. With time-sliced 'when demons', the Atari permitted a technically primitive but intellectually deep form of multi-programming under user control. The four software sprites attempted to replace the expensive TI graphics hardware with simulated capabilities. The research lab was axed before their developmental projects came to fruition.
- The Coleco Adam had the best mix of hardware and software function for education use, but the manufacture and assembly of the machine was beset with problems of quality control that were insurmountable.
- The MSX microcomputers, some of which are the best Logo-capable systems commercially available today, are not imported into the United States because the major European producer Phillips believes (rightly, I suspect) that the education market has been saturated with Apple IIs and IBM PCs.
- The best generally available system for use with small children till now has been the Apple II with a plug-in sprite board containing the TI-99 graphics processor. The two main advantages provided by Apple Sprites were an increase in the memory size, permitting more complex

collections of procedures to be assembled, and the addition of a drawing capability for the sprites. Recently, the board and software were discontinued, for both technical and marketing reasons.

This record will not convince anyone of the grand success of the private sector in doing any more than making and losing money. With such volatile markets, very little that takes thought or time can get done. Someday we will have a stable computer product permitting the development of good educational software for young children. That day is not yet. If better systems come along, will they — like the MSX — fail either to reach the market or to sell because the enthusiasm and capital of the public and the education systems have been used up? It is quite possible that future opportunities have been polluted through temerity and over-selling.

An Explanation: The Medium Has No Consumable Content

The disappointing impact of computers on education may be partly explained by the lack of content addressable with the technology. Consider, in contrast, the video cassette recorder. VCRs have reached a 'take-off' point and now are present in over 30 percent of American homes. A key element in the success of VCR technology — not only in the market but also in user satisfaction with it — is the existence of a massive stock of material which the VCR brought to a new level of accessibility. As a 'follow-on' technology, VCRs reproduce for resale the production of 70 years of film and TV with marginal conversion costs.

What existing material do micros have accessible? Ideas? Yes, but they must be recoded for each new system unless microcoded emulation of predecessor machines becomes common. More to the point, existing larger systems and minicomputers typically have different purposes than did micros purchased for education. To offset this limitation, conversational programming languages suggested the possibility of extensive programming by end-users. What precisely that meant and what has evolved from that hope is our next theme, Computer Based Microworlds.

A CONSTRUCTIVE ALTERNATIVE TO GETTING TEACHED [15]

The broader availability of technical training and its vigorous application have created an explosion in the quantity of knowledge available. Too often the rate of knowledge growth outpaces the ability of teachers to absorb and communicate what is known, and skills developed through schooling are obsolete or irrelevant before students are in a position to apply them. Beyond the arena of instruction waits another problem, pervasive but less well recognized: commonsense knowledge is becoming harder to acquire. We are all served by tools more complex than we understand. The objects we depend on 'contain no user serviceable parts'; if they did, few of us would have the experience to know what to do with them. A second source of impenetrability is the increasing complication of life by extrinsic rules, even at the simplest level. As an everyday example, consider how the imposition of percentage sales taxes makes simple addition of small purchases harder. The decreasing accessibility of common sense knowledge makes the instructional contribution to cognitive development even more critical than it has been in the past.

The reforms of yesterday have been significant and effective, even if not entirely adequate to cope with the problems of today. The long lectures of the past are now sometimes circumvented by work with concrete materials, thanks to the followers of Montessori. Teachers do now ask 'How can we present material in ways more congenial to the developmental level of the pupils?' Piaget's effort to focus on the activity of the pupil remains a positive and potent force in education. Following him we ask the different question, 'How can we instruct while respecting the self-constructive character of mind?' Granting the good will of teachers and the effectiveness of past reforms, instruction is still typically frontal lecture in form. Teachers still teach. The children still 'get teached', whether they learn or not. The reasons may derive from institutional efficiencies, as Bauersfeld has suggested (in an invited lecture at Purdue University, 1987), but I argue here that today's problems in education have their roots within the views of mind and learning from which we generate curriculum. We need today a constructivist alternative to pupils' 'getting teached', a genetic vision of knowledge and its growth that is at least as explicit and well articulated as the standard view, specifying

- components of knowledge
- interrelation of knowledge components
- functioning of knowledge components
- the emergence of behaviour from the interactions of components
- processes of development (observed and ideal)
- methods of evaluation derived from the view but recognizing the legitimate interest of society in evaluation of the process and results.
- actions and options available to educators.

---

15. 1987 Unpublished.

A Constructive Alternative to 'Getting Teached'

A view of knowledge in which skills are seen as decomposible into a series of procedures (sub-skills) leads to a focus on the logic of prerequisites in curriculum. This may be an error, as suggested by this simple example. In the elementary grades, addition instruction is often sequenced by the magnitude of addends. Teachers have told me 'We don't add any sums higher than 12 in the first grade.' Yet it is only logical to focus on the addition of single digit sums within a specific scheme of representation. Children may know very well that 15 cents and 15 cents make thirty cents or that four quarters make a buck. Different aspects of knowledge are more or less salient according to the scheme of representation involved. A focus on the varieties of representations and their relation to human learning (drawing on studies in Artificial Intelligence and the Cognitive sciences) will provide better guidance for generating curriculum. Curriculum design requires a logic of psychological genesis, not the structured logic of the domain expert.

Local Clusters of Empirical Knowledge

The way to knowledge lies through the fields of ignorance. There is no single path. People typically develop familiarity with a domain through a limited experience of its various possibilities (we can say they experience some aspects of the domain as a microworld). The development of disparate bodies of knowledge (call them microviews) based upon the experience of microworlds is guided by personal action and social interaction. Only later, if ever, do people achieve a unified comprehension. Integration of knowledge derives from later experiences of which two kinds (at least) appear possible:

- rational reconstruction of prior knowledge through reflection
- discovery of an especially apt, concrete model

Such an especially apt model, even though encountered after other experiences, can through its simplicity and good fit help explain the nature and operation of objects and processes in more complex and less obvious situations. I call such a concrete model a (temporally) post-cedent logical ancestor. This kind of cognitive reorganization derived from the internal construction of a post-cedent ancestor would be expected to dominate the learning of young children, inasmuch as rational reconstruction may remain uncommon except in circumstances where formal capabilities are well developed. When there exists a cluster of cognitive structures derived from varieties of experiences relating to the same kind of knowledge (as experiences with counting, and coins, and measure may all relate to processes of addition), a post-cedent ancestor would be more generally named the nucleus of a microview cluster and the process of internalizing such a nucleus would be cluster nucleation. What would make a nuclear microview central? Aptness as a crisp representation of the relevant knowledge is a first answer. Simplicity would make the microview easier to remember in detail and easier to think with. A cluster nucleus would present a more 'thinkable model' for a domain than would less lucid representations. It would dominate its cluster-members by its efficiency in thought. The nuclear model finally would come to serve as a ground of explanation for their processes as well, and this is the relation which gives it the power to advance reformulation of earlier experiences and the integration of disparate experiences into a coherent, augmented area of knowledge. If we express this in terms of a geographic metaphor, the nucleus of a cluster could be seen as a regional capital or the central city of a metropolitan area, in communication with its earlier established empirical domains as suburbs. Such a geographical metaphor can help us discuss how such clusters can relate to one another.

Structured semantic networks

On the ground, cities and suburbs are connected by local roads and rail lines. Major cities today also are interconnected in more immediate ways, by air or express trains. If we imagine that these cluster nuclei, these mental capitals, are interconnected, we have a graphic image for knowledge in the mind as a structured semantic network. If we adopt such a vision for guidance in thinking about knowledge within individuals, the critical questions to be asked are first, how does such a network grow and second, what are the interrelations of the development of such personal knowledge with the social context?

Genesis in the Cognitive Network: psychological issues

Why should it be the case that different schemes of representation are important in education? One reason is the Galton phenomenon: some people think predominantly with words, some with images, some with kinesthetic feelings; most of us think in mixed modes which alternate and interact variously in different domains of experience. Another reason is that multiple representations covering different aspects of a 'common domain' permit the expression of a more robust and adaptable set of responses to externally presented problems than any single formulation would permit. The nucleation of such a cluster by the dominance of one single mode (because its best model is somehow more fit than others) would integrate and strengthen its structure. One conjecture for the larger scale organization of mind is that until such nucleation is achieved, a cluster's interconnection to and integration with the broader cognitive network would not be stable. A corollary of this conjecture is that networks of 'nuclei' alone would not be a desirable outcome of instruction because they could not by themselves form a robust, flexible, and coherently integrated network.

Genesis in the Cognitive Network: sociological issues

The way to knowledge lies through the fields of ignorance. Why should one begin the journey? How can one value what neither has been experienced nor understood? Abstract or future advantages may be important to some adults, but human engagement is the primary motive for children, and it remains primary for many adults as well. Conventions are shared knowledge about what we do together and how we do it. We all accept conventional knowledge and, in bits and pieces, come to understand the function and logic in detail of the various things we do. A child may, for example, be quite happy to take turns at beginning games of tic tac toe with a playmate while lacking completely any sense of the relative adverting adhering to that first move. There may be many different ways of gradually coming to understand the rationale for accepted practice. Instruction may be one. Observing others and the consequences of their action is another.

Working out encountered problems may lead to a purely internal discovery. The essential situation is, however, that society provides frameworks of interaction with discoverable meanings; the engagement with these frameworks leads to their later exploration and comprehension in detail.

Educational Implications and Directions for Research

This vision of mind as a structured semantic network offers the hope of solving some problems. If the focus on multiple representations of knowledge in different modes of experience argues that a broader base of empirical experience is needed for stability of learning, it also presents a concrete proposal about what makes for such stability. Further, the conjecture that cluster nucleation is a prerequisite for stable integration of local domains of knowledge into the larger cognitive network provides us guidance as educators. The hypothesis itself is a formulation by which we can judge whether any student should or should not be able to integrate new learnings into what is already known. If, on the other hand, it requires a deeper penetration of what a pupil knows to provide guidance for his activities, that is a sign of the increasing depth of our appreciation of cognitive development, however much in fact it increases the practical burdens of instruction.

The question of sequence in curriculum comes now in a new light. Doubtless there is a sense in which knowledge of one level is prerequisite for later learning. However, within a common domain of experience, prerequisite knowledge sequences may be largely irrelevant if empirically rooted microviews are built up through everyday experience-induced associations and through the adoption of conventional knowledge from social interaction. Within the terminology of Vygotsky, one might say that prerequisites are unimportant within the zone of proximal development. What is a prerequisite for stable understanding is a breadth of empirical information which can be rationalized and comprehended through the development of a post-cedent logical ancestor in cluster nucleation.

If we focus closely on what sort of thing a nuclear microview might be, the primary characterization is that it should be a 'thinkable model', one fit to the domain and efficient enough that it can serve as the ground of thought experiments — those very reflections which will bring about the rationalization of the local cluster and create its stability. One implication for education is that we should try to catalog and articulate known models which might be able to play such a role. With respect to empirical knowledge and the experiences on which it is based, one may inquire of disparate microworlds about the extent and limitations to their variety, and also explore how they are interrelated with each other and nuclear models.

Aiming to build a structured semantic networks in pupils' minds requires the development of a more structured view of knowledge. Some models are more important than others. With this proposal, we have a principle for judging which are more important and why they are more important — without diminishing at all the requirement for sufficient breadth of experience that potential nuclear models can have some base of material to function with and reorganize. Finally, given that one may imagine a flexible and extensive scheme for representing human knowledge as a structured semantic network, would it be possible to reorganize our view of what is known — say the contents of encyclopedias — into a form which would be compatible with this vision of human knowledge? Could one imagine pupil workstations in which the students would have representations of knowledge (their own and the worlds') which would help them compare their knowledge network for a domain with other possible organizations and extensions? If such is possible, should the potential be explored? Could it be exploited as an method of evaluation? How else would it be exploited? Exploring such issues is one part of my research agenda. I believe it holds promise both for significant work in educational and psychological research and for our societies' attempts to cope with the knowledge intensive world of today and tomorrow.

DESCENDING UPRIGHT AMONG STARING FISH [16]

The primary tension in education is between a society intent on the transmission of its values and knowledge and an individual learner, with distinct and not-necessarily-related interests and commitments. The design of computer-based microworlds is one strategy for reducing this tension by involving the learner in an engaging activity from which one may discover the notions and values of the society. But what is the knowledge embodied in a microworld and how is a user to discover it? And how does this process go forward? And what guidance can a designer find? I develop three themes below, drawing inspiration for the particular approach taken from some literary examples, from some Logo microworlds, and from other ideas of artificial intelligence.

Creativity and Constraint

Yazdani (1989) describes the process of story writing as an author's presenting a multi-faceted description of an imagined world under the constraints of seriality of the text medium. The author achieves artistic effects by controlled revelation of the world view through ordering of selected elements and the texture of expression. Educators and microworlds designers might likewise inquire what are the constraints of our medium against which we struggle to realize our art.

J. R. R. Tolkein, author of the heroic fantasies 'The Hobbit' and 'The Lord of the Rings', one of the most popular writers for the literati in this half century, is a world class creator of virtual worlds. Tolkein's achievements and ideas can help illuminate the challenge before the would-be microworld designer. In an academic lecture, Tolkein described his sense of the roots of fantasy in fiction:

> 'The incarnate mind, the tongue, and the tale are in our world coeval. The human mind, endowed with the powers of generalization and abstraction, sees not only green-grass, discriminating it from other things (and finding it fair to look upon), but sees that it is green as well as being grass . But how powerful, how stimulating to the very faculty that produced it, was the invention of the adjective: no spell or incantation in Faerie is more potent . . . The mind that thought of light , heavy, grey, yellow, still, swift, also conceived of magic that would made heavy things light and able to fly, turn grey lead into yellow gold, and the still rock into swift water. If it could do the one, it could do the other; it inevitably did both. When we can take green from grass, blue from heaven, and red from blood, we have already an enchanter's power . . . But in such fantasy, as it is called, new form is made; Faerie begins; Man becomes a sub-creator . . .'

Tree and Leaf

16. 1993. In *Rethinking Roles of Technology in Education* (Estes & Thomas, Eds.), pp. 767-769. This presentation proposal was accepted as a keynote talk at the 10th annual International Conference on Technology and Education.

But varying qualities is a form of creativity with which we are quite familiar. With the addition of a single variable, a SQUARE procedure can draw a figure of varying size; with a second variable the SQUARE becomes a POLY procedure; with a third it becomes POLYSPIRAL. These exemplify changing the values used in a process.

Changing the process itself leads to new creations, a new microworld with its own unusual beauties. When the increment of the POLYSPIRAL procedure is applied to the angle value instead of to the side-length of figures drawn, the POLYSPI becomes the INSPI, capable in its turn of its own independent elaborations and semantics. Changing a process creates more variability (with new kinds of confusion and chaos) as well as new kinds of order. POLYSPI-like designs were made before computing. I doubt that this is true of INSPI designs. So there is something new under the sun.

The creation of new things is more striking than the attribution of aberrant qualities. Most of the specific creatures of Tolkein's fancy can be seen as mixtures of qualities. But there is one new creation comparable in novelty to the INSPI where one can examine the process by which the creature became who or what it is: Smeagol (aka Gollum, the riverine hobbit gone-wrong). In this specific sense, different character development through varied experiences is the literary analog of process modification creating INSPI.

What are the constraints? For the literary genres, the processes are worked out in tales, the telling of which takes time. For computer microworlds, processes are less time-constrained. They go forward faster and can be repeated. In literature, the revelatory process is development in time. In computer microworlds, the revelatory process is an unpacking of component parts through analysis in detail.

Fate and Learning

The primary satisfactions of literature derive from aroused expectations and their resolution by the end of the work. One measure of the quality of a literary work is the sense of necessity developed as the story unfolds. If we seek to design microworlds through which people can learn without instruction, we should be able to specify what is the deep content that ultimately will be discovered by people who have the experience and do not miss its meaning. What is 'fated' to be discovered? What is the equivalent of 'fate' in a timeless medium? Here is one answer to consider. One element of cognitive power is the ability to deploy alternative descriptions of circumstances and problems; furthermore, this deployment is enhanced by integration of the different perspectives made possible by the different descriptions. Consider increasing complexity in Logo turtle geometry as an example. One of the best slogans for the Logo microworld ideal is 'no threshold; no ceiling.' One can make a circle with the simplest composition of primitives. One can make a 3-dimensional projective sketch of the Piazza San Marco, if you know how. One should not assume, however, that traversing that path is trivial simply because there is no threshold. There may be giant steps along the way. Compare a circle's description as a Logo procedure with a Cartesian equation of a circle:

REPEAT 24 [FORWARD :steps RIGHT 15] $X*X + Y*Y = 25$

One can make the Cartesian circle into an ellipse by adding non-zero and nonidentical coefficients to the X and Y terms. How does one make the Logo circle into an ellipse? It is possible but not quite so easy.

The first point is that different descriptions are useful for solving different specific problems. A second point is that one better understands both descriptions of objects when the descriptions are brought into contrast. Multiple descriptions permit the relativizing of each one involved. This is equally true for simple descriptions and complex ones. Beginning with turtle geometry — realized and embedded in hardware systems implemented in Cartesian reference frameworks, represented by the X-Y plane of reference for a video display, one is destined to learn about both descriptions of space and objects and therefore also about their interrelations. This is a 'fated' learning outcome. This is what a microworld user will discover if there is interest enough and time.

There is a second answer to the question of what is ultimately to be discovered in a microworld: the interrelation of structure and function of its elements. Consider the fact that Logo is a procedurally-structurable, recursively-interpreted language. These are the primary features of its function. Notice also that its primary data structure is a list, each of whose elements are either symbols or other lists. Once when discussing Logo procedures as data-structures, a colleague remarked the insight noting, 'Ah! It is no accident that Logo is both a list-structured and procedural language.' Exactly so. Because Logo data-structures are recursively interpreted lists of lists, Logo procedures can be defined as structures permitting recursive invocation limited only at the time of interpretation.

Illusion and Comprehensibility

Nabakov's observations on some objectives and techniques of writing appear prominently in *Transparent Things,* most notably his appreciation of the critical issue of the relationships between the surface and depth of descriptions. His first chapter focuses on the challenge of exposition under the constraint of maintaining an illusion of the seeming reality of the present time. He says it this way:

> 'When we concentrate on a material object, whatever its situation, the very act of attention may lead to our involuntarily sinking into the history of that object. Novices must learn to skim over matter if they want matter to stay at the exact level of the moment. Transparent things, through which the past shines.

> 'Man made objects, or natural ones, inert in themselves but much used by careless life . . . are particularly difficult to keep in surface focus; novices fall through the surface, humming happily to themselves, and are soon reveling with childish abandon in the story of this stone, of that heath. I shall explain. A thin veneer of immediate reality is spread over natural and artificial matter, and whoever wishes to remain in the now, with the now, on the now, should please not break its tension film. Otherwise the inexperienced miracle-worker will find himself no longer walking on water but descending upright among staring fish . . .'

Transparent Things

What he says about his art seems to be at least as relevant to domains that are timeless as to those that are fugitive — for the following reason. We people don't seem to be very good with details and with complexity. If we sink into an analysis of details, we will lose not our sense of the now (Nabakov's concern) but of the here — where we are and how that fits in other schemes. This happens all the time to programmers. Either we cram into dense procedures more detail than Aristotle could master or we create networks of relations that branch out beyond the view our editing screens give us onto the field of our existing procedures. If we find ourselves working with a medium whose constraint is not time but management of a multitude of levels of interrelations, what does it mean to think of Nabakov's goal of maintaining an illusion, not breaking the 'thin tension film of the now'? My vision of an answer to this question is technical, an interface design suggestion for programming language implementations. I suggest that a program editor for a complex, layered, structure of linked descriptions should be implemented with at least three 'views': the procedure of current interest (with full text displayed in some readable form); the calling layer (possibly displayed in some reduced font-size mini-window, and the called-objects layer. Such an editor display — automatically created and with relevant text segments maintained visibly in registration — would be an analyst's tool for keeping with the 'here'. Selecting the superordinate or subordinate window would move the content of that window into the central focus window and re-enter into registration the appropriate corresponding layers in the hierarchy of structure, even as footnotes are managed by text processor applications.

If we cast our minds back to earlier days of the AI community, we will remember that the choice always needed to be made between the strategies of depth first or breadth first in searching of large information spaces. The different effort we make in education, understanding and communicating information more than searching for it, our appropriate contrast should be between issues of depth and issues of the surface, where the maintenance of coherence and comprehensibility across the fringes of an arena of interest is our best analog of maintaining the illusion produced by the magicians of language. A flexible banded editor might help us do that.

Bibliography

Minsky, M. *The Society of Mind*, New York, Simon & Schuster, 1985.

Nabakov, V. *Transparent Things*, Greenwich, CT. Fawcett Books, 1972.

Tolkien, J. R. R. *Tree and Leaf*, London, Unwin Books, 1964.

Yazdani, M. 'Computational Story Writing,' in *Computers and Writing*, Williams and Holt (Eds.) Norwood, NJ. Ablex, 1989.

THE ROLE OF MICROTHEORIES IN MICROWORLDS[17]

Practical matters are often in advance of the theoretical questions that are of greater interest to some of us. And indeed, if you look around at any education conference, you will see marvels of modern technology available — but one of the questions we should always ask is 'What does this mean? What does this all amount to? What is really profound in this body of work?' The touchstone that I use, the guide that I follow in trying to answer this question, in respect to educational issues, comes from some questions put forward by Jean Piaget in a book he wrote for UNESCO entitled *The Science of Education and the Psychology of the Child*. Piaget said that we can not claim to really understand what we are doing as educators unless we can answer three questions: What is in the child's mind? How do our actions change what is in the child's mind? And why do some changes persist for a long time while others do not? Of course, you know the notions of constructivism, and the notions of constructionism as formulated here try to provide some sorts of answers to that question. My own research tries to look in exquisite detail at questions of what's in the mind and how it changes over time. But I would like to say something else about that. I think I have a contribution to make here. I would like to talk a little bit about the way these word worlds relate to a child's language knowledge. And how microworlds relate to what children do.

Let me take the following starting point. Monday we heard Seymour Papert joking about grammar. 'Should we teach children grammar so they can speak better? That's perfectly silly.' Of course it is. If you 'can spell all the words you use and your grammar's as good as your neighbours,' what more do you need? What is it one learns from playing with a BEACH microworld? The child learns that there are two classes of words in the world. There are object-names, such as SUN or CAR or TRUCK. Then there are action words, the words that change things. What are we really teaching the child? If you are only dealing with one word at a time, it's hard to say that you are dealing with parts of speech. But let's look a little closer:

Apple Sprite Logo	State Variables
State Variables	State Changers
OBJECT	TELL :number
SHAPE	SETSHAPE :number
COLOUR	SETCOLOUR :number
POSITION	FORWARD :number
	BACK :number
HEADING	RIGHT :number
	LEFT :number
SPEED	SETSPEED :number
PENSTATUS	PENUP
	PENDOWN
	SETPENCOLOUR :number

17. 1993. Unpublished. This text is part of the keynote presentation as delivered at the 10th International Conference on Technology and Education.

We have here a short description of the set of state variables that completely describe everything there is to say about a Sprite Logo Object. It has a number, it has a shape, a colour, location, and heading. What we are doing in a sprite Logo Word World is segregating words of the computer language and the natural language into names for objects and state variable changers. Does that take us very far? Perhaps not very far, but it moves us in an interesting direction.

The CITY Word World

The microworld scene shown here (an early sketch of Tech Square, home of the MIT Artificial Intelligence laboratory) is one whose objects are controlled by Logo language phrses. The word NEW determines that a new object will be created. If you want to have more than one object of a specific type in your word world, you have to be able to distinguish between them. That's what adjectives do for nouns. For example, consider the phrase 'THE NEW BLUE GIRL.' The word BLUE modifies the following word GIRL; together they specify the shape and colour for a single object. When you can use adjectives, you can have a red girl and a blue girl, and others as well. It is possible — even easy in Logo word worlds — to justify for a child greater complexity than is possible in microworlds controllable by one word at a time. When sprite Logo first was available, one could not get very far with a TI-99 because there was precious little memory in the computer. But Logo sprite systems and LogoWriter systems have much more memory available now. Let me show you how one might go ahead to actually parse something such as this phrase:

Suppose we have a phrase 'the red girl walks fast.' What would we like the sentence to do? First, to specify the active object and then to change it's state. By writing procedures for the specific words, anyone can make that happen. In this example, what does the word 'the' do? Does anybody know? Well, surely a five year child will not know. So it has my favorite procedure 'TO THE' — which does absolutely nothing: it outputs whatever is input to it; it passes the buck. We can distinguish between sprite objects of the same shape by colour differences. The word RED defines the value of a global variable which is used for testing against a two part data structure containing a sprite number and a colour. Thus one can tell at any point whether we are talking to a red girl, a blue girl or yellow girl or a green girl. We can do this with elementary Logo procedures. In the same spirit of radical simplicity, you need not distinguish between WALK and WALKS unless you want the difference to make a difference. A very simple set of procedures is all you need to parse

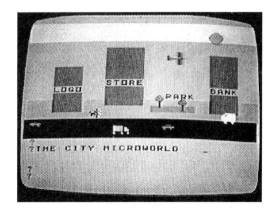

sentence level statements in this Logo word world.

Are we teaching the child grammar? The person who makes such procedures learns grammar of a sort. What sort of grammar is it? And how does it relate to the 'real thing' that grown up 'serious' people study. Here I think we get to the key issue of of Logo's value in education. As a child proceeds to build things like this, sets of procedures, the child is beginning to construct in her mind a microtheory of the domain — a microtheory to go with the microworld. And what is that microtheory about? It specifies what are the objects of the microworld, what are the relations between the objects in the world and how specific ones relate to each other.

About Different Kinds of Theories

Let's talk a little more about the notion of a microtheory. We hear a lot about microworlds. But what about theories. In my recently published book, volume two of Artificial Intelligence and Education, the ideas I'm describing right now appear in the first chapter, entitled 'Shared Models: the cognitive equivalent of a lingua franca.' It begins with a discussion of what you might call a common sense theory of what theories are about. It has four components; four types of theories are dealt with: perspectives, common sense theories (minimal models), technical theories (simple or as elaborate as quantum electrodynamics), and presentational theories, the kinds of simplified stories we offer lay-people or children to give them a flavour of what a technical theory is all about.

Let's start with an example of a perspective. The world, for the longest time, was something we thought of as the centre of the universe. And, of course, many of us still do. Once people got off the surface of the planet, it became very hard not to see that what was most important about the world was not that it was so big or capacious but that in fact served as a container for the biosphere in which all of us live. Though it's somewhat peculiar to think about it this way, the earth is kind of a jar — but with the contents on the outside. Strange characteristics for a container; but with implications relating to the fragility and stability of the environment and the possibility of evolution. A simple observation, such as that one, embodies a perspective.

Sarkhar's Theory of Social Cycles

Let me give you an example of a common sense model, a specific one which — if we are going to talk about changes — is not inappropriate. For the past couple of years there has been a fad of predicting financial ruin. There is a fairly popular book lately called 'The Coming Great Depression of the 1990s.' In that particular book, the author advanced a theory, a cyclical theory, of the development of society. He says that when you have a time of trouble, you get a revolution, and what happens in a revolution is that the Army takes over. Rule by the military is eventually replaced — because military people are often not so flexible as others — is replaced by intellectuals taking over and getting power; they dominate the country or region. But of course intellectuals are too much caught up in ideas and pay too little attention to details. Those people who pay attention to the small details, the bankers and administrators eventually dominate the world. And what do they do? To amass all the fortunes and power of their region of the world, they grind down everybody else. They drive soldiers and intellectuals down into the lower classes, so that once again society has trouble and revolution. This is what I consider a minimal model. It is essentially a common sense theory for thinking about phenomena that are too important to let pass, but for which we can have no better theory than the kind of thing represented here.

About technical theories: I suppose you already know what those are about, so I won't say much about them. These are all the theories of modern science.

Presentational theories — what are those? They are simplifications used to introduce and explain technical and common sense theories.

How MicroTheories Work in MicroWorlds

Now what is a microtheory? Well, with respect to a microworld, it is a theory of what goes on in the microworld. And since the microworld itself is a made-up, presentational model, whether made by an educator, a parent, or a software designer, the situation is one where the child is developing piecemeal a theory for something that has already been simplified.

My speculation is that the distance between a child's microtheory for what is happening in a microworld and the ultimate knowledge about what is going on in the microworld, that difference is much less than it would be for a child constructing microtheories about what is happening in the larger world. In a sense then, the possible educational gain of microworlds comes from a more intimate fit between possible microtheories and the way the microworld really works.

Ultimately then, the main thing that a person gets from working with a microworld is the experience of doing a kind of virtual science, of saying 'Here is something interesting enough to be worthwhile explaining. I'll come up with my best shot, try it out; if it doesn't work, well we'll debug it and improve our theory.' That approach is in the best traditions of science.

A further observation I can make is that we are looking at intermediate kinds of objects. We really don't care with respect to any microworld what the child's ultimate knowledge is. But the interesting thing here is the notion that microtheories are kinds of intermediate theories. The reason there might be something deep here is that this resonates with Piaget's notion of the grouping as a kind of precursor structure that does not yet have the full competence and status of a mathematical group. The grouping is a way station on the path to the ultimate knowledge that one would like to reach. So these microtheories for microworlds are intermediate structures . . .

I would like to draw to a conclusion if I may, then. As you can imagine, I am leaving out a lot here, fascinating to me, perhaps a little less so to you. The essential message I have been talking about with microtheories is that we want to look at the intermediate structures. Why is that important? Let's think about life. We all know how it begins and where it ends. All of interest happens in between. I would say to you that in cognitive development, despite our great haste to have children grow right smack up and become ace scientists or mathematicians or writers or whatever, it is better to let them have the choice and freedom to follow their own path and become their own authentic beings. One element of authenticity is that their minds should be stocked more with their own personally worked out theories than with ideas adopted from others but never understood. Such is the greatest gift we can give to any of the young people who come under our influence as educators . . .

Psychology

Case Studies Materials and Analyses
THE DEVELOPMENT OF OBJECTIVES[1]

'. . .the more one examines life the firmer becomes the conviction that it contains no well-rounded plots and that a good deal of what we do has a higgledy-piggledy nature, slapstick in tone, which forces us either to be greatly sad or highly hysterical. Philosophy is merely the parlor interpretation of unplanned pandemonium in the kitchen. The philosopher attempts the Herculean when he tries cataloguing chaos.'
Walt Kelly – (Epilog to 'Ten Ever Lovin' Blue Eyed Years with Pogo')

Introduction
This chapter explores a person's developing objectives, tracing the pattern of their changes through analysis of a limited empirical corpus. The issue confronted here is creativity in respect to objectives. That goals dominate activity is a central dogma of current work in the study of intelligence. However, any person who showed the goal commitment typical of artificial intelligence programs would be judged a monomaniac. Human commitment is typically of a more limited sort. Consequently, I prefer to describe people as having not goals but objectives, indeed, large collections of objectives.[2] In special circumstances some people do develop commitment to and struggle to achieve very difficult ends; such behaviour would be properly characterized as goal driven.

My specific endeavor here will be to recount and explain some details of how a seven year old child drew the picture of a house and its setting. My general purpose is to find and present specific sources of guidance, i.e. what led the child to do one thing rather than another. The two principles of creative projection I uncover and examine are simple elaboration, that is, applying some working procedure to some slightly more complex case, and objective formation proper through the frustration of an attempted elaboration. Tracing the developing activities of the project raises important issues about how problem solving in the current task domain relates to earlier experiences. The value of

---

1. 1977. Unpublished. Subsumed as Chapter 1 of *CECD* (1985). See also the text of 'On Not Planning' in the introduction to this collection.

2. In precise use, the word 'goals' generally implies struggle and hardship in achieving some end; the contrasting word 'objective' implies the attainability of the end. These and other contrasts are laid out in extensive detail in Webster's Synonomy.

working through this analysis and its introductory material is uncovering a view of mind which is then applied to the problem of learning in the remainder of this book.

Background Of The Data Collection

I had two purposes in preserving a better record of interactions with children; first to understand better the specific path of learning and second to record their reactions to programs I developed for their use. The work was not an 'experiment' in the sense of being fashioned to test some hypothesis. This particular project began with my asking my son, Robby, aged 7 years 5 months, (7;5) that he test a new drawing program and give me his reactions. (See Figure 1.1) At the end of the project, I had an audiotape record of a multi-day computer project. The material is suitable for an analysis of objective development because the boy followed his own direction within the loose constraints set by the computer medium and the programmed environment. The story of how Robby made this drawing will not be presented chronologically but rather in an order chosen to highlight the ideas which the case material exemplifies. We begin with presentation of several related and simple cases of elaboration and the natural limitations of the process. Let us start then with a simple idea, but in the middle of a story.

The DRAW program offered the menu of shapes in Figure 1.1 for a child's selection.[3] The expectation was that children would enjoy assembling designs of the menu into whatever shapes suited their fancy. When a child completed a shape, he directed the program to generate a Logo procedure for recreating that shape by specifying its name.

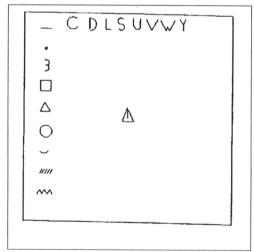

Figure 1.1 - Menu of Shapes

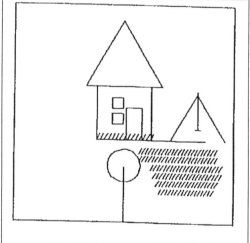

Figure 1.2 - H7GS: ' House and seven grasses'

My intention was that DRAW function as an introduction to programming for children. DRAW uses procedure names with inputs to specify the size of the designs. For example, 'BOX [20]' makes a square 20 turtle steps on a side and 'BOX [20 100]' makes a rectangle 20 turtle steps high and 100 turtle steps wide. Robby was provided with a list of procedure names for shapes in the menu, but the lack of clarity about how inputs were applied to shapes created some of the problems and even interesting incidents in the development of H7GS (the name Robby gave his scene).

Cases of Elaboration

The Basic Example

Near the completion of the drawing shown in Figure 1.2, Robby said he wanted to put some grass near his house. After several trials, exploring the effect of the input parameters on the turtle's action, Robby completed the first line of grass at the base of the house. He then undertook the yard, first with three lines of grass (after which he saved his work as H4GS — House and Four Grasses) and then completed, with three more lines of grass, his final product, H7GS. In the explication of changes in Figure 1.2, notice the stepwise progression and changing of one element at a time.

An initial success and six elaborations: The scene was made over three days in working sessions of approximately an hour's duration each. During the development of the scene, the shape menu was also on the computer display. The spaces above and to the left of Robby's scene were filled by the menu shown in Figure 1.1. The details of successive elaborations in use of 'HAIR' procedure to make grass are as follows:

Initial success: grass at the base of the house.

ELABORATION	DETAIL
1	grass low on screen: changing initial turtle location
2	a little longer (changing an input variable value)
3	a little longer still; saving work on a disk file
4	grass moved left (near the tree)
5	moved left, made longer; no good, too close to tree.
6	repeated higher (farther from tree) saved as H7GS.

In this environment, elaboration is the process of repeating the execution of a successful procedure with some small variation of its application, for example in the locaton of the turtle or the value of an input variable supplied to the procedure.[4] With the grass of H7GS, the process of elaboration was terminated by exhaustion. There is no more room for grass; in this specific sense the application of the procedure to this little task domain is complete. The child's progressive mastery of the use of the procedure in the environment has turned a procedure, at first successfully executed in one specific case, into a tool usable more freely within a small domain of application. This is a very concrete form of generalization. Such a process of elaboration is not limited to task

---

3. The program was inspired by the drawing techniques of Ed Emberley (1972).

4. See the extended citation Tversky and Kahnemann: On Anchoring with Variation.

domains using computer procedures. For example, if one tells a child that numbers greater than twenty are formed by concatenation of twenty with the well-known smaller numbers, he should not be surprised that the child puts together what he's been told and begins counting with twenty-one and proceeds through twenty-nine, twenty-ten, twenty-eleven, etc. With this counting example, the child focuses on the most salient element and varies the adjunct terms. Although 'achieving mastery through consolidation of a working procedure' may be one reason behind the everyday phenomenon of elaboration, there are surely others. I am less interested in reasons for elaboration than in the creativity of the process.

Figure 1.3 - Paper Plans

Consequently, I choose here to set out some other examples which reveal the impact of concrete experiences on the process.

Repeating a Successful Procedure to Achieve a Complex Concrete Objective

Early in the project, Robby noted some of his intentions in the sketch of Figure 1.3. In general, his plans revealed a process of repeating a successful procedure with a minor variation to achieve a richer, concrete objective, one more complex, more full of detail, more like the everyday world in which he lived. For example, the house he first produced has overhanging eaves as did the carriage house in which we lived at the time. The dormer windows — a dominant aspect of his planning — reflect forcefully the influence of the presence of such windows in that house, as well as being duplications with reduced proportions of the HOUSE itself. The detail of the windows — their being made of four panes — also reflects this casual inspiration of the created object by the concrete experience of everyday life.

Two aspects of the paper plans are noteworthy. First is the repetition of basic shapes on a diminishing scale. Thus the house shape itself is replicated in the dormer window. The square of the house storey next appears as the window and then as the individual glass panes. The second aspect is the concreteness of the drawings in the sense that his plan shared several specific features with the house we lived in. Finally, notice at this early planning stage the appearance of the grass motif which was only completed at the end of the project. See the text for a discussion of the role of deferred objectives in this project.

Blocked Objectives

I felt it necessary to dissuade Robby from undertaking these specific additions to his house because of all the complicated positioning that would have been required to achieve the dormers-with-four-paned-windows. He himself decided that making a doorknob for the door would be too tedious (he imagined here making a series of twenty four 'forward and right' commands). Finally, the grass which he later added as the finishing touch of his H7GS design first appeared in this sketch (the five slanted lines with three arrows from them). I suggested to Robby using the HAIR procedure to make the grass he wanted. Robby adopted the idea and elaborated it: 'I could put three grasses in here so it looks like a yard.'

If objectives are blocked, some appear to be lost but not all of them. We know from the final design of figure 1.2 that Robby ultimately achieved his objective of making a yard. The characterization of elaboration as one process of objective generation is accurate, but it is not the whole story. We now examine in detail how this simple objective of making a yard became deferred and by what sort of objective it was replaced. The reason we do so is to develop a richer sense of the interplay of multiple objectives over a long time scale and, hopefully, a simple model which adequately describes that interplay.

Deferred Objectives

After I explained how to use two input variables to specify the height and width of a door, Robby expressed a desire to make a park, 'Before we go into the fancy stuff, why don't we put in the grass?' He pointed to his chosen design in the shape menu, and I told him the procedure name was SAW. Neither of us knew what relation the specific input bore to the size of the figure. Robby decided to execute SAW [10]. The object created was a single sawtooth of size smaller than the turtle-cursor. He erased that and tried, at my suggestion, SAW [100]. Robby wanted grass extending from the house to the edge of the screen. What he got surprised us both.

Robby: Hey! That's one big blade of grass.
Bob: Oh . . . you know what happened, Rob? This SAW procedure tried to make the grass 100 turtle steps high. That's not what you wanted . . . I think you'd better erase that . . . Go ahead, Rob, rub it out.
Robby: No, it's going to be a playground.
Bob: Oh . . . I get the idea. [This is not a suggestion, but my empathetic grasp of what his motives were.] You want to keep that, like the swing set out back in Guilford [the town we formerly lived in].
Robby: Yeah.
Bob: We can still put some grass in.
Robby: No. It's going to be a tar playground.

The tenacity with which Robby protected this accidental addition to his house was shown even more forcefully in what followed. He could not see any good way to get the turtle to the top of the 'swing', save trial and error. I suggested erasing the swing and re-creating that appearance by executing TRI [100], because I knew that the turtle would finish the procedure aligned under the top vertex of an equilateral triangle. From such a position, reaching the vertex would have been simple. Refusing this suggestion, Robby proceeded to the vertex by moving and turning the turtle little by little, reaching it precisely but in his own way at his own pace. Thence he drew the swing and seat of Figure 1.2.

Demon Procedures and the Symbolic Achievement of Frustrated Objectives

Robby's adoption of adding a swing to his house can be described as the activation of a demon procedure. In the lexicon of Artificial Intelligence, 'demon' names a procedure which becomes active under the fulfillment of specific conditions. Think of Maxwell's demon, a little man who watches a strictly limited set of conditions and leaps into action when those conditions indicate the opportunity is right to effect his objective. Robby's 'swing demon' was created by our moving to Massachusetts. At our former home, the swing set was Robby's delight. When we moved, he expected to disassemble it and bring it with us. The unforeseen obstacle was the resistance of our new landlords; they would not permit such a swing on their property. I propose, then, that Robby's adding a swing to the HOUSE he had constructed, when he saw its achievement as being within reach, amounts to a *symbolic realization* of a prior, frustrated objective. I specifically disavow making the Freudian claim that such symbolic realization satisfies whatever frustrations are entrained in an objective's failure.

```
OBJECTIVES        SOURCES            DEMONS                                 ACHIEVED
Encode a House    Programming        HOUSE                                  —
                  Project            |
Bring Swing Set   Moving             |  SWING  —                            —
First Square      HOUSE demon        X  |                                   yes
Bigger Square     Bob                |  |                                   yes
Add roof          HOUSE demon        X                                      yes
Add eaves         Elaboration           |                                   yes
Window            Elaboration           |  WINDOW                           —
Door              Elaboration           |  |  DOOR                          —
4-pane window     Elaboration           |  |  |                             —
Dormer window     Elaboration           |  |  |                             —
Door              DOOR demon            |  |  X                             —
Door knob         Elaboration           |  |  |                             —
Grass             Rob (procedure)       |  |  |  GRASS                      —
Yard (of grass)   Elaboration           |  |  |  |  YARD                    —
Door              DOOR demon            |  |  X  |  |                        —
Grass             GRASS demon           |  |  |  X  |                        —
Swing set         SWING demon        X                                      yes
Tree (of yard)    Elaboartion              |  |  |  |                       yes
Person (of tree)  Elaboration              |  |  |  |                       —
Window            WINDOW demon             X  |  |  |                        yes
Grass             GRASS demon           I  |  X                              yes
Window            WINDOW demon          X                                    yes
```

Window 2	Elaboration				yes
Door	DOOR demon	X		yes
Window 3	Elaboration				—
Yard	YARD demon		X	yes
Seven grasses	Elaboration			yes

'X' indicates that the objective surfaced and either was achieved or deferred. This chart is produced from a detailed analysis of the material summarized in the text. See in the text 'A
retrospective account' for an explanation of the source of the HOUSE demon.

Figure 1.4 - Inception and fulfillmenet of deferred objectives

My proposal is different, that the symbolic realization of prior frustrated objectives
explains a significant portion of those everyday objectives which a person adopts as he
operates in a relatively unconstrained task domain.

The Demon Objectives Proposal

This proposal — call it the DEMON OBJECTIVES proposal — implies first that there
might be a multitude of objectives which could be activated at any time. This is very
troublesome. One might ask whether it be possible to make any sense at all of behaviour
— in terms of the operation of such demon procedures — given their potentially
enormous number. It IS possible to do so. Figure 1.4 exhibits such an analysis in detail of
the components of the design H7GS.

The Demon Objectives proposal is troubling most especially because with the 'symbolic
realization' of objectives almost anything can symbolize anything. Such vagueness is
possible that any interpretation might work. It is at this point that I must invoke a
commitment to empirical detail as the guidance which can save us from the excessive
fancy of a theorist's imagination. If one examines what is unusual about the interpretation
of objective formation implicit in Figure 1.4, he will notice that it depends especially on
two factors: first is the unusual closeness, in a problem solving study, of the experimenter
and the subject (no non-intimate of the subject could claim such understanding without
ridicule); second is the time scale as a factor of enormous signifcance.

To clarify the importance of time scale, I present here a second demon driven
interpretation of objective formation, one based on related material from a protocol taken
in an earlier project with the same child. It also introduces a new issue of major
importance. Robby's attempting to apply a successful solution to the next more complex
objective in that earlier project encountered an unanticipated obstacle and generated a
demon — an objective he failed to achieve and which was deferred for activation at some

later time. I propose that Robby's choice of drawing a house as his initial and primary objective in H7GS derives from the following specific failure in a previous project.

A Retrospective Account - A House that Failed

I told Robby I was going to make a procedure for him to try on his next visit to the Logo lab. I wrote TRI, a procedure for generating an equiangular triangle of 100 turtle steps on a side.[5] Robby was a little confused as to my purposes but followed step-wise my drawing the figure on our chalkboard and my encoding the procedure on a 3x5 card. I followed TRI with TINY, which drew a similar triangle of 30 units side measure.

TO TRI	TO TINY	TO FOX
FORWARD 100	FORWARD 30	CLEARSCREEN
RIGHT 120	RIGHT 120	SETHEADING 90 TRI
FORWARD 100	FORWARD 30	LEFT 60 TINY
RIGHT 120	RIGHT 120	RIGHT 60 FORWARD 70
FORWARD 100	FORWARD 30	LEFT 60 TINY
RIGHT 120	RIGHT 120	HIDETURTLE
END	END	END

Thereupon I told Robby the idea was to make a FOX out of these two triangles, in the way he had learned from reading Ed Emberley's books. This caught his interest. We began FOX.[6]

We simulated on our home blackboard the action of a Logo computer turtle. I arranged initial conditions so that at the completion of TRI the turtle was horizontal at the left vertext, pointing across the top of the head. To put on the ear we had to have him point differently. 'How much is half of 120?', Robby asked me, then said the turtle must 'LEFT TURN 60' after my answer. What do we do next? Robby: 'TINY'. His decision to turn left 60 degrees worked. The FOX had one ear. We returned the turtle to the horizontal, went forward 70 turtle steps, did a left turn 60, and invoked TINY. Our FOX was complete. Robby showed his mother the procedure we had 'planned out' for our next trip to Logo and brought her to the chalkboard to see the FOX we had drawn.

Robby's triangle

5. The Logo procedures encoded throughout the text conform generally to that of Apple Logo. Where departures are made (usually for historical reasons), I will make it clear. Since Logo is a high level language, the differences between various implementations with comparable machine features are minimal.

6. Employing the figure assembly techniques described in Ed Emberley's books, Robby's practice was to make elaborate and extensive drawings at nearly every opportunity. His figure assembly skills were well developed.

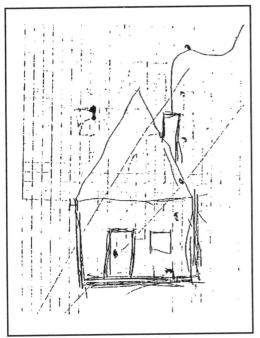

Figure 1.5 - A house that failed.

My objectives were completed, but Robby developed his own.

An Unexpected Elaboration

Robby asked me for a 3x5 card so he could write a procedure for a HOUSE. It is hard to be certain why Robby chose a house as his next project, but it is not unreasonable that, having worked through a FOX picture by assembling two triangles, Robby was attempting to create a house from a triangle and a square. One could judge this objective to be the next more complex task, thus a simple elaboration. I tried to help, but Robby said he wanted to do it alone. As I was leaving the room, he asked how much was half of 90. This question echoed his earlier query when attempting to figure out how much the turtle should turn before drawing the TINY ear. Half of 120 was, by chance, a good choice in that case. Half of 90 was not so lucky a choice in this second case. When I returned from some chores, I found on the chalkboard a triangle, with Robby standing puzzled before it.

Drawing of a House That Failed

Robby asked if 40 was the right length for the slope of the roof. I informed him that by choosing 45 degrees at the horizontal vertices he had gotten himself into a tough problem — not even I could tell him what the right number was just by looking at the triangle. He argued that 40 should work because 'when you make triangles out of tinker toys, if you use two blue ones for the side, you use the next bigger size, a red one, for the longer part; and 50 is like the next bigger size from 40'. Should I have told him about the square root of 2? I did say that with triangles, the next bigger size for the side depends on the angle, that 45 degrees made things tough but that 60 degrees was a good number and that's why the FOX had worked out so well. Robby was clearly in over his head. He decided he was going to stop because the problem was too hard and he had to leave for a birthday party. He folded his work and threw it in the trash whence I retrieved it later. You can see his drawing of the house he failed to encode in Figure 1.5.

The main points of similarity between the failed-house in this figure of Robby's earlier programming project and the house of H7GS are: general proportions, existence of a door and window (and the doorknob which Rob also failed to get in H7GS); the scribble at the bottom of his drawing may have re-appeared as his first successful use of the HAIR procedure to represent grass.

Shadow Domains - a Central Postulate of This Work

In this incident, one can see exhibited the guidance of problem solving within the task domain (Logo programming) by values appropriate to what I call a 'shadow domain'. Logo commands are typically formed by an operation (WHAT to do) and an operand (HOW MUCH of it). Note that Robby had a good sense of operations in that domain. He knew about going forward, about turning, about making procedures, but his use of these ideas was imperfect, in the sense of how to apply them to this specific problem. What recourse had he? He chose to operate in the task domain with operand values derived from the shadow domain, as his explicit analogy makes clear: he assigned distance values in this new domain, Logo language programming, on the basis of relations applying in a shadow domain, in this case the play world of tinker toys, to which he assimilated his coding judgments. Should this surprise anyone? Is not an operand — the how much or how many of an action — the finer specification of choosing what is to be done? If one is familiar merely with the operations of a domain, is it not reasonable that judgments of quantity and relation might still lag behind familiarity with operations? In precisely this sense and at such a specific point, the values of a shadow domain could be used to guide judgments in a task domain.

To understand problem solving in a task domain, one must be sensitive to existing shadow domains — whatever they are and however many they may be. There exists some more profound relation that must be considered in the problem solving environment than a simple assignment of external objects to internal categories. This more profound relation is an expression of the fundamental problem-deforming character of mind. The impact of such guiding knowledge on problem solving MUST be considered and CAN be considered; THIS IS A CENTRAL POSTULATE OF MY WORK. Let us now attempt a deeper characterization of these shadow domains and the development of objectives.

Reflections

Shadow Domains and Cognitive Structures

We have seen how this little shadow world of 'tinker toy' play entered into one child's problem solving in a programming task domain. One could label such a thing analogy and let it go as something vaguely understood. I choose, however, to pursue the character of such shadow domains by a more extended analysis of this example. Consider first that the guidance of problem solving solving by past experience CAN ONLY BE through the cognitive structures of mind. The child has constructed within his mind symbolic descriptions of his past little worlds of experience — call such a structure a microview[7] — which is useful not only in tinker-toy play but also as a model which provides guidance to him for solving newly encountered problems in different task domains. Three characteristics of this tinker toy microview stand out as especially noteworthy: the concreteness of the objects of the world; the usefulness of the knowledge about them for guiding problem solving; their procedural genesis.

---

7. The character, development, and interaction of such microviews is explored through the empirically based analyses of *CECD*. A compact overview is presented in Chapter 7 of that work.

With respect to concreteness, note that the rods not only have well defined properties of length and assembly-relations, they are also specified by their colour coding. The salience of such accidental properties as colour (for objects whose most important relations in normal play use are geometrical) implies that microviews may be more experience bound and particular than is logically necessary. An implication of this fact is that the use of such microviews with particular problems encountered may be highly idiosyncratic. If the child preserves too much concrete detail of his past experiences, his problem solving attempts could be more hindered than helped by such guidance. Is not this all too often the case?

The Generation of Hypotheses from Simultaneously Active Microviews

The use of one body of knowledge, e.g. the tinker toy microview — to provide explicit guidance in problem solving in a different task domain, programming in turtle geometry, emphasizes its model-like character. Robby called upon his knowledge about tinker toys — and that of number sequences simultaneously — to form an hypothesis about what might be reasonable operands for turtle geometry commands. At least two observations are appropriate here. First, such a style of problem solving helps explain the genesis of hypotheses in fact, whether or not one can feel logically entitled to use the information.[8]

This observation raises serious questions about the value of any description of problem solving which focusses on a single task domain. If shadow domains play an important role in problem solving, if the invocation of knowledge appropriate to the microviews constructed from earlier experience guides problem solving behaviour in novel situations, any study of problem solving sharply focussed on a task domain alone is vulnerable to the criticism that the task itself may inhibit the characteristic operations of natural intelligence. Secondly, if new microviews are constructed within the mind through problem solving experiences and if the shadow domains of prior microviews guide problem solving behaviour in novel situations, can it be doubted that there must be a very potent 'genetic' influence of prior experience on the development of new cognitive structures?[9] This in turn suggests that it might be fruitful to think of the mind as having a control structure of invocable knowledge which embodies the genetic path of descent.[10] To the extent that any description of mind — however precise and formal — cannot encompass such an organization of knowledge, it is inadequate to represent human mentality even in the relatively simple area of problem solving. Any theory which undervalues the functional and developmental importance of such an organization of structures will misguide those who follow it, no matter how great its other virtues may be.

---

8. There is a major issue here, the validity of induction, which like a hidden shoal I would prefer to avoid. Note in the appendices of *CECD* the extended citation 'Goodman: On rightness of rendering' his reference to frantic attempts to justify the process of induction. Prefer, if you can, his more balanced view.

9. I use 'genetic' here in the specific sense of Piaget's genetic epistemology; I have no intention of raising or arguing in this place any questions of the relative influence or experience and biological inheritance.

10. What this might mean in practical terms and how one might gather evidence for or against such a conjecture are central issues dealt with in Chapters 2 through 5 of *CECD*.

Generalization and Classification

We can say a procedure becomes progressively generalized in application as it is used first with one variation then another. Thus a concrete procedure used within a task domain becomes a tool applicable over the range of that domain.[11] But the microviews in the mind may be more than collections of procedures. They have — or at least seem to have — existential implications. How can it be the case that a procedure could serve a classificatory function? To the extent that a procedure has become a tool which functions over a limited domain, the question can be put to it whether or not a specific object would serve a specific role in the functioning of the procedure. The question 'Is X a kind-of-thing?' can be reduced to 'Will X work in your procedure which applies to such kinds-of-things?' This is a commonplace question, one which every problem solver asks when seeking substitutes caused by some material shortage which blocks achievement of his objective with some ongoing procedure.

Generalization and Objective Formation

Given that one can understand how a provided procedure such as SAW, which Robby used for making grass, could be made into a tool through progressive variablization of salient inputs, we might next ask how created procedures such as HOUSE could also be turned into tools. The HOUSE procedure is context-bound in the following senses. Consider the HOUSE as portrayed in the picture of H7GS (Figure 1.2). That HOUSE is composed of a large square and triangle with a door and two windows as essential features; call that HOUSE 'HDW' (for HOUSE-DOOR-WINDOW). 'HDW' does not exist independently of the specific design in H7GS. For the HOUSE 'HDW' to exist as a tool, its embodiment in a procedure would require extraction from the context in which it developed as a construct. Creation of such a tool would show generalization as context de-sensitization. Robby did not show this form of behaviour. No one should be surprised at failing to see such an event: one should expect such generalization to take some time and to wait on the adoption of an objective of greater scope where the development of such a tool would be useful.

Context Desensitization

A second, specific sense in which the HOUSE is context-bound is in respect of scale, i.e. the HOUSE, in however many instantiations it might appear, would always be the same size. Let me exhibit some Logo instructions to variablize a HOUSE, thus turning this object into a tool:[12]

---

11. If one pushed a vision of the child as scientist, one might want to argue that he is 'testing an hypothesis' about the application of his theory to a particular case. A slightly weaker position is that the child is exploring the range of application of his procedure. This is still 'scientific' in the sense of many physical laws, such as Hooke's Law of elasticity, which are valid only over the range of circumstances to which they are found to apply. More importantly, this view emphasizes the abductive rather than inductive character of the inferences involved. See, however, my final character of Miriam italicized at the end of 'A cognitive profile' in the appendix (p. 221 of *CECD*).

12. A short technical note. The procedures invoked here, BOX and TRI, were written to take inputs as lists and implement default values for variables not specified; consequently, their syntax is quite non-standard.

```
TO HOUSE.CONSTRUCT          TO HOUSE.TOOL :HOWBIG
BOX [100]                   BOX [ :HOWBIG]
PEN UP                      PEN UP
FORWARD 100                 FORWARD :HOWBIG
PEN DOWN                    PEN DOWN
TRI [140]                   TRI [ (7 * :HOWBIG/5) ]
END                         END
```

As an overview of the process of making tools from objects in this domain, we should expect the developmental sequence to consist of at least these three steps: creation of a concrete object for a specific purpose; context desensitization of the procedure which produces the object; use of the procedure as a tool by its invocation from a higher level of control. The purpose, either explicit or implicit, of such an endeavor is to create components for some project of larger scope — which could only be imagined as possible given the achievability of its components.

Implicit in these forms of context desensitization, implicit in the repeated use of a procedure as a tool, is the creation of structure through the invocation of the procedure from a higher level of procedural control.[13]

The Unified Generalization Proposal

I propose that the process by which a concrete procedure is transformed into a tool is the same process by which a demon is created, that the failed objective capable of symbolic realization is the cognate of the tool created from the achieved objective. Let us call this idea the 'unified generalization' proposal. Let us look more closely at the parallel. If one notices that any objective implies a structure, a temporal and serial structure of the process of pursuing that objective. First, actions achieved by procedures serve objectives. The structure of all actions have beginnings, middles, and ends. The simplest such action structures, wherein the middle has no significant complication, proceed nearly directly to achievement of the objective. The simplest elaborations are of such a form. When that process occurs (whatever it may be) which transforms the serial structure of pursuing an objective into components of control structure, there is no reason to suppose that objectives should be immune from the context desensitization that is implicated in generalization. This is precisely what symbolic realization of objectives requires. If you compare the little procedures for the HOUSE.CONSTRUCT and HOUSE.TOOL, you will notice that it is precisely the objective achievable by the procedure that is changed. In this specific sense, the symbolic realization of a demonic objective does not appear markedly different from the generalized application of a procedure which has been transformed into a tool. At this level of description it is possible to unify the problems of generalization and objective formation. A schematic textual representation of the unified generalization proposal is presented in the box of the caption.

---

13. This is a central theme of *CECD*; its more precise exposition and its role in learning appear more explicitly in chapters 2 and 4 of that book where it is discussed as the elevation of control. See also in *CECD* the extended citation 'Papert: On the elevation of control.'

BEGINNING:
An initial objective becomes active
- when its procedure appears achievable in a domain
OUTCOMES:
The initial objective succeeds:
- this leads to a new objective through elaboration
- the procedure becomes a more generalized tool.
The initial objective fails:
- this leads to a new objective through demon formation
- the objective of the failed procedure becomes variablized, that is, symbolically realizable; at its furthest extreme, this permits detachment from the local context and procedure which created it.
CONSEQUENCES:
Any new objectives can become an initial objective.
The range of a procedure's efficacy is determined.

A Creative Closed System

A system such as represented in the box above is a creative, closed system. Objectives proliferate, some to be achieved after deferral, others to be permanently lost. Such a formulation shows how ideas and objectives may develop in a specific way in an individual mind. Nothing implies, obviously, that all objectives are determined exclusively by operations in such a closed system. For example, different bodily needs can provide starting points for diverse families of elaborated objectives (hunger, sex, etc.). Beyond the achievement of objectives, there may also be other motives for mental action. A second class might be represented by curiosity, seen as a primitive inclination to explore imperfectly understood phenomena; a third class might be purely expressive, as the poet G. M. Hopkins asserts:

> Each mortal thing does one thing and the same:
> Deals out that being indoors each one dwells;
> Selves - goes itself; *myself* it speaks and spells,
> Crying *what* I *do* is me: for that I came.

Constraining the behaviour one examines by pre-setting objectives, as in typical laboratory experiments, inhibits the surfacing of those processes which reflect the nature of mentality as revealed through its self control. The kind of analysis represented by the body of this paper, to the extent that it applies to behaviour less constrained than laboratory samples, is truer to the nature of the mind. However unsatisfactory the conceptual machinery for coping with the analysis of such challenges as Robby's HOUSE, restricting oneself to simpler problems will lead to solutions entirely inadequate to represent important processes of the natural mind. If we fail to tackle such problems as Robby's HOUSE (which is constrained by the medium more than by any objective), we miss a major component of mentality, perhaps THE major component. We might even see demon-driven structures as a searching of domains so limited that nearly all demons are inhibited. We might see isolated problem spaces constructed by experiments. We will miss not only solutions, but also profound problems of mentality.

How General Are These Ideas?: 'Bricolage'

One may ask, given that these notions are built on a few ideas and illustrations, whether or not the characterization of mind is sufficiently general to warrant interest and exploration. Against the goal-dominated activities of programmed intelligence, I hold out a contrasting characterization of human action, based on a much broader base of diverse cognitive study than analyses of my children's problem solving.

Claude Levi-Strauss describes the concrete thought of not-yet-civilized people as 'bricolage'[14], a French word naming the activity of the bricoleur (a man who undertakes odd jobs, a sort of jack-of-all-trades, or more precisely, a committed do-it-yourself man). The essential idea of bricolage is the looseness of commitment to specific goals, the idea that materials, structures, and competences developed for one purpose are transferable, can very easily be used to advantage in the satisfaction of alternative objectives. Levi-Strauss's appreciation of bricolage is sufficiently profound to be worthy of both quotation and extended examination.[15]

> ' . . .The bricoleur is adept at performing a large number of diverse tasks; but, unlike the engineer, he does not subordinate each of them to the availability of raw materials and tools conceived and procured for the purpose of the project. His universe of instruments is closed and the rules of his game are always to make do with 'whatever is at hand' . . . *in the continual reconstruction from the same materials, it is always earlier ends which are called upon to play the part of means* . . . This formula, which could serve as the definition of *'bricolage'*, explains how an implicit inventory or conception of the total means available must be made . . .so that a result can be defined which will always be a compromise between the structure of the instrumental set and that of the project . . . The bricoleur may not ever complete his purpose but he always puts something of himself into it . . .'

Planning versus Bricolage

In this description, one can appreciate the opposition of planning (the epitome of goal-directed behaviour) and the opportunism of demon-driven bricolage. This idea seems an idea profoundly antithetical to the goal-driven commitments of cybernetics and artificial intelligence. Observe, however, that the two are not discontinuous, that all activities can be seen as a mixture of the dominances of the polar tendencies represented here. The second point, not the less important, is that the relationship is not directional: there is no reason to suppose that planning is a more nearly perfect form of bricolage. If some inclusion relation must be sought, one could easily view planning as a highly specialized technique for solving critical problems whose solutions demand scarce resources.

---

14. For more detail, see the Extended citation at p. 250 in *CECD* 'Levi-Strauss: On Bricolage.'

15. Pp. 17, 21 in *The Savage Mind*, University of Chicago Press, 1966.

Broader Considerations:

Control Structure of the Mind

Over the past century, we have witnessed a widespread abandonment of the concept of 'free will,' an idea useful to individuals and society but one for which there is no sensible proposal at mechanical levels of description. Theorists of mind have striven to replace the individual who directs his thinking with some other alternative. Freud introduced fragmentation of the person into three active and competing homunculi: the individual becomes the body housing the Ego, Id, and Superego. For Freud, the apparently integral personality is a projection by society and the self on the resultant behaviour of these three primtitive forces and their processes of interaction.

Minsky and Papert, in the *Society Theory of Mind*, push the fragmentation and competition of the Freudian vision to its logical completion in the attempt to banish from the mind any trace of a mysterious homunculus.[16] Instead of three struggling fragments of self, they proposed societies of agents — each agent so simple it could be represented by a comprehensible computational process. For me, the image of mind as a society of computing agencies did not make satisfactory contact with the issue of how a person can feel himself to be related to the many subordinate processes from which others might see his behaviour to emerge. Levi-Strauss's characterization of bricolage seemed to fill this critical need — relating a computational theory to a more human image of man — and to go considerably beyond it.

Bricolage as a Model for the Self-Construction of Mind through Interaction

To the extent that bricolage, and not planning, is the best characterization of objective-related human behaviour in everyday situations, introducing the idea of bricolage into the AI community could permit the development of machine intelligence with some creativity in generating goals.[17] But further, and much more importantly, if behaviour is seen as driven by a bricoleur's objectives and if one constructs his own mind out of concrete experiences, then the metaphor might be extended to bring Piagetian mental self-construction (currently the best theory of human learning) within the range of a non-demeaning mechanical vision of mind.

The Functional Lability of Cognitive Structures

Students of anatomy have named the adaptiveness of structures to alternative purposes *functional lability*. Such functional lability is the essential characteristic of the bricoleur's use of his tools and materials. I propose that bricolage can serve as a metaphor for the

---

16. A research program and an assemblage of ideas while I was their colleague, the society of mind theory represents the intellectual backdrop against which my work may be seen as the major empirical investigation of learning developed in that MIT community during the late 1970s. Minsky continues his effort to produce a work which will make these ideas generally accessible as a theory.

17. An example bearing on this contention is the program AM which has succeeded in inventing the idea of number. The program is described in the thesis by Douglas Lenat, 'AM: an Artificial Intelligence Approach to Discovery in Mathematics as Hueristic Search.' For a perspicuous analysis of the successes of that program, see 'Why AM and Eurisko Seemed to Work,' by Lenat and Brown (1983 AAAI conference).

relation of a person to the contents and processes of his mind. Bricolage, as a name for the functional lability of cognitive structures, emphasizes the character of the processes in terms of human action and can guide us in exploring how a coherent mind could rise out of the concreteness of specific experience.

Bricolage presents a very human model for the development of objectives, for learning, and even a model for the interaction of the texture of experience and the symbolic descriptions through which people think. This represents not a mere metaphor in some superficial sense but a radical idea.[18] Every new idea is a metaphor; what is important is its fecundity. An idea becomes a radical metaphor precisely to the extent that its ramifications are found to be richly productive, in practice, in other domains. Functional lability is witnessed diverse other areas as well, for example in the process of physical evolution, and in the development of civilization. Consider these important examples.

Functional Lability — In The Evolution Of Flight

How did dinosaurs turn into birds? A team of researchers at Northern Arizona University proposed an explanation for the development of powered flight which appears to be a significant breakthough in our understanding of this major evolutionary change.[19] It is valuable for my purposes as a clear example of functional lability which emphasizes both the step-wise adaptedness of precursors and the locus of creativity.

A number of people have believed that powered flight derived from soaring as the membranes of tree dwelling gliders somehow changed into muscular wings. The details of this scheme comprise the arboreal theory of flight. A competing theory, the cursorial theory, has been much strengthened by the breakthrough of Caple, Balda, and Willis. This team created a series of models of successive forms of 'proavis' and then established the progressive adaptedness of each of these models by coupling appropriate aerodynamic arguments with a cost-benefit analysis of specific behaviours. A sketch of their assumptions and arguments is as follows.

The Physics of Running and Flying

Assuming first that the ancestors of birds were insectivorous dinosaurs, the theory measures good adaptedness with the criterion of 'foraging volume,' the space within which the creature might capture bugs in a given time. The greater the foraging volume, the better a creature could compete. Since bipedalism produces a higher reach and speed covers a greater area, one or both should be expected to develop. Well articulated, supple movement would provide more effective penetration of that foraging volume, as would the ability to jump at any point in a running course, so the well balanced control of movement by itself would favor those creatures which possessed it. These issues of balance and control become increasingly important as running speed increases. The location of considerable mass in a biped's forelimbs which could extend far beyond the

18. A philosopher I once knew, Huner Mead, aethetician and student of Susanne Langer, argued often with me the point that every philosophical system begins with a radical metaphor, a root from which it grows, branches, and is nourished.

19. My version is based on the article 'How Did Vertebrates Take to the Air?' by Roger Lewin in the Research News section of *Science* (July 1, 1983). The original by Caple, Balda, and Willis appeared in the *American Naturalist* (**121**, 455 (1983)).

radius of the body would provide significant control. The conclusion is that 'wings' developed because of the adaptive advantage of better balance in the air and on landing after a jump, not for flight.

Any flattening of these balancing forelimbs would provide lift,[20] thus permitting the extension of this increase in foraging volume through gliding on limbs already powered to exercise control of attitude. A similar effect would be achieved by extension of proto-wings through the elongation of scales and their transformation into feathers. The effect of lift would be to increase stability and thus permit greater running speed, and thus greater lift again, both of which extend further the predator's foraging volume.

Summary: Positive Feedback

In summary, three different physical changes lead to positive increases in foraging volume; bipedalism, increased running speed, and controlled jumping at speed. Because of the physics of the world, limbs extended to control the trajectory during a high speed jump experience lift. Since this lift increases with increasing speed and since it also increases the stability of the running creature, a positive feedback condition develops where more speed produces more lift and this in turn produces more speed. The creature takes off. Once in the air, those very limb movements which facilitate trajectory control, when coordinated, serve as the power stroke of flight.

Where does the Miracle Occur?

The character revealed in this example of evolution is one where opportunistic systems are constrained into paths of a step-wise development which permit coupling of physical effects of the milieu. The magic comes from the functional lability of physical structures (the leg becomes an arm becomes balancing mass becomes an airfoil) in a world where serendipity is possible and development irreversible.

Functional Lability — In The Invention Of Writing

The Sumerians of Mesopotamia are usually credited with being the first people to write texts, about 3000 B.C. The writing system had two basic character types: objects used as counters, numerical signs, were pressed into a clay surface; all other signs, pictographs and ideographs alike, were incised with the pointed end of a stylus. This invention is surely one of the central events in the history of civilization. It is possible to advance well reasoned arguments that make this creation comprehensible. More specifically, with the domestication of plants and animals around 8500 B.C., as Schmandt-Besserat observes:

> 'The new agricultural economy, although it undoubtedly increased the production of food, would have been accompanied by new problems. Perhaps the most crucial would have been food storage. Some portion of each annual yield had to be allocated for the farm family's subsistance and some portion had to be set aside as seed for the next year's crop. Still another portion could have been reserved for barter with those who were ready to provide exotic products and raw materials in exchange for

---

20. Lift is the common name for the Bernoulli effect, the pressure differential created by airflow around an asymetrical convex object. If such an object, an airfoil, is flat on the bottom and curved on the top, it will experience net pressure up.

foodstuffs. It seems possible that the need to keep track of such allocations and transactions was enough to stimulate development of a recording system . . .'[21]

The recording system which satisfied these needs, one where specific clay tokens represented quantities, was very stable. It spread thoughout the region of western Asia and remained current there for four thousand years. The second major step followed another cultural landmark, the emergence of cities . . .

> 'The development of an urban economy, rooted in trade, must have multiplied the demands on the traditional recording system. Not only production, but also inventories, shipments and wage payments had to be noted, and merchants needed to preserve records of their transaction . . .'[22]

The Replacement of Tokens by Symbols

Most significant seems to have been the development of token-based contracts. These contracts are represented now by clay envelopes, usually sealed with the marks of two merchants, hardened by baking, and containing within them the numeric tokens representing the amount of goods exchanged. Such a contract in hand, a middle-man could transport goods from one city to another with a guarantee to all that neither the shipment nor the terms had been altered. But, since the contract was validated by remaining unopened, one could not tell what it said without destroying it; consequently, it became customary to impress on the outside of the envelope the shapes of the tokens contained inside. The tokens were pressed into the clay envelope with a mnemonic intention based on one-to-one correspondence; the marks they made came to represent the contents of the envelope. The external markings were not invented to replace the tokens sealed within the clay envelopes, but that is what, in fact, happened. And this replacement of tokens, signs of things, by symbols — the impressions they made in a soft clay surface — was the beginning of writing.

The Flowering of Effects — from Adaptive Development

According to this scenario, writing was not invented to transmit ideas; but in the history of the West it has been a most powerful force in doing that, the primary means by which man has been able to extend communication beyond the circle of his immediate acquaintance, both in space and time. The functional lability of written symbols permitted a flowering of effects to derive from the adaptive development of writing's precursor, an accounting function, in response to a sequence of specific needs.

I see in this cultural example, and in Jacob's vision of evolution[23] the same processes of bricolage whereby an active agent applies pre-existing resources to new problems — through which process he defines what is novel in the problem and extends by modification his earlier resources. Occasionally these newly modified resources have a far wider application than their precursors. Such functional lability, developed through

---

21. This citation and general view is derived from 'The Earliest Precursors of Writing' by Denise Schmandt-Besserat in Scientific American, June 1978.

---

22. Schmandt-Besserat, op.cit.

23. See the extended citation at p. 253 in *CECD* 'Jacob: On Bricolage in Evolution.'

application to particular problems, is the root of creativity in evolution, culture, and personal development.

We can bring this broad ranging claim down to earth in the case of cognitive development by trying to penetrate more deeply into the Piagetian notions of assimilation and accommodation.

Bricolage as Problem Deformation: C. S. Peirce and Abduction

People frequently confuse 'abstract' with 'generally applicable'. What one DOES could apply generally and merely seem abstract if problems in the external world are deformed to fit processing by highly particular structures of the individual mind. Piaget named such a process of problem deformation 'assimilation,' taking that name at various times both from an alimentary metaphor and processes of linguistic change. If we move in the direction of more logical descriptions, the most apt way to characterize such a mind's logic in action is as proceeding less by deductive or inductive logics than by what C.S.Peirce named 'abduction.'[24]

> [Abductive inference] . . .is where we find some very curious circumstance, which would be explained by the supposition that it was a case of a certain general rule, and thereupon adopt that supposition.

Peirce's theory of types of inference: simple examples
DEDUCTIVE INFERENCE
- the rule: All the beans are from this bag are white.
- the case: These beans are from this bag.
- *implied* result: These beans are white.

INDUCTIVE INFERENCE
- the case: These beans are from this bag.
- the result: These beans are white.
- *implied* rule: All the beans are from this bag are white.

ABDUCTIVE INFERENCE
- the rule: All the beans are from this bag are white.
- the result: These beans are white.
- *implied* case: These beans are from this bag.

Peirce's terms rule, result, and case translate into a more concrete vision of the evolving mind as follows. The 'rule' becomes a cognitive structure, a model of a situation, what is known in the mind. The 'result' is the problem situation actually

---

24. Peirce, the major American philosopher of the nineteenth century, wrote popular articles as well as more technical work. His most accessible work, well represented by the essay 'The Fixation of Belief' is both profound and charming. The idea of abduction sketched below was introduced in his essay 'Deduction, Induction, and Hypothesis.' A technical analysis of his developing ideas of logical fundamentals may be found in *Peirce's Theory of Abduction* by K. T. Fann.

confronted. It presents immediate data such as 'these beans are white.' The implied case is the interpretation of the problem through the model.

Abduction is prior to Deduction and Induction
Abduction is prior to deduction and induction. This formulation emphasizes that a primary aspect of problem solving is the adopting of a hypothesis about 'what's what.' The perspective from which you view a situation determines what problem you imagine you are attempting to solve. This is so less by choice than by necessity: one can recognize the unfamiliar only by first misapprehending it as something familiar, then progressively distinguishing it from things actually familiar in the past. Thus, the core of abductive inference in human problem solving is the deformation of problems to fit the recognizing processes of models in the mind.

The best computational embodiment of such a view of mind is presented in Sussmann's HACKER system (Sussman, 1975), wherein a mental 'programmer' perfects old programs and assembles new ones with the guidance of failure information from its previous mis-appreciations of presented problems. Similarly, the Merlin system (Moore and Newell, 1973) matches a target/goal description against stored descriptions by some higher-level process making terms variable until partial equivalence is achieved at some level of variation. In contrast, the essential element of my vision of the evolving mind is that a number of active descriptions apply themselves simultaneously, each performing its best match/deformation, and those with sufficiently good match to the specific problem go forward while other competitors infer nonsense and inapplicable results. It is the difficulty of applying generated conclusions that defeats the parallel effort of the less successful competitors.

Convergence
With such a vision of mind, it is possible to understand how generally applicable skills arise from the coordination of diverse structures based upon particular experiences with processes that are more like abduction than generalization.[25]

Bricolage, as a name representing the functional lability of cognitive structures, with its focus on the interaction of pre-existing tools and available materials, helps to explain the power of the particular in determining the course of development. Here is a profound convergence, permitting a unification of points of view through which the form of evolution of species, the rise of civilization, and the pattern of development of the individual mind can be seen as the parallel results of the same sorts of historically determinate processes.

Bricolage and Cognitive Structures
What are the practical advantages of discussing human activity as bricolage in contrast to goal driven planning? The first advantage is that it is more natural, a more fit description of everyday activity than planning is. The second is that it is more nearly compatible with a view of the mind as a process controlled by contention of multiple objectives for resources than is planning, which seems to call for a single centre of decision or a chain of decisions in a pre-ordered form. The final and most important

---

25. Chapters 2 and 4 of *CECD* show extensive, detailed examples of how such ideas can be applied in describing a specific mind and its development.

advantage permits a new vision of the process of learning. Bricolage can provide us with an image for the process of the mind under self-construction in these specific respects:

- if the resources of the individual's mind are viewed as being like the tools and materials of the bricoleur, one can appreciate immediately how they constrain our undertaking and accomplishing any activity.
- not only constraint comes from this set of limited resources; also comes productivity, the creation of new things — perhaps not exactly suited to the situation but of genuine novelty.
- the mind, if seen as self-constructed through bricolage, presents a clear image of the uniqueness of every person:
  • each will have developed his own history of conceptions and appreciations of situations through which to make sense of the world.
  • each will have his personal 'bag of tricks,' knowledge and procedures useful in his past.
  • each will have his own set of different, alternative objectives to take up as chance puts the means at his disposal.

If viewed as claims, such statements are not easy to prove. However, they provide a framework for investigating learning which could be valuable by NOT demeaning human nature through assuming it is more simple than we know to be the case. With such an intention, it is reasonable to ask if these ideas can be applied to a specimen of behaviour — one able to sustain extended analysis — so that we may return with a richer and more precise application of how the development of objectives and learning create the self-constructed mind.

Implications for Method

The image of bricolage, when extended from a description of behaviour to a characterization of typical human thought, suggests how to explore human behaviour for evidence about mind. It gives hints of what to look for in the search for the psychologically real (concrete experiences and their sequelae). It emphasizes the importance of following an individual's selection of activities and the need for sensitivity to culture in tracing the development of mind on a Piagetian scale of development. Given that such observation has provided a fecund method to study the development of objectives, should it not be extensible for the exploration of such issues as how the fragmentary character of experience affects the mind and how significant learning happens in concrete situations? After this analysis of Robby's project, such questions generated 'The Intimate Study' of my daughter Miriam's learning, the case analyzed in detail in 'Computer Experience and Cognitive Development'.

A RESEARCH PROPOSAL FOR THE INTIMATE STUDY[26]

Charles Peirce argued that research in physics is of three kinds: first, the making out of new phenomena; second, the investigation of their laws; third, the measurement of constants. If the science of learning is to be like physics at all, should it not be so in permitting this latitude among the legitimate aims of research?

Peirce goes further in valuing as most important the making out of new phenomena. An example from current controversies will make clear why I find his judgment congenial. Though students of the mind from one stance or another may quibble over Piaget's formulations of development, none will deny him foundational status in the modern study of mind precisely because he discovered the regularities of ignorance.[27]

I part company from Peirce when he avers that the discovery of new phenomena is largely a matter of chance and when he makes that most dangerous of speculations, 'the new phenomena which now remain to be discovered are probably only of secondary importance.' My view comes from a contemporary vision of doing science which in part Peirce inspires, but in which he could only partly share and a vision wherein the critical issue is the relationship between data and theories.

Data and Theories

We are fortunate to have lived in a period of rapid scientific change, one consequence of which is that process itself has come under scrutiny and been rendered more nearly comprehensible. Our climate of opinion now takes for granted that essentially sociological perspective on scientific change advanced by Kuhn. And if such micro-cultural relativism leaves one uneasy, as it does me, there is still the profound ideological antidote of Peirce's vision of truth as the convergence of opinion over time in the community of minds. Gould[28] has described the recent paradigm shift in geology (i.e. to the general acceptance of continental drift as a consequence of the plate tectonics theory of geodynamics) as a pellucid example of scientific change. The essential points of his description reveal the interrelation of data and theories in most important scientific work.

Cast your mind back 20 years. Recall those popular books by Velikovsky, Earth in Upheaval, and so forth, wherein he argued astrophysical explanations for data no other

---

26. 1977. Unpublished. This text has been subsumed as an appendix to chapter 2, 'Evolving Datacase Designs,' in *CS&C* (Lawler and Carley, 1996).

---

27. How ironic that, much as Einstein's 'invariance theory' became 'relativity,' Piaget is popularly known for discovering 'conservation.'

28. See 'The Continental Drift Affair,' Natural history February 1977

theories could explain (e.g. peculiar distributions of African-like fossils in Scandinavia, etc.). He argued unconvincingly that astrophysical events had triggered continental migrations because there was no conceivable mechanism on earth to explain how continents of granite could plow through the seas of basalt underlying the great world oceans. He was ridiculed and the data to which he called attention were dismissed.

Gould recounts how a few mere years ago a new theory of geodynamics, proposing a mechanism which was capable of explaining the gradual separation of continents, raised again to prominence these data Velikovsky had invoked. The new theory swept the field of geology so that it is now a different science from what it was. The reason was not Velikovsky's data. The coerciveness of the plate tectonics theory derives from a prediction of the relevance of a new class of data (the directional magnetization of patterns of deep sea core samples), the discovery of this new phenomenon, and the lack of any conceivable mechanism other than sea-floor spreading for interpreting the results found. The pattern of change is this: a new theory is proposed which demands examination of new data; those new data exhibit phenomena which are interpretable only in terms of that theory; the new theory, in rendering one of several prior theories a consequence, selects between what had been previously competing interpretations of older data.

The computational theory of the self constructing mind will play a role in the science of learning analogous to that of plate tectonics in geology. I expect to find in the class of data I am now collecting sequences of events which will be interpretable as the interaction of concrete representations of ideas with specific events in terms of the progressive elaboration of those concrete ideas (debugging to meet new environmental requirements) and insight through analogy (abstraction of procedural control structure through substitution of terminal values and lowest level procedures). I believe these data will not be interpretable any other way.

Such data as I now gather may be vulnerable to criticism because they are of my daughter. One might note that geologists studied sea-floor spreading in the mid-Atlantic, not in their own back yards. Why do such a study as mine is? I would ask a similar question: why did geologists not first study sea-floor spreading on the moon? This lame joke is meant to suggest the important issue is not interpersonal involvement but the even more primitive question of what is the whole phenomenon to be explained and under what conditions is it possible (or impossible) to collect those data which are relevant to explaining that phenomenon. The geodynamicist must explain one mechanical system, the earth. There is only one earth and that is relatively convenient to observe. I believe one mind is a complete system to be explained. If it is necessary in tracking concrete development to observe that mind in all its settings and situations, it is not a mere convenience but a requirement that the mind be available to observation nearly all the time. For a researcher to win parent's confidence and gain permission for such a pervasive study would be most difficult and most likely impossible. I conclude it is a practical necessity that such a study be of one's own child.

If one argues further that the geologist takes core samples near the mid-Atlantic ridge, not everywhere, I admit freely that the analogy breaks down. The selective principles in my observation and data recording focus first on the locating the actions, objects, and situations to which may be plausibly ascribed specific ideas in Miriam's mind; second, on observing the way Miriam's ideas change at a low level of detail to permit plausible inferences about the immediate or proximate causes of these changes.

In conclusion these few words: men have long argued over the relative import of intrinsic and extrinsic factors in development. With the newly specific ideas of artificial intelligence, I hope to trace the interaction of psyche and settings to see how of the concrete world we encounter:

> *Nothing of him that doth fade*
> *But doth suffer a sea-change*
> *Into something rich and strange —*
> *the human mind.*

HULA HOOP ANALOGIES (Vignettes) [29]

One of the most active foci of developmental incidents so far has been Miriam's use of the hula hoop. Four separate incidents come together as activities centred on this toy.

How we came to buy a hula hoop

Our family was having dinner at the house of a Cambridge friend. My children had been playing with Jenner (my friend's 5 year old daughter) during the late afternoon. When I arrived from the lab, I found the three children, two bikes, and a red-white-and-blue striped hula hoop on the sidewalk. Since it fell my lot to put the toys away, I noted it well.

Because Miriam suffered some confusion about right and left turns in using SHOOT (see, for example, Logo Sessions 1 and 3), I decided to undertake 'playing turtle' with the game (i.e. playing SHOOT with the floor taking the place of the display screen and Miriam and me taking turns being the turtle and being the turtle commander) Which we did in Logo Session 3. With this intention, I manufactured a hoop from some polyethylene tube lying in a pile of oddments in the music room. The hoop was adequate for playing turtle, but not as a hula hoop (Miriam attempted to so use it). Miriam suggested that we buy one at the Coop. (We had walked there the day before to buy the puzzles for Logo Session 2). Miriam had not seen any hula hoops at the Coop. When I asked her if she knew whether or not they were sold there, she said, 'Maybe.' Other lab members had seen them on sale there, so we agreed to get one from the Coop before our next session.

The following Monday snow kept us from walking to the Coop. I asked Miriam if she would mind my buying the hula hoop the next day before she came to MIT. Miriam agreed to that on condition that I buy one with red-white-and-blue stripes. I argued the Coop might not have such a kind. In that case, Miriam responded, she would have to pick one out. Luckily, Jenner's hoop had been purchased at the Coop also.

5/12/77 — The Lemon Twist

I had purchased the hula hoop in the morning and was setting up the music room for our later use when one of the boys in an on-going class from CAPS (the Cambridge Alternative School Program) asked if he could use the hula hoop. After doing a hula, he let the hoop fall to the floor, slipped a foot under the hoop, and rotated it about one leg, raising the other foot so that the rotating hoop would not strike him in the ankle. I was impressed; I had never seen anyone do that with a hula hoop. But I had seen Miriam do a similar thing with one of her toys, the Lemon Twist.

---

29. 1977. Unpublished.

The Lemon Twist has been one of Miriam's favorite active toys for some time. Having seen it advertised on a TV commercial, she bought one with her own money. (This was the first such purchase she ever made). The toy has a hard plastic lemon at one end, connected to a small loop at the other by a piece of tubing about 18" long. A child slips one foot through the loop, then kicks in such a way as to cause the attached lemon to swing around that leg. I remember the day last spring when Miriam bought the toy, her first trials, her showing it to older friends, her watching them, and her slowly developing skill.

This afternoon Miriam was delighted to find her new hula hoop. It was perfect, even having the marble inside as did Jenner's. I mentioned to her the boy from CAPS, how he made it go around on his leg. Miriam put her foot under the hoop and kicked it a few times. 'Like that?' Obviously not. 'I don't know how he did it, Miriam, but he made it work just like your lemon twist.' With two or three tries, Miriam was able to make the hoop circle her leg several times at each execution.

5/12/77 — Doing the Hula

Despite Miriam's success with the foot centred hula twist, she was unable to keep the hoop from falling down. She holds the hoop with both hands in front and a part of it against her back. She throws it in one direction or the other, moving her trunk in no clear way (it's very hard to see any pattern because the hoop falls so quickly).

Over the following days, several people showed their skill in the Logo foyer. (Playing with the hoop was a favorite pastime on Miriam's breaks from our sessions). Sherry Turkle claimed having once been champion of Brooklyn and gave a demonstration. So did Donna and many of those who wandered through. Miriam improved rapidly. Her later description of how to keep the hoop from falling: 'It's easy. Just keep pushing your belly in and out,' I believe puts at the surface what she saw as significant in her observations of others' practice.

5/12/77 — The Bicycle Analogy

During a break from Logo Session 7, Miriam discovered that the hula hoop will stay upright if rolled. For the past several days, maybe the past two weeks, Miriam has attempted to ride her bicycle without training wheels. She received one hint, one good piece of advice from Jim, our neighbour: if you try to go fast on the bike, it will stay up. Miriam has succeeded through doing that.

When I asked her now why the hula hoop stays up instead of falling over, she said, 'Well, because I make it go fast.' When I asked if there were anything else she knew like that, Miriam replied, 'Yeah, sure. The bike.'

5/19/77 — Ping Pong Balls

Miriam continued playing with the hula hoop at Logo throughout this week. Since she is willing to watch other people and listen, adults incline to show her the things they enjoy and can do. This has caused me a problem. I will elaborate.

At the beginning of the project, Miriam underwent a number of experiments to permit the probing of her skills and understanding. One of these experiments involved showing her how to make a ping pong ball slide away and then return as an initially imparted backspin overcomes the impetus of its forward projection. (This experiment is described in The Grasp of Consciousness, Piaget (1974 French, 1976 English)). Since the time of that experiment, Miriam has been, whenever she has a ping pong ball at hand, making it slide away and spin back to her. She has shown this game to friends in the play group. The back spinning phenomenon is clearly one that engaged her interest.

A secondary intention of mine in buying the hula hoop was to conduct with Miriam a follow-up experiment to explore how easily she could generalize her ping pong ball knowledge to the similar back spin phenomenon with a hula hoop.

As I passed through the foyer a few days ago I heard Donna say, 'Miriam, did you ever see this?' as she set the hula hoop on the floor with its circumference vertical. I asked Donna not to show Miriam the back spinning. Today, before our session began, Miriam was doing the hula in the foyer. She and Glen were apparently too noisy for the good order of the office, so while Miriam joined me in the music room, Glen went into the Learning Lab to play with the hula hoop. When Miriam and I came out for a break, Sam (an 8 year old) said, 'Hey, Miriam, did you ever see this?' Glen had just been demonstrating back spinning to Sam. I stopped Sam's explanation, explaining to him and Sam that Miriam and I were going to do an experiment about that and I did not want them to explain it to her now. Miriam and I left for sodas.

A while later as we re-entered the Learning Lab, Miriam, whom I was carrying at the time, glanced through the opening door, then excitedly turned to me and said, 'Daddy, did you see what Glen just did?' I put Miriam down in the music room and asked what Glen had done. Miriam explained clearly enough to show that she had seen his back spinning the hula hoop. I turned on the tape recorder beginning again the transcription of Logo Session 10.

Bob	Wait a minute. No, I don't understand. You said he rolled something and made it come back?
Miriam	A hula hoop.
Bob	He did. How did that happen?
Miriam	I don't know. I think it went (a gesture in the air—unclear) like this.
Bob	It did what?
Miriam	I think it went like that (gesture again), then it rolled and came back.
Bob	Well, wait a minute. Let's see if I can get the hula hoop and you can explain what happened. (Bob brings in the hula hoop)Now, what happened?
Miriam	It went like that (here Miriam gestures with the ping pong ball back spinning gesture on the edge of the hula hoop). Like that (repeating the gesture). I don't know how he did it.

(This gesture represents the only procedure Miriam knows creating a comparable effect; Miriam assumes Glen used some such procedure but is uncertain).

Bob   Why?. . . I saw you pushing on it, the back of the hula hoop.

Miriam   Yeah. (Miriam repeats the gesture several times).

Bob   I get it. Have you ever done anything else like that?

Miriam   Yeah.

Bob   What?

Miriam   The ping pong ball.

Bob   That's absolutely right, Miriam. I find that very striking. Did you ever see anybody else do that with a hula hoop?

Miriam   Unh-uh.

Bob   Glen, would you come here for a while please? Miriam saw you doing this (spinning the hoop) for the first time she has ever seen anybody doing it. She figured out how it worked and why. So it doesn't matter if Miriam sees it happening all over, now. (spins the hula hoop). Did you see it go out the door and come back?

Miriam   Yeah. (Miriam tries once and is interrupted by talk). Hold it. I know. I'm going to do it. (Miriam tries backspin and succeeds, laughing). It rolled backwards that time.

Bob   That's a direct, analogous extension of our work with the ping pong ball.

Relevance

The problem I mentioned at the beginning of the last incident receives its fourth illustration; after the end of Logo session 7, while I gathered my paraphernalia for our trip home, Miriam played with the hula hoop outside the music room. Marvin saw Miriam playing and said, 'Miriam, have you seen this good trick yet?'

Thus, over the course of a few days, while the materials were at hand and Miriam was sensitized to the phenomenon, in four separate cases she encountered situations of potential informal instruction (if you count Sam's attempt and Glen's demonstration as separate). Can one control such exposure? I believe such attempts would fail, as this attempt of mine failed, because a lively intelligence, sensitized to an engaging phenomenon, will notice its manifestation with only the slightest exposure. Since controlling exposure is not possible, especially in a rich environment and an active culture, the problem becomes methodological. How to be in the right place (for me, with Miriam) at the right turn (when an insight occurs); how to recognize a significant development and document its occurrence in detail sufficient to support subsequent analysis and interpretation. I believe the design of this project, as an intensive, protracted, naturalistic study of a bright child in a supportive environment during a recognized stage of rapid development, focuses on a rich domain of developmental data. The breadth of this study with respect to a child's life in the home, at play with friends, and under tutelage (at Logo), being both intrusive (thereby perturbing the structure of her mind) and extensive (opening to observation situations not usually attended to), offers a better hope of following the fine structure of developing ideas than does any method limited to sampling ideas in separate minds. The recognition of significant developments is circumscribed by my sensitivity: whether that is adequate remains to be seen. The coupling of selective observation with mechanical recording and immediate transcription is my best answer to the documentation aspect of the problem.

Beyond the issue of methodology highlighted by these incidents, raised to theoretical prominence are the issues of analogy (how what is learned as a concrete action is extended to situations where the same action control structure effects a comparable result), the importance of sensitivity to phenomena (that periphery of effects, as Piaget has it, from which cognition proceeds to the centre of explanation through the hypothesis of a known action), and the contrast of learning through analogy with learning through the progressive elaboration of not-yet-adequately-structured descriptions. These issues are raised but not to be addressed here.

HOUSEKEEPING CORNER (Vignettes) [30]

5/24/77

Since Miriam started recounting where she spends her time in kindergarten (see Vignette 12), it has become clear that she spends most of her time in the 'housekeeping corner.' When I've been in the kindergarten class, I've usually found myself playing with blocks, or making designs and elaborate towers from Cuisenaire rods. Miriam has frequently played otherwheres. I have seen her there, curled up in the baby carriage, but I've had no good idea of what games she and her friends invented for that location.

That question received a major clarification today while Miriam was stringing beads for necklaces. I had given her a Bic pen cap to poke the string through the beads. After she learned the cap was from an exhausted pen, Miriam began this conversation: (M is for Miriam, B for Bob)

M: Can I keep the cap?

B: Sure.

M: Thank you. Tomorrow I'm going to take it to school.

B: The cap?

M: Yeah.

B: What for?

M: Because we usually play Doctor, there in the housekeeping corner.

B: Un-huh.

M: And we give each other pretend shots.

B: Oh my goodness. You're not really going to poke anybody with that, are you?

M: No (you silly Daddy).

B: But that will be your needle?

M: Yes. Sometimes we use pencils.

B: I hope nobody ever gets hurt.

M: We don't.

B: Good. . . I think that's kind of funny. That you have a house-keeping corner and you play Doctor. Is that because everybody likes giving shots?

M: Yeah.

B: Does anybody like getting shots?

M: No. We always run away from the Doctors.

B: Well, who's the Doctors. . .or does it change?

M: It changes. We run away 'cause we don't want our shots.

B: Yeah.

M: We always have it in the summer. We run away because we don't want it and the door's always open in the summer.

B: You mean the door to the kindergarten? Or the housekeeping corner, a pretend door?

---

30. 1977. Unpublished.

M: A pretend door to the housekeeping corner. It's always open so we run right out.

One fact, of possible relevance in initially suggesting the game to the children though not at all accounting for its continued interest, is that Dara's mother is a nurse. Dara and Maria are the two girls Miriam most plays with in kindergarten.

After we focused a while on the beads, I resumed the theme of the housekeeping corner by attacking the game of 'Doctor'.

B: I still think it's kind of silly that you play Doctor in the housekeeping corner. Do Doctors come to houses or something?

M: Sometimes they do.

B: Don't you ever play anything else? Or is it always shot giving?

M: We like the Doctor but sometimes we play House of the Wicked Witch.

B: Wicked Witch? How's that go? I never heard of that. Is that like something from the Wizard of Oz? Or a different wicked witch?

M: From the Wizard of Oz.

B: Does anybody know the song or what?

M: I and Dara know the song.

B: You and Dara?

M: And Maria.

B: How's it go? 'La la the wicked, la la the wicked witch, la la the wicked witch is dead'? No? That's not the song?

M: No. It's about the Wizard.

B: Oh. We're off to see the Wizard?

M: Yeah.

B: The wonderful Wizard of Oz?

M: Yeah.

It's clear that my wicked witch was she of the West upon whom did fall Dorothy's house. In retrospect, I'm sure the children think more of the Witch of the East, she commander of flying apes and pro-foundly allergic to water. No dancing Munchkins for them.

5/27/77

Miriam arranged for Dara to come play at our house today. Because Miriam expected to come to Logo, I asked her if she intended to bring Dara with her and wondered whether Dara would want to come. Miriam responded that she could get Dara to come to Logo by telling her it was a good place to play Wicked Witch. I had no idea why this was so.

Dara and Miriam at lunch told me a little more of Wicked Witch, not clearly perhaps but enough to reveal what sorts of sides and tensions exist. They mentioned that the boys build spaceships in the kindergarten and should they be left unattended, the girls play Wicked Witch, swoop down on the spaceships, and keep the boys away. This, I saw too late, was relevant to Logo's being a good place to play Wicked Witch. Robby and Sam have been playing war games in the Learning Lab, building barricades or trenches from unoccupied chairs. When Miriam and Dara seized the momentarily unoccupied trenches, I realized from the commotion how Wicked Witch was being applied at Logo.

Gretchen informs me that while the children played at home, most of their time was spent playing Doctor in the tree fort.

Relevance

Both Doctor and Wicked Witch are highly mobile fantasies which appear to be role centred with improvised skits focussed on dramatic actions: giving and getting needles; seizing somebody else's place. From outside the kindergarten, the setting dependence of the games I speculate to be primarily in the nature of a space allocation. The girls play in the housekeeping corner. They use it as their home base for whatever fantasies they can construct with a sufficiency of roles for themselves.

MAKING JOKES AND ONE CHILD'S LEARNING[31]

Scholarly work tends, in this period of professional specialization, to seek theoretical depth as its first objective. There are other possibilities worth pursuing as well. This collection of material relating to learning and humor comes from a broader effort called 'The Intimate Study'. Breadth of coverage was a consequence of my primary commitment to following the development of a child wherever her behaviour and learning might lead. The method of analysis has been to proceed as deep as the data collected permit, with the technical objective of using that material as a foundation for the creation of computational models of knowledge and learning. The primary analyses of that broader study appear in Lawler (1985); the movement in the direction of cognitive modelling is represented by Lawler and Selfridge (1985), and Lawler (1987). The four central analyses of 'The Intimate Study' are about Miriam, my daughter. The extensive detailed data collected in the study of her thinking and the attempt to use it all in interpretation represent an effort to tighten up and exploit methods of idiographic study to permit empirically based descriptions of cognitive structures. The four primary analyses of Miriam's learning form a unified exploration of how local changes in cognitive structure result in significant large scale effects. Other analyses, such as this study of her humor, have different but related objectives.

The Intimate Study was inspired in part by a suggestion of Flavell's (1963) to blend Piaget's focus on knowledge structures with the ecological emphasis of Barker and Wright (1955) and undertake 'a type of research endeavour which has not yet been exploited: an ecological study of the young child's mundane interchanges with his workaday world.' Because the study was not about a great man's thought but merely about the marvel of a normal child's learning, it depends for its general interest in a technical way on arguments about the lawfulness of psychic phenomena advanced by Kurt Lewin. He argued that *the individual case does not merely illustrate the general law; it embodies the general law.* If mental phenomena are lawful in a strong sense, as physical phenomena are, one can arrive at the general law through detailed interpretation of the particular case (Lewin, 1935). The primary objective of 'The Intimate Study' was to produce a corpus which could be analyzed in such a way as to advance our understanding of learning.

Humour should have a role in such a study, and not merely because it is of interest to all of us. Humour often emerges from the juxtaposition and interplay of multiple points of view. Learning also often derives from the conjunction and clash of pre-established knowledge structures. For this reason, studies of humor and learning can illuminate each other. The difficulty of collecting information about human thinking makes the study as challenging as any among those not strictly impossible. The idiographic method has been, so far, under-used in studies of humour:

---

31. 1977. Unpublished. Published as 'Making Jokes and Learning,' *Humor* (Elsevier, 1989).

'We would argue that our relative ignorance of the bases underlying individual variations in children's humour partially stems from a certain methodological myopia. Overconcern with empirical generalization has led many researchers to over-emphasize the value of the nomothetic and differential research strategies, and to downplay the utility of the idiographic aproach. While we agree that generalizability is important, and ultimately the goal of any humour theory, we believe quite strongly that in-depth case-study analyses of humour, which is the core of the idiographic approach, are extremely valuable and deserving of greater attention. If nothing else, they would appear to be a potentially rich source for the generation of testable theoretical ideas. (One should never forget that Freud's unparalleled theory of personality and Piaget's equally impressive theory of cognitive development originated from intensive case studies of a small number of individuals.)'

Brodzinsky and Rightmyer, 1980

My hope for this paper, based as it is on a limited collection of humorous material embedded in a very detailed case study, is that it will inspire those with richer topical collections of material to pursue analyses which will tell us more about the way that uniform laws of development lead to individual differences in various circumstances.

CONSTRUCTING KNOWLEDGE FROM INTERACTIONS [32]

'Human beings do not only interact with objects and natural phenomena . . .but also, and in a primary sense, with other human beings.'

H. Sinclair (1989)

Mme. Sinclair focuses our attention on the profound issue of how interaction and self-construction relate to one another. In presenting an approach to this issue which I have found productive, I will begin with a few general observations and then go on to some concrete stories of development, drawn from very detailed and meticulously analyzed corpora (in Lawler, 1985, 1986).[33] My preferred descriptions, through which I bring such general issues down to concrete cases suitable for examination, are functionalist in orientation and ultimately computational in technique. Let me illustrate the role of control knowledge in developing behaviour with a simple example before going on to consider two complex examples of mathematical learning, involving the integration of disparate varieties of mathematical knowledge.

Learning to Control Interactive Protocols

The Articulation of Complementary Roles

At the age of two, my daughter Peggy imitated the other members of her family. She began to imitate the knock-knock jokes of her sister Miriam (8 at the time), this way:

Peggy: Knock-knock.
Bob: Who's there?
Peggy: (Broad laughter).

That first night, Peggy plied her 'joke' upon me time and again. Eventually, for variety, I said 'Knock-knock,' but she did not reply. I tried many times. Even though she sensed something was expected of her, she *did not* reply. I would say she *could not*.

Early the next morning I heard Peggy talking to herself in her crib:

Peggy: Knock-knock.
Peggy: Who's there?
Peggy: (Laughter).

At breakfast, Peggy's first words were 'Knock-knock,' and I responded appropriately, saying:

Bob: Knock-knock.
Peggy: Who's there?
Peggy: (Laughter).

---

32. 1990 Journal of Mathematical Behaviour, vol. 9, pp. 177-192.
    1991 Republished in *Transforming Early Mathematics Education* (Steffe & Wood, Eds.) Erlbaum.

33. Central arguments bearing on the importance of the case method may be found in Lewin (1935) and in Langer (1967).

at 6;0

```
  10      |3|2|4|        2 2 8 5 7
+ 20    + |2|1|2|      + 4 7 3 4 5
----     -.--.--        ---------
1200      |5|0|9|        7 0 2 0 2

 (a)       (b)             (c)
```

at 6;9

```
   |3|8|          |3|8|          |3|8|
 + |3|4|        + |3|4|        + |3|4|
   --.--          --.--          --.--
   |6||12|        |8|1|          |9|9|

    (a)            (b)            (c)
```

Figure 1.   Figure 2.

That same afternoon, Miriam confirmed my observation, 'Dad, Peggy can say `Who's there." I consider this a simple, lucid example of processes in the articulation of complementary roles.

Elements of the Example:

A learner with a relatively inferior comprehension is engaged socially with more comprehending people — in this case focused around what is literally a script for a joke's telling. During the engagement, social demands push at the boundaries of comprehension of the person with the undeveloped perspective. The learner attaches to herself uncomprehended 'routines' of engagement (in both the theatrical and programming senses). The process may be friendly or not so — but it is more aptly and generally described by that wide ranging class of intimate relationships that characterizes the interactions of a small society, the home. This first type of process I call *homely* ('home-like') *binding* .

The second type of process, *lonely discovery*, occurs when the learner is deprived of social engagement — left to her own devices — and uses those devices to re-enact the uncomprehended experiences, compensating for the solitude by simulating the role of the other actor. This simulation of the other actors imposes a real demand for the distinction between roles and their relations lacking in the initial engagement. My name for this pervasive and repeated sequence of homely binding and lonely discovery is *the articulation of complementary roles*. In such cases, the relation between social experience and personal construction is that more integrated discriminations are required for controlling or directing multi-role enactment of interactive protocols than are required for acting in them. These incidents provide a succinct example of how the articulation of complementary roles creates new control structures in the mind.[34]

This empirical material and its interpretation create a puzzle for instruction. Learning occurred not because it was socially directed but as a compensating adaptation to the deprivation of social interaction. Fantasy rescued the child from loneliness; the more complex requirements of interaction with one agent simulating another as well as acting

---

34. One can not argue coercively that this single incident must have been the sole generator of such a change. If, however, particular experiences are the foundation for cognitive development, then some one among them must have been the first. This experience clearly exhibits a set of characteristics which seem essential to the process.

out her own role engendered the construction by the individual of skills of sufficient generality and lability that they could function effectively in other domains of life. How one should represent such knowledge and its changes is a complex question, one which these observations by themselves provide insufficient guidance to permit us to resolve.

Integrating Related Knowledge Structures

An Introduction to Paper Sums

This story is about a child's learning to do additions whose unit sums crossed a decade boundary. In this specific sense, it relates to 'carrying'. (In the development of the particular child, it also was crucial to her later learning to do vertical form sums in the Hindu-Arabic notation.) At the beginning of the study, Miriam then 6;0 (six years, zero months), was unable to add 10 plus 20 on paper in the vertical form. When I asked her the question 'How much is ten plus twenty?', Miriam answered with confidence, 'Thirty.' Her response to the first sum presented in Figure 1 (a) was quite different. 'I don't know . . . twelve hundred?' (After this confusion, vertical lines were used frequently to emphasize column alignment.)

Despite instruction that she should not 'read' the individual digits but should add within the columns and assemble a result from the columnar sums, for (b) of Figure 1 Miriam summed the addends to 'five hundred nine' [2+1+4+2 = 9]. She received instruction for solving problems such as (c) of Figure 1 by a procedure I call 'order-free adding' — based on the very simple idea that it doesn't matter in what order one sums column digits so long as any column interaction is accounted for subsequently. After preliminary instruction, the typical problem presented two multi-digit addends in the vertical form. Her typical solution began with writing down from left to right the column sums of well known results. Next, Miriam would return to the omitted subproblems and calculate them with her fingers. When this first pass solution produced multi-digit sums in a column — a formal illegality, as I informed her — Miriam had to confront the interaction of columns. I instructed her to cross off the ten's digit of such a sum and add it as a 1 to the next left column, that is, to 'carry the one.' With less than two hours of such instruction, Miriam succeeded at solving sums with two addends of up to ten digits; but she realized no significant gain, for the procedures were subject first to confusion and then to forgetting.

An Analysis: Rules that Don't Make Sense

Why were Miriam's initial skills with paper sums vulnerable? Consider the three representative solutions of Figure 2.

The first, (a) of Figure 2, shows no integration of columnar sums; the second, (b) of Figure 2, shows a confusion over which digit to 'put down' and which to 'carry' (with an implicit rule-like slogan behind the action). If you don't already understand the meaning of the rule 'put down the N and carry the one,' why should you prefer that to a comparable rule, 'put down the 1 and carry the N' [as in (b) above]. Miriam was confusable in the sense that she chose, with no regularity and no apparent reason, to apply both these rules. Although frequently instructed in the former rule, she did not remember it. The rule-like formulation made no direct contact with her underlying microview structures. Without support from 'below,' the rule could not be remembered. Microview is a term I use to specify a particular species of schema, one whose principal component is a collection of pattern matching procedures and whose functions are executed by a cascade of activation when a pattern is adequately matched. Microviews are postulated to embody very local knowledge and to compete with one another in a race to solve problems as they interpret them. Thus, a verbal query 'How much is 25 plus 10?' could be solved by counting from 25 on fingers or in terms of US coin equivalences. The specific character of solutions emerging as behaviour provides evidence about which structure among those known to exist won the race in a given instance. At the time of this incident, Miriam's arithmetic competence is describable as embodied in a COUNT-view (based on mastery of one-to-one correspondence), a MONEY-view (based on coin relationships), and a DECADAL-view (based on manipulation of numbers as multiples of ten; her unusual knowledge derived from particular experiences with computer-based materials at the Logo project). These three microviews form a cluster, related as components of her mental calculation repertoire.[35]

Miriam eliminated her confusion by inventing a carrying procedure that made sense to her, shown in (c) of Figure 2. 'Reduction to nines' satisfied the formal constraint that each column could have only a single digit in the result by reducing to a 9 any multi-digit column sum and 'carrying' the 'excess' to the next left column. (38 plus 34 became 99 through 12 reducing to a 9 with a 3 carried.) Miriam's invention of this non-standard procedure (at 6;3;6) I take as weighty evidence characterizing her understanding of numbers and addition in the vertical form. (The latter we will discuss shortly.) About numbers we may conclude she saw the digits as representing things which ought to be conserved, as did the numbers of the Count microview. The achievement of columnar sums by finger counting or by recall of well-known results further substantiates the relation of paper sums to numbers of the Count view. Let us declare, then, that these experiences led to the development the *Paper-sums* microview, a cognitive structure that is a direct descendent of the Count view.

Miriam did not understand 'carrying' as being at all related to place value. The numbers within the vertical columns did not relate to those of any other column in a comprehensible way. Despite my initial criticism of 'reduction to nines' — by asking if she were surprised that all her answers had so many nines in them — Miriam was strongly committed to this method of carrying. For Miriam, at this time, vertical form addition had nothing to do with the Money or Decadal sums she achieved through mental calculation. 'Right' or 'wrong' was a judgment applicable to a calculation only in the terms of the microview wherein it was going forward. I conclude then that the Paper-sums microview shows a line of descent from Miriam's counting knowledge, diverging with respect to those other microviews which involved mental calculation.

The more general final point is that what made sense to Miriam completely dominated what she was told. Why is it that the rule she was given didn't make sense?

---

35. See Chapter 2 *CECD* for more data and analyses.

How can we recapture a sense of what that must have seemed like? To her, a number represented a collection of things with a name: '12' was a name by which reference could be made to a collection of twelve things. Digit strings may have seemed to her as words do to us, things which cannot be decomposed without destroying their signification. If you divide the word 'goat' into 'go' and 'at,' you have two other words not sensibly related to the vanished goat. Similarly, from our common perspective, if you don't see the `1' as a `10' when you decompose a `12' into a `1' and `2', you lose `9'. Unless you appreciate the structured representation, the decomposition of 12 can make no more sense than cutting up a word. What appears as forgetting in Miriam's case is an interference from established processes; what makes sense in terms of ancestral cognitive structures dominates what is inculcated as an extrinsic rule. (I don't claim to offer a theory of forgetting. Competition from sensible ideas of long dependability is a very good reason, however, for forgetting what one is told but can't comprehend.)

The Carrying Breakthrough

The 'carrying problem' was not restricted to Paper-sums and in fact began its resolution through integrating the microviews of mental calculation. Although she could add double digit numbers that involved no decade boundary crossing, like 55 plus 22, Miriam's Decadal view functions failed with sums only slightly different, such as 55 plus 26. Sums of this latter sort initially produced results with illegal number names, i.e. 55 + 26 = 70:11 ('seventy-eleven'). In playing her favorite computer game, however, precision was not required. Miriam's typical 'fix' for such a calculation problem was to drop one of the unit digits from the problem and conclude that 55 + 26 = 76 was an adequate solution. She could, of course, cross decade boundaries by counting, but for a long time this Count view knowledge was not used in conjunction with her Decadal view knowledge. Miriam's resolution of one species of carrying problem became evident to me in her spontaneous presentation of a problem and its solution (at 6;3;23). She picked up some of her brother's second grade homework and brought it to me (M: for Miriam; B: for Bob):

M: Dad, twenty eight plus forty eight is seventy six, right?
B: How did you figure that out?
M: Well, twenty and forty are like two and four. That six is like sixty. We take the eight, sixty-eight (then counting on her fingers) sixty-nine, seventy, seventy-one, seventy-two, seventy three, seventy-four, seventy-five, seventy-six.

Here was clear evidence that Miriam had solved one carrying problem by relating her Decadal and Count microviews. When and how did that integration occur?

Integrating Disparate Microviews

We were on vacation at the time. I felt Miriam had been working too hard at the laboratory and was determined that she should have a rest from our experiments. I was curious, however, about the representation development of her finger counting and raised the question one day at lunch (at 6;3;16):

B: Miriam, do you remember when you used to count on your fingers all the time? How would you do a sum like seven plus two?

M: Nine.

B: I know you know the answer — but can you tell me how you used to figure it out, before you knew?

M: (Counting up on fingers) Seven, eight, nine.

B: Think back even further, to long ago, to last year.

M: (Miriam counted to nine with both addends on her fingers — leaving the middle finger of her right hand depressed.) But I don't do that any more. Why don't you give me a harder problem?

B: Thirty seven plus twelve.

M: (With a shocked look on her face) That's forty-nine.

Something about this problem and result surprised Miriam. I recorded this situation and her reaction in the corpus; I did not appreciate it as especially significant at that time. My current interpretation focusses on this specific incident as a moment of insight.

Characterizing the Insight

Precisely what was it that Miriam saw? In the Decadal view, the problem 'thirty-seven plus twelve' would be solved thus, 'thirty plus ten is forty; seven plus two is nine; forty nine' — a perfect result. Miriam had recently become able to decompose numbers such as 'twelve' into a 'ten' and a 'two'. This marked a refinement of the Count view perspective. If we imagine the calculation 'thirty seven plus twelve' proceeding in the Count microview — with the modified perspective able to 'see the ten in the twelve' — Miriam would say 'thirty seven [the first number of the Count view's perspective], plus ten is forty seven [then counting up on her fingers the second addend residuum], forty eight, forty nine' — also a perfect answer. We are not surprised that the Count view answer is the same as that of the Decadal view, but I believe the concurrence surprised Miriam. One can say that Miriam experienced an insight (to which her 'shocked look' testifies) based on the *surprising confluence of results* from apparently disparate microviews. `Insight' is the appropriate common word for the situation, and I will continue to use it where no confusion is likely. Since its range of meanings is too broad for technical use, I introduce a new term, the elevation of control, as the technical name for the learning process exemplified here. The *elevation of control* names the creation of a control element which subordinates previously independent microviews, in the sense of permitting their controlled invocation; some experiences of insight are the experienced correlates of control elevation.

The character of control elevation is revealed in the example. The numbers involved were of the right magnitude to engage Miriam's Decadal microview. Also, she had just been finger counting (a Count view function). If both microviews were actively calculating results and simultaneously achieving identical solutions, the surprising confluence of results — where none should have been expected — could spark a significant cognitive event: the changing of a non-relation into a relation, which is the quintessential alteration required for the creation of new structure.

The sense of surprise attending the elevation of control is a direct consequence of a common result being found where none was expected. The competition of microviews, which usually leads to the dominance of one and the suppression of others, also presents the possibility of cooperation replacing competition. So we see, in the outcome, Decadal beginning a calculation and Count completing it. This conclusion, however much based on a rich interpretation, is an empirical observation. Where we *expected* development in response to incrementally more challenging problems, we *found* something quite different: cognitive reorganization from the redundant solution of simple problems.

The elevation of control, a minimal change which could account for the integration of microviews witnessed by Miriam's behaviour, would be the addition of a control element permitting the serial invocation of the Decadal view and then the Count view. Let us declare at this moment of insight the formation of a new microview, the SERIAL view.[36] Although the Serial view is achieved as a minimal change of structure, its integration of subordinated microviews permits a significantly enhanced calculation performance, one so striking as to support the observation that a new functional level of calculation emerged from the new organization. This is especially evident where knowledge is articulated by proof. Consider this example (at 6;5;24).

Miriam and Robby, himself no slouch at calculation, were making a clay by mixing flour, salt, and water. They mixed the material, kneaded it, and folded it over. Robby kept count of his foldings. With 95 plies, the material was thick. He folded again, '96,' then cutting the pile in half, flopped the second on top of the first and said, 'Now I've got 96 plus 96.' Miriam interjected, 'That's a hundred ninety two.' Robby was astounded, couldn't believe her result, and called to his mother to find if Miriam could possibly be right. Miriam responded first, 'Robby, we know ninety plus ninety is a hundred and eighty. Six makes a hundred eighty six. [Then counting on her fingers] One eighty-seven, one eighty-eight, one eighty-nine, one ninety, one ninety-one, one ninety-two.'

We can see the Decadal well-known-result (90 plus 90) as a basis for this calculation and its relation to her counting knowledge. Both these points support the argument that Miriam's new knowledge was specifically of controlling pre-existing microviews. Robby was astounded — and we too should try to preserve a sense of astonishment in order to remain sensitive to how small a structural change permits the emergence of a new level of performance.

---

36. One wants to avoid the creation of something from nothing. See in this connection the discussion of 'relational conversion' in *CECD* (Chapter 7). In *OCL*, I advanced the same argument, first that the boundaries between microviews are defined by networks of 'must-not-confound' links which function to suppress confusion between competing, related microviews; second, that the conversion of these repressive links, established by experience, to more explicit relational links, generates 'new' control structure at moments of insight. The creation of inhibiting relations between microviews to suppress confusion does the real work of structural creation. The relational conversion, in which an inhibiting relation is turned into one of richer semantic content, permits the smooth transformation in functional capability to another behaviour over what otherwise would appear to be an unbridgeable gap.

Integrating Knowledge From Diverse Sensory Modes

Early papers of the MIT Logo project claimed that design producing procedures written in Logo would be more comprehensible to children because one could simulate the drawing agent (the light turtle on the video display) by moving through space with her/ his own body. For many children, this was not obvious. The light turtle lived in a vertical world, they in a horizontal one. Miriam played in a variety of 'turtle navigation' games which led to her familiarity with a set of angle values and useful relations (90 plus 90 equals 180). She also spent considerable time playing with design generating procedures, such as the well known Logo polyspiral procedure:

```
to polyspi : side : angle : change
forward : side
right :angle
polyspi (: side + : change) : angle : change
end
```

Miriam enjoyed making designs, colouring them, and sharing them with her friends. She became familiar with specific values of angles that would make her favorite designs; but these 'angle' values bore no apparent relationship to her other experiences. During the core six months of 'The Intimate Study', Miriam did not give evidence of understanding how angles and movements of turtle navigation related to angles and designs produced by repetition in the video context. She could use repetition, but there was no evidence she understood it as she so obviously did in this later incident: Turtle on the Bed (6;11;15)

> As I worked at my bedroom desk, Miriam offered to sit in my lap, but I turned her down. She moped a little, then crawled onto my bed and began to move and spin in a most distracting fashion. 'What are you doing? You're driving me batty!' I complained. Requesting a pen and a 3x5 card, Miriam drew on it a right rectangular polygonal spiral to show what she was doing in her 'crawling on the bed game.' Her verbal explanation was that she was 'making one of those maze things.'

Whence came this connectedness in her knowledge of serial physical action to pattern? My best answer is as follows.

Cuisenaire Rods and Polyspiral Mazes

When one day the children pestered me to play with some Cuisenaire rods I had brought home from the lab, I agreed on condition that we begin with a project of my choosing. My proposal was this: after they sorted the rods by colour (and thus by length as well), I would begin to make something; their problem was to describe what I was making and what my procedure was. I began to construct a square maze of Cuisenaire rods. After I· placed four rods, I asked the children what I was making. Robby answered immediately, 'A swirl, a maze.' Miriam chimed in with his answer. At that point, I asked Robby to hold off on his answers until I discussed my questions thoroughly with Miriam. Having placed eight rods, I asked the children if they could describe my procedure. Miriam could not, at first, but when I focused her attention on the length of each piece, she remarked: 'You're growing it bigger and bigger.' Upon questioning, she noted the increment was 'one.' After Robby added rods of length nine and ten, Miriam justified his action by arguing, 'It goes in order . . . littlest to biggest,' and finally described my rod selection rule as 'every time you put a rod in, it should be one bigger than the last one.' Miriam understood well the incrementing of length, but she showed considerable difficulty with the role of turning in the angles in my rods maze.

When I set down the eleven-length (the orange and white pair of rods), I did not orient it perpendicularly to the previous length. Miriam declared the arrangement incorrect but had trouble specifying precisely what was wrong. When she rearranged the rods to place them correctly, she simply interchanged the location of the orange (10cm) and white rods (1cm). From this action, I infer Miriam considered the placement incorrect because two rods of the same colour were adjacent to each other — but not because the one rod was colinear with the preceding one. Here I asked Robby to explain what I should have done:

R: You should go a right 90. It could be orange, right 90, white orange.

B: And what should I do after the next orange?

R: You probably could do an orange and red.

B: (Placing the new rods colinear with those preceding)

R: Hold it ! You should do a right again.

B: Oh. Miriam, what should I do next?

M: A right 90, green and orange.

B: Next?

M: A right 90, purple and orange.

This is the point at which Miriam brought together in a comprehensible relation the steps and result of a maze generating procedure.

Several aspects stand out. Miriam received extensive guidance. Second, Miriam worked with a familiar objective and familiar objects, and applied familiar operations. (*This* experience was clearly important for Miriam, specifically in establishing this sort of knowledge as very personally owned: in later years, whenever offered Cuisenaire rods to play with, constructing a polyspiral maze surfaced regularly as her objective of choice.) These experiences of the rods-maze and turtle on the bed appear to have integrated and thus culminated the development of Miriam's knowledge about iteration. The preceding incident about addition focussed on microviews which had much in common. The turtle on the bed incident presents a concrete linking experience as a possible basis for interconnection between essentially remote clusters of microviews. *Essentially remote* refers here to Turtle Navigation's being related primarily to walking and Computer Design's being related primarily to seeing, thus being descended from different sensori-motor subsystems, ie. locomotive and visual.

The central issue of human cognitive organization is how disparate and long-developing structures become linked in communication to form a partially coherent mind — such as we experience personally and witness in others. The framework used here discriminates among the major components of the sensori-motor system and their cognitive descendents, even while assuming the pre-eminence of that system as the basis of mind. Imagine the entire sensori-motor system of the body as made up of a few large, related, but distinct sub-systems, each characterized by the special states and motions of the major body parts, thus:

Body Parts	**S-M Subsystem**	**Major Operations**
Trunk	Somatic	Being here
Legs	Locomotive	Moving from here to there
Head-eyes	Capital/visual	Looking at that there
Arms-hands	Manipulative	Changing that there
Tongue/ears	Linguistics	Saying/hearing whatever

Much of the activity of early infancy specifically involves developing coordinations between these five major sensori-motor sub-systems. Such a fundamental organization in the development of coordinated systems might be assumed to ramify through all descendent cognitive structures developed from interacting with the experiences of later life.

The rods-maze microview closed the unbridgeable gap between turtle geometry Navigation microviews and the Design cluster by playing a mediating role. The local character, the task-specific binding of Miriam's learning in the rods-maze incident, implies that it was not developed analogically (i.e. from her turtle geometry experiences) but *de novo* from more primitive components of the sensori-motor system. If descended directly from the coordinating scheme which results in hand-eye coordination, the rods-maze microview was effective as mediator for two reasons, which can be brought forward in this simple comparison expressing the activity of the primary agents in these microviews:

Locomotive	**Mediating**	**Visual**
I move from	You (hand) move	That(thing) goes
here to there	from here to there	from here to there
Body as agent	**Hand** as remote agent	**Eye** as active agent

The primary difference between the active programs of the human locomotive and visual subsystems is the level of aggregation which is significant for their functioning. The body lurches forward, step by step. The eye recognizes an image as an entity by circulating repeatedly in the pattern of a closed loop, a 'feature ring,' which defines that object in memory. The *feature ring* is a complex recognition procedure, which represents the saccades of eye focus and the possibility of recognizing features. Its primitive elements can be described as similar to the movements of the locomotive system, going forward and turning right[37]. Because of years of developed hand-eye coordination, the eye can recognize the pattern that emerges from what the hand does whereas it can not recognize so simply (if at all) the pattern that emerges from the path of body movement through the plane. The rods-maze experience was able to function mediatively between descendents of the locomotive and visual sub-systems because the hand, as the familiar agent for manipulating remote objects (say little toy dolls some of whom may be thought of as self or other), can make the bridge between an action of movement which a body might make and one which can be coordinated with visual results.

---

37. See chapter 5 in *CECD*, or Noton and Stark (1972).

The Channelled Description Conjecture

The body-parts mind proposal serves the function here of separating groups of cognitive structures on a large scale. Some cognitive structures are descended from ancestors in the locomotive sub-system and others from ancestors in the visual sub-system. If there is body-based disparateness, what leads to subsequent integration? The progressive organization of disparate structures and sub-systems proceeds from the needs of the individual as a complete being. The achievement of an individual's goals requires the cooperation of disparate cognitive structures and sub-systems of such structures, e.g. crawling to get some desired object requires the use of arms, legs, and vision. Focussing as it does on the descent of cognitive structures from ancestors in the motor sub-systems, the body-parts mind proposal definitely favors the activity of the subject in the creation of cognitive structures over the impression of sensations on the mind. In this specific sense, the proposal is fundamentally compatible with Piagetian constructivism.

Even if the mind is a network of information structures comprised of the same types of elements, one need not conclude that it is uniform. Microviews are shaped both by their specific descent from body-defined sub-systems and by their interconnection possibilities in terms of those sub-systems. The connections between late-developed cognitive structures mirror — and are guided by — the interconnection possibilities of the sensori-motor system which are first explored and described in the motor programs developed during the sensori-motor period of infancy. This idea, which I name the *channelled description conjecture*, is not an hypothesis which was posed for experimental confirmation; rather, it is a ground of explanation found useful in making sense of knowledge Miriam developed and failed to develop during her many encounters with geometry during 'The Intimate Study'.

The Power of Ideas and Cognitive Structure

The question of what constrains the possibility of some ideas being powerful and others not so is the crux of the channelled description conjecture. Concrete embodiments of ideas are personally owned because they are not remote from the shaping structures of the soma itself. Experiences such as those of the rods-maze are powerful precisely because they provide the links between late developed structures and the coordinating schemata (the primary integrations of the sensori-motor sub-systems achieved during the sensori-motor period). They are important because they link the concrete structures of body knowledge to the more abstract descriptions of external things that blossom in maturity as the cognitive network of the mind.

In strong form, the channelled description conjecture proposes that ONLY those concrete embodiments of ideas which link together descendents of disparate sensori-motor subsystems can be powerful; it claims that such models are the correlate in concrete thought of the correspondence schemata of the sensori-motor period and that on them depends the developing coherence of the individual's cognitive structure. Further, such microviews provide the bases of construction of the more extended cognitive nets of developed minds, functioning as the ancient cities, the geographic capitals of personal importance. In contrast with a goal-oriented attempt to link feelings and thoughts — as upon a basis of disparate need systems proposed in ethology, or with a Freudian focus on the conflict between competing, even conflicting homunculi in the mind — the channelled description conjecture proposes a third model of basically disparate structure: the mind is not uniform because the body, the effector agent of the sensori-motor system, is not uniform. This view is better characterized by a pun of Wallace Stevens, 'my anima likes its animal,' than by either the needs or conflicts of the other mentioned alternatives.

The role assigned to coordinating schemata bears on VonGlasersfeld's observation (1989) of their role in the naïve assumption of the reality of external things. In his view, the correspondence of schemata in diverse modalities leads to the unwarranted inference that we can know about external things them-selves. In my view, the later descendents of these coordinating schemata are primary mediators in the construction of cognitive coherence. If the assumption of the knowability of external things is an illusion (as we have all believed since Kant), it is a very strong weakness, one perhaps partly explicable by the coherence creating function which I ascribe to multi-modal correspondences.[38]

Where Do Our Ends Begin?

What makes men happy is loving to do what they have to do.

This is a principle upon which society is not founded . . .

Helvetius (De L'espirit)

How do we begin to think about the challenge of fitting society's goals to those of learners? *How can we instruct while respecting the self-constructive character of mind?* Here is a view of the development of goals I derived years ago (from Lévi-Strauss and François Jacob) as an extension of the notion of bricolage.

Claude Levi-Strauss describes the concrete thought of not-yet-civilized people as *bricolage*, the activity of the *bricoleur* —a sort of jack-of-all-trades, or more precisely, a committed do-it-yourself man. The core idea is looseness of commitment to specific goals, with the consequence that materials and competences developed for one purpose are transferable to the satisfaction of alternative objectives:

'The bricoleur is adept at performing a large number of diverse tasks; but, unlike the engineer, he does not subordinate each of them to the availability of raw materials and tools conceived and procured for the purpose of the project. His universe of instruments is closed and the rules of his game are always to make do with 'whatever is at hand' . . . In the continual reconstruction from the same materials, it is always earlier ends which are called upon to play the part of means . . . The bricoleur may not ever complete his purpose but he always puts something of himself into it . . .'

(from The Savage Mind, pp. 17, 21).

One can appreciate the opposition of planning (the epitome of goal-directed behaviour) and the opportunism of bricolage. Of course, the two are not discontinuous;

---

38. For an attempt to apply such ideas directly to educational issues, see Lawler (1989) or (1996).

all activities can be seen as a mixture of the polar tendencies represented here. Second, the relationship is not directional: there is no reason to suppose that planning is a more nearly perfect form of bricolage. One could easily view planning as a highly specialized technique for solving critical problems whose solutions demand scarce resources.

Bricolage and Cognition

Students of anatomy have named the adaptiveness of structures to alternative purposes *functional lability*. Such functional lability is the essential characteristic of the bricoleur's use of his tools and materials, so bricolage can serve as a metaphor for the relation of a person to the contents and processes of his mind. This emphasizes the character of the processes in terms of human action and can guide us in exploring how a coherent mind could rise out of the disparateness of specific experience. What are the practical advantages of discussing human activity as bricolage in contrast to goal-driven planning?

1. Bricolage presents a human model for the development of objectives; it is a more natural, thus a more fit description of everyday activity than planning.

2. It is more nearly compatible with a view of the mind as a process controlled by contention of multiple objectives for resources than is planning.

3. The most important advantage is *a new vision of the process of learning*. Bricolage can provide us with an image for the process of the mind under self-construction in these specific respects:

- if the resources of the individual's mind are viewed as being like the tools and materials of the bricoleur, one can appreciate immediately how they constrain our undertaking and accomplishing any activity.
- not only constraint comes from this set of limited resources; also comes creativity, the production of new things — perhaps not exactly suited to the situation but of genuine novelty.
- the mind, if seen as self-constructed through bricolage, presents a clear image of the uniqueness of every person:
  - each will have developed his own history of conceptions and appreciations of situations through which to make sense of the world.
  - each will have his personal 'bag of tricks,' knowledge and procedures useful in his past.
  - each will have his own set of different, alternative objectives to take up as chance puts the means at his disposal.

If viewed as claims, such statements are not easy to prove. However, they provide a framework for investigating learning which could be valuable by *not* demeaning human nature through assuming it is more simple than we know to be the case.

Acknowledgement

This paper draws heavily on examples published in Lawler, 1985. It will appear in the forthcoming book Transforming Early Mathematics Education, (Steffe and Wood, eds.) along with other papers presented at the Sixth International Conference of Mathematics Educators, Budapest, 1988.

References

Jacob, François (1977) 'Evolution and Tinkering'. *Science*, 196, pp.1161-1166, 10 June. Republished in *The Possible and the Actual*. New York: Pantheon Books, 1982.

Lawler, Robert W.(1979) 'One Child's Learning'. Unpublished PhD Thesis. MIT.

Lawler, Robert W. (1985) *Computer Experience and Cognitive Development*. John Wiley, NY.

Lawler, Robert W. et al. (1986) *Cognition and Computers*. John Wiley,NY.

Lawler, Robert W. (1989) 'Sharable Models: The Cognitive Equivvalent of a Lingua Franca'. *The Journal of Artificial Intelligence and Society*, Vol. 3, 1. Springer, NY.

Lawler, Robert W. (1996) 'Thinkable Models'. *The Journal of Mathematical Behaviour*, Ablex, Norwood, NJ. Forthcoming.

Langer, Susanne. (1967) See 'Idols of the Laboratory'. In *Mind: An Essay on Feeling*. Johns Hopkins, Baltimore.

Lévi-Strauss, Claude. See 'The Science of the Concrete'. In *The Savage Mind*. University of Chicago Press, 1966.

Lewin, Kurt (1935) 'The Conflict between Galilean and Aristotelian Modes of Thought in Contemporary Psychology'. In *Dynamic Psychology: Selcted Papers of Kurt Lewin*. McGraw-Hill.

Noton and Stark. (1971) 'Eyes Movements and Visual Perception'. In *Scientific American*, 224, 6.

Sinclair, Hermine. (1989) 'Learning: The Interactive Re-Creation of Knowledge'. In Steffe and Wood.

Steffe, Leslie & Wood, Terry (1989) *Transforming Early Childhood Mathematics Education*, Lawrence Erlbaum, Hillsdale, NJ.

VonGlasersfeld, E. (1989) 'Environment and Communication'. In Steffe and Wood.

Computing Tools for Case Study Analysis

CASE: A CASE ANALYSIS SUPPORT ENVIRONMENT[39]

Abstract

The synergy between hypertext tools for organizing large, heterogeneous databases and functioning models as explanations of processes may permit us to address a class of problems remaining largely bypassed and undervalued in the study of human learning. If these 'power tools for the mind' permit us better to manage and model complexity, they may bring within our grasp a series of problems long considered beyond the reach of well articulated understanding. One such cluster of problems centres on how cognitive development of the individual relates to particular interactions. Case study has long been an effective tool in unravelling the more intricate patterns of human behaviour and development. Its focus on individual behaviour leads to the detailed observations necessary to understand an individual's performance. As contrasted with methods which attempt to 'hold all else equal,' case study traces in detail the path of change, and so it is the method of choice in studying learning. Technology has enhanced the dependability of case study materials: videotape permits capture of enough of a context to permit later interpretation in detail. This blessing is a burden in disguise, for there is no balanced development of techniques of analysis. Computers can facilitate the analysis of case material to redress that imbalance. One may hope their use will introduce a new period in the study of intelligence, one where cognitive scientists will have at last the tools to study the development of knowledge in its full particularity.

An Example of a Case Study Corpus

Since significant learning appears from processes which are extended in time, its understanding depends upon a multitude of interactions between what is in the individual's mind and the accidents of everyday experience. This stance has led me to study and record the cognitive development of one of my daughters from the time she was 18 weeks old through the sixth year of her life. The targeted theme of this study is the interrelationship, if any, between the development of language skills and knowledge and spatial knowledge. Every week we have videotaped experiments and our play together; we supplemented those mechanical records with extensive naturalistic observation. The total number of tapes comprising the corpus is 240 (each containing, typically, three experimental sessions). For the first three years, the experiments divide into sets with two different foci. The first is a continuing series about Peggy's developing

---

39. 1982. Unpublished. Subsumed in the collection of papers for the First National Hypertext Conference (Chapel Hill, 1987), this text was later also published in *Hypertext: The State of the Art* (Intellect, 1990) and also subsumed in Chapter 2 of *CS&C* (1996).

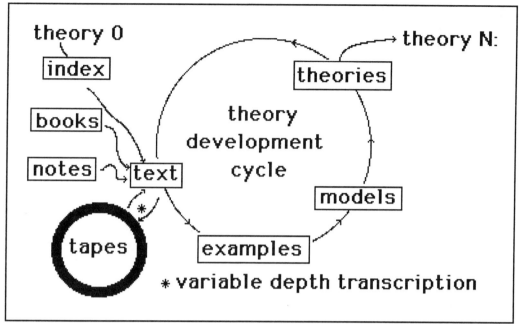

Figure 1: CASE, a Case Analysis Support Environment

object knowledge; this material relates to literature of the Piagetian paradigm and is intended as a calibrating spine of the study. The second set of experiments is more a miscellany, each one drawing its inspiration from what my wife or I could notice as most potentially fecund in the child's behaviour. Some incidents of the naturalistic observations are striking in themselves, such as the child's climbing up to a tea table — when she had not yet walked — and pushing it across the floor, walking behind it. Other observations were driven by quasi-regular reflection, and they tend to focus around my theoretical concerns, such as the interplay of language production and other dimensions of development.

Using Hypertext to Cope with an Extensive Corpus

The information captured in so rich a medium as videotape is beyond all hope of transcribing completely in any serial symbolic form, such as text based protocols. Any theory which initially selects the material to be transcribed must be a preliminary, imperfect theory — but its selection criteria will screen out possibly critical information. We can begin, however, with partial transcriptions and use the file updating capability of computer based storage to extend the transcribed corpus at need. Call this strategy variable depth transcription. The researcher records what he imagines as relevant, with such pointers to source material as to make its deepening at need a matter of course. As his analysis leads to improved theory, that theory will suggest the need for deeper analysis of parts of the corpus and their more extended transcription. The extended database will then suggest enhancements of the theory. A positive feedback loop is established. Hypertext facilities now existing and under development permit such an approach. They need to be applied to two problems: recording important details and their interconnections in on line databases; and developing functioning models of cognitive structures and their changes, based on the empirical material of the corpus. These are the objectives of the CASE project.

Data Files:

Index: A bi-directional index of text files contents; this is a list of themes and purposes, on the one hand, and a list of activities and results on the other.

Text: By episodes with scenes: for scenes, a summary description; for episodes, a summary description with variable depth transcription of action and dialogue.

Examples: Related behaviours: for each discriminated behaviour, the file will contain an archetypical example with its 'link-set' — pointers to all other located relevant occurrences (in the literature as well as in the specific study; the purpose is to provide a minimally abstract of the exemplified behaviours.

Models: Speculative, ascribed functional schemata: these are to be the minimal models necessary to function over the set of related examples; the file will indicate model sequences and correspondences with other models in the file.

Theories: Theories of model development: the possibilities this file presents are: describing the minimal changes necessary to cover examples of significant development; the possibility of holding in different states of development alternate theories relating to the corpus; further, to the extent that the models and theories can be made functional, it will be possible to engage in regression testing of theory changes by applying them over the set of models and examples.

Progress to date with the CASE project has been extensive but limited in kind. The original objective of this research was to explore the use of hypertext systems as a tool for advancing the analysis and modelling of detailed case studies. The conceptual focus was two-fold, on developing a database and psychological analyses, and on exploring the utility of hypertext for tasks involving the administration of complex bodies of information and even the development of and interconnection of functional models with them. Such remain the long term objectives of the research. In practice, to date the effort has focused on establishing the overall structure into which the case material will be fit over time. Significant segments of the corpus of naturalistic observations have been entered into the online database. We have followed this procedure:

1. information in the case corpus is brought on-line as ascii text files.
2. those files are imported to the Notecards environment where they are broken up into small text records (stored on individual cards).
3. an administrative structure is imposed on those records by storing them in hierarchically related systems of fileboxes.
4. thematic structures are imposed on those records by relating records in the notecards to one another with links whose type varies across a spectrum of issues.

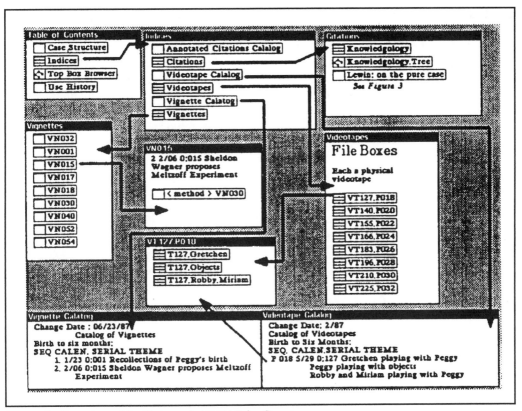

Figure 2: Overview of the Notecards CASE Files Structure

5. the conclusion is a network of database of records which the analyist can navigate and modify as his questions and knowledge change.

A First Implementation

The current Dandylion database, developed at the Army Research Institute for the Behavioural and social Sciences (ARI) in the first six months of the project, occupies more than 3400 pages of the Xerox hard disk storage (this is approximately 1,700,000 characters). Figure 2 shows a top level view of that database. The central structure of the database derives from three indices, or main categories of data. Videotapes represents a catalog of the videotape corpus. Vignettes is a catalog of notes and short stories based on naturalistic observation. Citations is a reference list of the books that I have read or might read that I think should be relevant to analysis of the corpus.

Bushy Trees

The vignettes catalog in Figure 2 is a list of themes in the vignettes of naturalistic observations in the database. This text entered the database as an ascii file. The vignette database itself is a filebox of notecards, each of which contains text manipulable by a WYSIWYG editor. Each vignette card is created with text selected from the vignette catalog, cut, and pasted into a notecard. As needed, text of individual vignettes has been transcribed from the manuscript to a notecard and inserted in the vignettes filebox. The structure of the file is shallow and broad (720 notecards). The file is logically sequential, ordered by serial date from the day of the subject's birth. The sequence is explicit in the notecard labels though not in the physical organization of the database. For example, VN054 contains notes of motor development observed in the 54th day of the subject's life. Themes and issues that relate one vignette to another are represented by typed links threading the vignettes along a string of logical interconnection. The primary link types represent categories of infant development (motor, perceptual, cognitive, social) and study focal themes (language, physical objects, methodology). Since any protocol may contain information relevant to several themes, the threads interweave through the collection of protocols in a complex but comprehensible fashion.

Each sub-filebox in the videotape database of Figure 2 represents a single physical tape. Each videotape is divided into scenes (another subfilebox) named with a label of the form Tnnn.keyword, where nnn is the serial date in the subject's life and the keyword names either the other persons in the scene (a parent, sibling, or pet is typical) or the experimental materials used by the subject. Each scene is, as appropriate and as needed, further analyzed into thematically defined episodes which contain in turn sequences of actions, speech, and commentary by experimenters. Thus, videotape 'VT127.P018' in Figure 2 names a physical tape made on the 127th day of Peggy's life (and eighteenth week). The subboxes 'T127.Gretchen' and T127.Objects' specify scenes in which the subject was with her mother first and then with a specific collection of experimental objects. This database is also shallow and bushy, containing about 750 fileboxes representing scenes (each subdivided into episodes as well). The reason for this labelling is so that a simple lisp function can sort vignette and videotape card titles within a specific date range and order the material to support the correlation and interlacing of events noted in the naturalistic observation and recorded in the videotapes.

Progress and Limitations

The initial efforts in the first six months of this project were directed primarily towards familiarization with the system, database design, and the beginnings of database construction. Database construction took place in the Smart Technologies Group of the Army Research Institute for the Behavioural and Social Sciences, Washington, DC. The protocol material for the database was keyed online at a remote location as ascii files (now still available in this form), then mailed by arpanet to the laboratory at which they were integrated into the database by cutting and pasting text strings into notecards. At this point, I have available a structure with which I can begin the analysis and model building the corpus demands for its serious scientific exploration. Given that the database I'm constructing is very large and detailed, it should be no surprise that progress is slow, especially now that the effort has turned toward analysis of videotaped experiments. A beginning has been made in the analysis of videotape materials, but only at the top level of observation. The current phase may best be described as corpus adminstration. It is becoming clear that the effort will go forward in three waves which, although they will overlap, will follow this natural sequence. Corpus administration, corpus exploration, theory construction. The primary feedback loop ultimately will range between theory construction and corpus exploration, but before that can begin there must be a critical mass of material under review and at least partially online. Achieving that critical mass is the heart of the current effort. Since the psychological analysis needed to construct decent models of material in the Peggy corpus will take years, it should be no surprise that I have a need to work with other models now. During several years, I worked with Oliver Selfridge to develop simple models of interactive learning and implemented them in zetalisp on a Symbolics 3600. For a variety of reasons, I decided to convert those models to run in Object Logo on a Macintosh computer. I am now attempting to connect those models to their corpus in a project parallel to the CASE project effort.

The Psychology of the Particular

Many social scientists stand in awe of general theories. They typcially seek an abstract correspondence which will generally permit predictions that will cover many of the specific events that interest them. For me, the primary value of a general theory is more down to earth, more like what an engineer needs; it is the aid a theory offers in understanding and solving particular problems, such as what enabled a specific person to learn some particular knowledge in a given context. Why are case studies focused on a single person worth paying attention to? I believe these methods and objectives will help us approach a new way of doing psychology.

Kurt Lewin argued (1935) that psychology is now an *Aristotelian* science and will become a modern or *Galilean* science only when researchers shift their focus from finding cross classificatory correspondences to developing explicit explanations for series of events in concrete cases. In short, human psychology will become a science only when it begins solving problems in concrete cases, as one does in reading computer memory dumps or exploring machine learning. Lewin's specific proposals failed to engender such a transformation (see chapter 2 in Langer, 1967), yet there remains the sense that his attempt was profoundly right — to move studies of mind from seeking correspondences to solving important problems in very specific and concrete cases.

The New Opportunity

If we can construct what Lewin refers to as 'the pure case' (a corpus with a sufficiency of information to explain adequately all questions on which it might bear) and extend the modelling successes of function-oriented psychology, this should impact both theory formation and how one teaches psychology. The CASE project is one experiment in this spirit. We are trying to:
- capture a detailed body of information

- convert that corpus to an on-line database via variable depth transcription
- link related events and model development within the corpus
- offer that linked database and access to the corpus materials to the scrutiny and further development by colleagues in order to enhance
  - development of alternative theories
  - application of our own theories to other cases/corpora

This method will also enhance the acceptability of the case study method by discriminating between the idiographic focus of the content of case studies and idiosyncratic interpretations of such studies. Such facilities will provide a kind of experimental workbench for students where they may undertake, as it were, a kind of apprenticeship in case study analysis under the tutelage of the case database developer.

Some may want to argue that such efforts are not scientific in the sense of permitting replicable experiments in other circumstances, but the effort is scientific in Peirce's broader sense — an attempt to approach some imperfectly understood but well defined reality through seeking the convergence of opinion based on serious and extended inquiry. That is enough for me.

There is no magic in either cognitive modelling or the use of on-line tools for managing data, but their synergy will permit us to address and solve some long-standing, important problems in cognitive psychology. It is the problems which give the tools their importance. It is the new tools which give us some hope of coping with the problems by sharing our information, analyses, and ideas.

References

K. Lewin. 'Aristotelian and and Galilean Modes of Thought in Contemporary Psychology.' In *A Dynamic Theory of Personality*: Selected Papers of Kurt Lewin, McGraw Hill, 1935.

S. Langer. 'Idols of the Laboratory.' Chapter 2 in *Mind: An Essay on Human Feeling.*, (Vol.1). John Hopkins Press, 1967.

C. S. Peirce. 'The Fixation of Belief.' In *Chance, Love, and Logic* (M. R. Cohen, ed.). Harcourt, Brace, and Co. 1923. 'Lessons from the History of Science. ' In *Essays in the Philosophy of Science* (V. Tomas, Ed.). Liberal Arts Press, 1957.

Acknowledgements

This work was undertaken through a senior research residency grant from the National Research Council at the Army Research Institute for the Behavioural and Social Sciences. My colleague, Joseph Psotka, director of the Smart Technologies Project at ARI,was extraordinarily supportive and helpful. His suggestions have made this work much better than it could ever have been otherwise.

Datacase Designs

DATACASES[40]

a project for the long term

Case study has long been recognized as a primary tool for exploration and theory development in the behavioural and social sciences. Given that case studies — in all their particularity and complexity — can not be replicated, their most productive scientific use requires that case study materials be maximally available for secondary analysis. The enhancement of recording technologies during recent decades has made significant strides in permitting such secondary analysis. Comparable advances in the area of interpretation are required; such appear within our reach, if not within our immediate grasp, through the well directed exploitation of computer technologies.

Exploiting Computing Technology for Secondary Analysis

The classic example of case studies used for the illumination of differently based interpretations is Robert White's 'Lives in Progress'. White provided interpretations of three of his case studies based on the biological, the psychodynamic, and the social and cultural views of man. That work is a classic for psychological education, primarily because it so well illustrates the theories. What is less well known is that White's remaining studies exist in archives at Radcliffe's Murray Research Centre. It is possible at this time, with sufficient knowledge, access, and support, to construct a new thing, a database of cases (call it a *DataCase*) organized around White's interpretations in his classic text but more thoroughly undergirding (and perhaps contradicting, even disconfirming) the notions published in his text. The first notion of a datacase then is that it represents a textual layer, interpretive in character and theoretically rich, supported by case detail both as exemplifications of notions and as existence proofs for phenomena. White's work can be made more available for secondary analysis through its embodiment in a DataCase. His work is important and exemplary in its commitment to multiple interpretations.

The on-line textual layer of the White Datacase could be created by scanning and re-structuring the text of White's book. The construction of the supporting layer, based on more extensive case study materials, would depend upon access to the archive of those cases.[41] The best candidate software concept for organizing such ill-formed records and relations into an information processing system is hypertext. A hypertext datacase will unify the database and text processing functions of information processing systems into a medium for supporting scholarly investigation of data-rich fields, such as the behavioural and social sciences epitomize.

---

40. 1990. Unpublished. Subsumed in Chapter 2 of *CS&C* (1996).

41. Lawler requested and received a visiting scholar appointment at the Murray Research Centre for the summer of 1991 to begin this work.

If DataCases also include the construction of epistemological models based on behavioural observation, they will exploit more fully the interpretive potential of computing. That is, simulation of processes comprise a third layer in a datacase. It is not possible to say, beforehand, that historically based studies are suitable for use as a foundation for the construction of epistemological models. White's studies were not collected with such an end in mind. Lawler's studies of his children's development were designed with such an intention, and their analysis has already led to some modelling studies.[42] One primary focus of this project will be the complete exploitation of Lawler's case studies for the construction of a three-layer datacase.

The Three-Layer DataCase

Lawler's case corpora currently include studies of three children, ranging in age from 18 weeks to 8 years. Other work is underway. The preliminary, partial textual layer of a datacase for Lawler's studies exists as the text of two books, in machine readable form, covering the early development of two children. The supporting layer exists as three corpora, much of which can be brought on-line with existing technology and considerable effort. The modelling layer exists in kernel form as a series of interactive machine learning programs, coded in a list processing langauge. The coverage of the text by the models is not complete; such should be considered the normal case — as it also should be considered the normal case that complete corpora are not covered by the text that purports to interpret their detail. A primary effort of this project will be the extension of this DataCase to cover the existing case corpora, including the study of the third child's developing knowledge of language and space and the functional modelling of existing and new interpretations where possible.

Special advantages of dealing with this material are at least two: first, the preferred position with respect to copyright (the principal investigator owns the material); second, as the designer and builder of this DataCase, the principal investigator will be in an ideal position to show other scholars how to exploit the material (both on-line and in the extended corpora) for their development of alternative interpretations.

Exploiting Scholars' Work for the Future

A second view of a datacase is that it comprises an encyclopedic summmum of a scholar's life and work, organized for its optimal exploitation by future scholars.[43] Piaget's extended corpus of writing and experimental work represents a major challenge to the

42. Lawler's studies are respected in a community of scholars who take developmental case studies seriously. Sheldon White has described Lawler's study of his daughter's cognitive development as ' . . .the finest single study of children's learning we have, in care, in detail, in breadth, and sensitivity of perspective . . .The work of 'The Intimate Study' stands as a model of the way a child's thinking should be examined.' Barbel Inhelder has noted that it is also ' . . . The first highly convincing synthesis of cognition science and genetic psychology. An innovative study which highlights the computational approach to new understandings of the growth of mind.'

43. It will not escape the notice of a perceptive reader that this book and its associated extended texts comprise a beginning of the Lawler Datacase in this second sense. See also the next essay on Digital Biography.

future for its thorough absorption and assimilation by scholars of today and tomorrow. Approaching the lifework of a such productive genius could be done different ways. One might, for example, focus on Piaget's creativity as an experimenter and form a catalogue of his empirical work.[44] Alternately, one might think of Piaget primarily as a theorist of mind and focus on theory development, begining a datacase around that theme.[45]

As with the studies by White and Lawler, special arrangements with respect to available materials and copyrights are very important. After extensive discussion with colleagues of Piaget's circle, it became clear that though significant unpublished materials exist, they are closely held by family and institutional colleagues who will choose to make use of those materials in their own time and in their own way. Such is their right, and one can only wish them the best of success at what will be a difficult labour. Perhaps some of these observations will prove of use in their community in due time.

The intention behind constructing a Piaget DataCase would be to bring his work into a form most suitable for future exploitation by students of mind. Since the future is still unclear however, this implies a need for maintaining the current structure and organization of the Piagetian corpus while admitting the need for later free-form linking, indexing, component extraction, and the development of tools for re-structuring based on ideas of future scholars. Various future reorganizations will be possible because there need be no single Piagetian DataCase. Much as commercial systems are 'backed up' by making copies that are kept over time, any Piagetian DataCase would be backed up — but differently because it would be copied and modified many times for various future purposes. The tree of possible reorganizations of the Piagetian corpus will blossom broadly. Time will tell which are the primary branches and what limbs will die and be lopped off. It is important that there be a well established root and bole lest future variations generate more chaos than creative exploitation.

Articulating the Knowledge of a Developing Science

At the end of his productive years, Norbert Weiner was approached by a younger mathematician who urged him to bring his knowledge to bear in organizing his own work for its best use by future students. Weiner preferred to spend his time working on harder, more personally interesting problems. Minsky, once *that* younger mathematician, agreed to join in *this* effort because the agenda is not so egocentric as construction of a monument to a man, it is rather one of exploiting today's technology to create a new tool

44. This approach has been followed by the Centre for Educational Research and Innovation of OECD, Paris, which commissioned development of an experimental catalog based on Piaget's work by Professors Pauli, Nathan, and Grize. Lawler began a joint project with OECD to bring their catalog of experiments on-line as a Macintosh hypercard stack. This project never attracted funding and has been deferred.

45. This focus is preferred by Piaget's close colleagues. H. Gruber, for example, who followed Inhelder in Piaget's chair at Geneva, focusses on Piaget's intellectual development in his book (with Vonèche), 'The Essential Piaget', subtitled 'An Interpretive Reference and Guide'. Lawler has discussed with Gruber construction of a prototype hypertext version of 'The Essential Piaget'.

for our scientific community.[46] The DataCase Minsky will begin simply — it has already begun in a modest way. Minsky's Society of Mind[47] comprises a textual layer of accessible introduction to themes in the nature of knowledge and its embodiment in mind, such as we know it now. Some essays point to the past, to what we know already. Other essays point towards to the future, suggesting new ideas for further development and evaluation. The 300 published essays in Minsky's book — a portion of the original essays available — can be extended, both with essays originally omitted from the printed version and with new work. The organization of material, sequential and chunked into chapters in the book, can be supplemented in the machine readable form by dynamically compiled, user-modifiable indices. The notions represented by the essays of Minsky's text can be supported or undermined by additional materials — from various sources — constructed as the underlying layer of a DataCase. Computational models of ideas, some already constructed by Minsky's students, can serve today as exemplifications of ideas. Minsky now holds copyright and editorial control over the content of his hypertext Society of Mind. He can offer his students the opportunity to extend his original text; he can offer them the opportunity to improve his original text. They can offer him aid in developing a shared, publicly articulated view of intelligence. Some day Minsky will yield control over editing the Minsky DataCase to others. It will become community property explicitly, as it is now implicitly. Then, perhaps even before then, variations of the Minsky DataCase should be expected to occur and develop in their own ways. Multiple variations will be the norm, not the exception; those variations, because occurring in machine readable form, will be more easily specifiable through machine embodied comparison of the DataCase variants themselves.

Where does the datacase go beyond commentary and extension? *Down*, to the detail of supporting materials; here is where the datacase earns its name as materials are linked into the structure of ideas to either support or disconfirm those ideas. *Up*, to simulations and alternate representations of the ideas and the evidence bearing on those ideas; models first will appear as demonstrations of notions appearing in the textual layer. Later, as more work is done on the themes of extending modelling to cover the notions of the textual layer, there will emerge a computational layer amounting to a functional redescription of the view of mind advanced by Minsky and his colleagues. Ultimately, the modelling layer will become a computational epistemology, one growing out of the human experience but open to more general characterizations of what mind is and might become.

The Interrelation of Multiple DataCases

These particular cases have not been advanced merely because they are convenient and thus possible to construct. The ideas and research have long been intimately related.

---

46. Though Minsky did once agree to participate in such a project, his active participation is less likely as time pases by. On the other hand, his personal efforts to bring his extended works to the public are in the same spirit, so the following text will stand as is, even though outdated in detail.

47. Published as a paper book by Simon and Schuster, New York, 1986.

Lawler's case studies were inspired by Minsky's observations on challenges facing the field of Artificial Intelligence (AI) in the mid-seventies. Neither the studies nor the results are trivially derivitive. One problem with mid-seventies theories of mind is that they were underdetermined — this is still true, in that one can represent functioning in many ways. Lawler's studies did not constrain theorizing in AI, nor was such their intention. They have however, suggested some non-obvious starting points for knowledge development and some mechanisms as effective which were not prominent in theory at the time.

Piaget and McCulloch, in an earlier generation, sensed the distant compatibility of biological and computational epistemologies. Minsky's Society of Mind began as a collaboration with Papert, for five years Piaget's mathematician. Symbol-oriented machine learning studies began in the sixties with the notion of procedural composition. Piagetian structuralism, requiring more complex structures to embody knowledge than the procedures and combined-primitives of the sixties, offered a richer vision of mind, in psychological terms, and thus appeared as an addressible, compatible challenge to early machine learning research: compatible because structural; addressible because computation offers a wealth of mechanisms for embodying structural development beyond simple composition. The challenge is profound; it has not yet been adequately met.

Piaget's case studies are an obvious inspiration for Lawler's studies. In contrast, however, note that Piaget's studies were based on the unified interpretation of case material based on three infant studies. Lawler's most thoroughly developed study was based on his second subject. (The work with the first subject could be taken as an extended, exploratory pilot study for the more detailed later study — thus influential in shaping the work but not integral.) Lawler's further studies involve interpretive work still underway and going beyond the initial study significantly in the range of themes and issues addressed — relating themes of language development with the Piagetian focus on knowledge about objects and space.

The ultimate intention of this project is to construct three primary DataCases, with the White DataCase as an important prototype. In this effort, the participation of Minsky and Lawler, scientists owning their own material, will be a significant advantage. Further, participating as designers and developers of the implemented DataCases, they will be the best situated persons to guide others in use of the facilities for secondary analysis, a primary focus of the effort. Their collaboration over the long term and into the future will undergird the attempt to interrelate their different DataCases and that of Piaget as well. The vision is inspiring, but the prospect is daunting. We will see what progress can be made.

Purdue University, March 1991

DIGITAL BIOGRAPHY[48]

Digital is the medium which encompases and subsumes all others — but *what is it for?* What uses or applications of digitial media can we create that will fully exploit its potential in service of the deepest of human desires?

> . . . Sin of self-love possesseth all my soul
> And all my every part . . .

> *(Shakespeare)*

> Each mortal thing does one thing and the same —
> Selves — goes itself; *myself* it speaks and spells,
> Crying *what* I *do* is me: for *that* I came . . .

> *(G.M.Hopkins)*

And each has a story to tell, the story of the life it has made.

In *The City and the Stars*, Arthur Clarke describes a world where people live, die, are reborn, and continue in this cycle through billions of years. In that world, the memories of an individual's past lives are restored to the reborn person after the twentieth year. When, tired of living, one returns to the hall of creation to end the current life, the person reviews the memories of past lives, including the latest one lived, and chooses what will be saved for recall in the next reincarnation.

What Clarke imagined as a necessary part of that cycle of birth and death, we can undertake today — in the sense of editing this life's memories to reveal and illuminate what has been most important to each of us as an individual. Multi-media control, non-sequential text, simulation, animation, extensive memory and quality video now permit individuals to begin to use the digital medium in a non-trivial, essentially artistic, and deeply personal task — recreating one's own vision and experience of life.

Who would want to do so and why?
Many, and for various reasons.

Who would pay?
The *wealthy* first, for themselves.

Then *organizations*, subcultures, even nations, wishing to honour their most distinguished members.

Then *the technically adept* with access to more limited resources.

Eventually and more generally, *those able to use tools* such as which will be created as the activity becomes popular.

Typically biographers make books, but they rarely do justice to people of genius. For example, in a recent book 'A Mind of her Own', a biography of the theorist of psychotherapy, Karen Horney, the author wrote a most engaging story, but as a study her

---

48. 1990. Unpublished. Subsumed in Chapter 23 of *CS&C* (1996).

story was severely limited. She told her audience about Karen, the person, but she left out Horney, the theorist.

Digital biographies, flexible enough to permit a reader to find the preferred depth, with components capable of function as well as presentation, can better do justice to the most remarkable among us.

What would be Done with such Digital Biographies?

For the individual as participating subject, digital biography would be an expressive act, an opportunity to render a vision of life and a sense of experience. For a biographer, it would be an effort of intellectual/social history. For society, one could think of such as archives for today and resources for tomorrow. Understanding individuals as creators of ideas can help in understanding the ideas themselves and their subsequent modifications. To the extent that such resources can permit better access for students to the original work of important thinkers and agents — even with later added annotations for clarification and guidance — their availability may improve students' appreciation of the application as well as of the structure of ideas in a community as it grows through time.

What would be Problems in Publishing Digital Biographies?

Publication separates into two issues: 'distribution' and 'annotation'. At any time, the limits on distribution would be technical (what hardware is accessible through which general access could be had), economic (who profits), and ethical (how does one deal with errors, misrepresentations, and distasteful truths?). The technical issues need not be confronted immediately — except that one would want to define specifications for or design a language for describing the relationships among the elements of the media in such a way that it would be only marginally dependent (if at all) on specific media or systems in which the biography would be instantiated. Economic questions would require negotiation as ever.

The ethical questions would probably have to be dealt with on a case by case basis at first until satisfactory norms evolve. This is so because the willingness of some people to share their views will depend on keeping secrets until their interests are invulnerable. On the other hand, if it is known that the truth will out in the end, misrepresentations of various sorts would likely be minimized except by the chronically deceitful. This is where annotation comes to the fore, because it will permit a kind of secondary public dialogue where the annotator will not have to invest years producing 'a work' to criticize mistaken points and argue against mistaken impressions.

Artificial Intelligence

THE TEXTURE OF BEHAVIOUR [1]

Taking behaviour seriously does not always permit the development of an explicit model of the behaviour, as this vignette[2] should convince you:

'On June 2, 1949, four-year-old Margaret Reid spent 28 minutes in the Midwest behaviour setting, Home Meal (lunchtime) . . .her behaviour was consistent with the standing behaviour pattern of the lunchtime setting. But this is by no means all. Margaret did 42 clearly discriminable and different things on the level of behaviour episodes during the 28 minutes. Here are 21 of the 42 actions, just half the total:

Rejecting lemonade; Recollecting pancakes eaten for breakfast; Cutting tomato; Helping self to noodles; Forecasting Bible School picnic; Challenging little brother to lunch eating race; Appraising combination of lemon juice and milk; Inquiring about Valentine's day; Coping with dropped napkin; Commenting on play of neighbour friend; Playing on words about Bible School picnic; Wiping something out of eye; Reporting little brother's capers; Dunking cookies in cocktail sauce; Telling about imaginary friends; Putting box of Kleenex on bench; Inviting parents to look into stomach; Soliciting mother's opinion on brother's eating; Using spoon as airplane; Chanting "Bones to Be"; Reporting on birthday greetings at Bible School . . .'

Barker and Wright then expand one of these incidents — Cutting tomato — into fifteen even more detailed action descriptions. How information processing models of today should approach material exhibiting such volatility is far from clear. In some instances, as Anzai and Simon (1979) demonstrate in 'The Theory of Learning by Doing', the analysis of limited-scope case material may proceed with admirable specificity. However, the orderliness of thought shown by their subject, a liberal arts college graduate, is not characteristic of the less regular thought of the child from whom every adult develops.

My study has taken a middle course between the analysis of limited scope experimental protocols and the overwhelming detail of a complete ecological study. By following the CHILD'S main interests and activities, the primary themes of her development were permitted to emerge sufficiently early on that they could serve as foci of documentation. Thus I could follow the learning of a single mind on its natural scale of development — that of months and years — while still preserving a sufficiency of material for detailed analysis where the pattern of development indicates the effort is justified; from these main developmental themes, I have chosen for extended analysis those which engage what I take to be central issues of the nature of mind. I believe there is no other so rich study of the cognitive development of so mature a child extending over so long a time and so explosive a period of mental growth.

---

1. 1984. Published in an appendix as an 'Extended Citation' in *CECD* (1985).

2. From *Midwest and Its Children* (Barker and Wright, 1955)

ABOUT THE NEXT PERSON YOU MEET [3]

'Tell me how to think differently about the next person I meet.'

Sheldon White

The study of the individual in a natural setting and the interpretation of behaviour there brings us directly to the case we want most to know about, ourselves. Because my work is focused on the learning of a particular child in particular situations, some people may wonder if it's so special that it carries no general relevance. Consider two criteria by which to make such judgments. Some experiences may be judged generally relevant because they involve kinds of events frequently encountered. Others may be so judged because they exhibit with unusual clarity or novelty events which are lawful. These suppositions are the main grounds of my empirical research:

- The individual case does not merely illustrate the general law; it embodies the general law.
- Through interpretation of the particular case in detail, we can arrive at the general law.
- If mental phenomena are lawful in a strong sense, as physical phenomena are, then the importance of explaining the concrete case must be granted from the beginning.
- If the phenomena of mind are lawful, it is reasonable to explore learning through the detailed analysis of an individual's learning.
- If the richness of the experienced mind is comparatively great, in terms of its ability to bring a multitude of perspectives to bear on the solution of any particular problem, documenting that richness of mind for even one person can be a considerable challenge .

I chose to study the learning of my daughter Miriam, because we were very close, I had known her long, and knew her well. For six months — beginning at her sixth birthday — we two and my eight year old son Rob worked as colleagues on a research project to document and explore my daughter's learning. This effort included the execution of quasi-standard experiments from the Piagetian repertoire, working sessions at the computer laboratory of the MIT Logo project, experiments at home, and naturalistic observation of Miriam's behaviour, thoughts, and feelings.

The basic corpus, consisting of the mechincal records of all experimental and working sessions (along with their transcriptions) is richly supplemented by the naturalistic observation. The primary themes of development emerged clearly, sufficiently early on, that they could serve as foci of documentation. From these main themes, I have chosen for extended analysis those whose development engages what I take to be central issues of the nature of mind. The modeling aims of my research have two bases:

- Functional structures are needed to represent problem solving behaviour. They also can represent knowledge.
- The genesis of new functional structures can be seen to emerge from the functioning of pre-existing knowledge structures.
- Exploring this dual thesis in detail is a central objective of my analyses.

---

3. 1984. Unpublished.

Cognitive Modelling

CO-ADAPTATION AND THE DEVELOPMENT OF COGNITIVE STRUCTURES[4]

Things developed for one purpose often can be used for something else. Systems, individuals, and even their component parts evolved under one set of environmental pressures may function well and with significantly different impact in changed circumstances. The general name for this circumstance is the **coadaptation** of structures.[5] The idea of coadaptation is extremely useful in explaining slatations in performance. I aim to produce a more articulate description of the role of coadaptation in the development of structures for thinking.

Within a function-oriented structuralist view of human learning, a central challenge is explaining the transition from from naivety to mastery. This is likewise a major issue for machine learning. We report here progress on that theme with programming experiments taking guidance from a human case study.[6] The domain is tictactoe (or noughts and crosses). The human case serves as the developmental prototype; it answers the question 'why this way?' The machine case serves as an experimental laboratory for asking 'how hard or simple might the development be?' The overall strategy has been to start with quite limited programs, reflecting specific important characteristics of immature thought, and have them get smarter by escaping from their original limitations. The performance objectives are to develop programs that will achieve primitive forms of abstraction, create internal reflections of external objects and processes, and learn without instruction.

---

4. 1986. In Procedings of the European Conference on Artificial Intelligence (1986).
    1987. In *Advances in Artificial Intelligence*, DuBoulay, Steels, and Hogg, eds. (Elsevier).

5. This is a technical use of the term, following Satinoff in *Neural Organization and the Evolution of Thermal Regulation in Mammals*, 1978, and Jacob in *Evolution and Tinkering*, 1977/1982. Satinoff notes:
    '. . .[M]ost, if not all, thermoregulatory reflexes evolved out of systems that were originally used for other purposes. To give just two examples of this, Cowles has argued that the peripheral vasomotor system, the basic system for changing blood flow at the surface, first served as a supplemental respiratory organ in amphibia. It then became a heat collector and disperser in reptiles (regulating the flow of heat from outside the body to inside) and finally a temperature regulatory mechanism for endotherms (regulating heat flow from inside the body to outside). Heath has argued that the change in posture from the sprawling stance of a reptile to the limb-supported posture of the therapsids, the mammal-like reptiles, and subsequently the mammals, and the consequent changes in muscular organization and muscle tension provided the basis for a high internal heat production. This illustrates *the principle of evolutionary coadaptation: a mechanism evolved for one purpose has as a side benefit an adaptive value in an entirely different system.*'
    For a profound and more general discussion of related views, see Jacob.

---

6. The case material used here is presented in detail in Chapter 4 of CECD.

From Anterior Structures to Mature Performance

Piaget's 'conservation' experiments are strong evidence that knowledge in the naive mind leads to reasoning surprisingly different from that in expert minds.[7] Such studies lead us to focus on the issues of what **are** the precursors of and the processes leading to mature performances. I have argued that in the human case mature skills can arise from small but significant changes in the organization of pre-existing, fragmentary bodies of common-sense knowledge[8] which represent the things of everyday experience and operations on them. If only one could specify the character and function of antecedent structures, he could explain large scale behaviour changes as saltations emergent from minimal internal organizational changes.

The Neophyte: particularity and egocentricity

Children's early cognition is usually described as 'concrete', a term which has two significant dimensions of meaning. The broader meaning is that the child's knowledge is based upon personal experience. It is in *this* sense that concrete knowledge is very *particular*, that is, depending on the specific details of the learner's interaction with people and things. Lawler's subject was observed beginning to play tictactoe strategically by imitating a three move plan for establishing a fork another child performed. The characteristics of her knowledge at that time were particularity and egocentricity. **Particularity**: when her sole plan was blocked, she was unable to develop any alternative.[9] **Egocentricity**: she did not attend to the moves of her opponent unless they directly interfered with her single plan. She was committed to her own objectives and unconcerned to the point of indifference about the plans of her antagonist.[10] In the setting of a competitive game, this was bound to change. But how, if a mind constructs itself from such beginnings, is it possible to escape the particularity and egocentrcity characteristic of early experiences? The journey from neophyte to master is a long one. One hope of the human study was tracing the path of such development. One objective of the machine study is constructing such a path.

Representation of Knowledge

The representation used to model Lawler's subject's naive knowledge, presented in detail in 'Learning Strategies through Interaction' by Lawler and Selfridge, 1985, has the parts necessary for adaptive functioning. Learning what to do is essential: GOALS are explicitly represented. Knowing how to achieve a goal is essential: ACTION PLANS are

7. See, for example, *The Child's Conception of Number*, Piaget, 1952.

8. Such an argument is detailed in Chapter 2 of 'Computer Experience and Cognitive Development', (*CECD*). The subject of that detailed case study will be referred to as 'Lawler's subject'.

9. The detailed background for the subject and the detail of this incident are presented at pp. 120-122 in *CECD*.

10. Piaget introduced this emphasis in the characterization of children's early thought in his early book *The Language and Thought of the Child*.

explicitly represented. Knowing when a planned action will work and when it won't is essential: CONSTRAINTS limiting application of actions are represented explicitly. The structure composed of this triad, a GAC (Goal, Action, Constraints), is our representation of a strategy for achieving a fork in tictactoe. Goals are considered as a three element set of the learner's marks which take part in a fork. This is the first element of a strategy. Plans of three step length, which add the order of achieving goal steps, are represented as lists. Constraints on plans are two element sublists, the first element being the step of

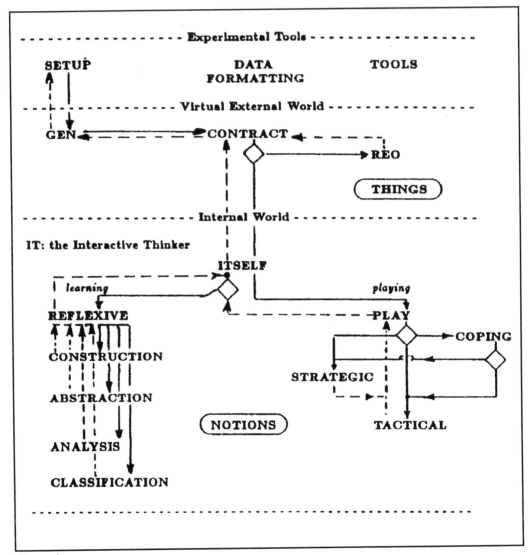

Figure 1

the plan to which the constraint attaches and the second being the set of cell numbers of the opponent's moves which defeated the plan in a previous game. In our simulations, REO (a relatively expert opponent) can win, block, and apply various rules of cell choice — though ignorant of any strategies of the sort IT is learning. Within the execution of our simulation, the structure of GAC 1 below will lead to the three games shown depending on the opponent's moves (letters are for IT's moves, numbers for REO's):

The representations and learning mechanisms are committed to cell-specificity; they are also self-centred, focusing on the learner's own plans and knowledge (as they must since, by principle, IT begins not knowing what the opponent will do; IT does not have the ability to model or predict an opponent's moves in any abstract way).[11] The result of learning simulations is a descent network which specifies all the goals and plans learned as modifications of the generating precursors of each.

Escaping from Particularity

If we ask where symmetry comes from in a world of highly particular descriptions, the answer MUST involve abstraction, but which form of those kinds possible? Abstraction by feature-based classification is the most commonly recognized form, but there are others. Piaget emphasizes a kind of abstraction, focusing more on *what one does* rather than on *what one attributes to external things* as a quality. This *reflexive abstraction* is a functional analysis of the genesis of some knowledge[12], as presented in Bourbaki's description of the generality of axiomatic systems:

'A mathematician who tries to carry out a proof thinks of a well-defined mathematical object, which he is studying just at this moment. If he now believes that he has found a proof, he notices then, as he carefully examines all the sequences of inference, that only very few of the special properties in the object at issue have really played any significant role in the proof. It is consequently possible to carry out the same proof also for other objects possessing only those properties which had to be used. Here lies the simple idea of the axiomatic method: instead of explaining which objects should be examined, one has to specify only the properties of the objects which are to be used. These properties are placed as axioms at the start. It is no longer necessary to explain what the objects that should be studied really are . . .'

N. Bourbaki, in Fang, p. 69.

Robust data argue that well articulated, reflexive forms of thought are less accessible to children than adults. The possibility that mature, reflexive abstraction is unavailable to naive minds raises this theoretical question: *what process of functional abstraction precedes such fully articulated reflexive abstraction*; could such a precursor be the kernel from which such a mature form of functional abstraction may grow?

---

11. The general commitment to egocentric knowledge representation has psychological justification in this specific case. Lawler's subject suffered the defeat above trying to achieve the victory of GAC 1 (the only strategy she knew), not attending to her opponent's move nor anticipating any threat to her intended fork.

---

12. Piaget contrasts reflexive abstraction with classificatory or Aristotelian abstraction (p.320 in *Biology and Knowledge*), demeaning the latter somewhat by referring to it as 'simple'.

The Multi-modal Mind

Let us discriminate among the major components of the sensori-motor system and their cognitive descendents, even while assuming the preeminence of that system as the basis of mind. Imagine the entire sensori-motor system of the body as made up of a few large, related, but distinct sub-systems, each characterized by the special states and motions of the major body parts, thus:

BODY PARTS	SENSORI-MOTOR SUB-SYSTEM	MAJOR OPERATIONS
trunk	**somatic**	being here
legs	**locomotive**	moving from here to there
head-eyes	**visual**	looking at that there
arms-hands	**manipulative**	moving that there
tongue, etc.	**linguistic**	saying whatever

We will assume the representations of mind remain profoundly affected by the modality of interactions with experience through which it was developed. One implication is that the representations built through experience will involve different objects and relations, among themselves and with externals of the world, which will depend upon the particular mode of experience. Even if the atomic units of description (e.g. condition action rules) are shared between modes, the entities which are the salient objects of concern and action are different; and in relation to each other only through learned correspondences. This general description of mind contrasts with the more uniformitarian visions which dominate psychology today. These major modal groupings of information structures are imagined to be populated with clusters of related cognitive structures, called 'microviews', with two distinct characters. Some are 'task-based' and developed through prior experiences with the external world; others, with a primary character of controlling elements, develop from the relationships and interactions of these disparate, internal microviews. The issue of cognitive development is cast into a framework of developing control structure within a system of originally competing microviews.[13]

Redescriptive Abstraction

I propose that the multi-modal structure of the human mind permits development of a significant precursor to reflexive abstraction. The interaction of different modes of the mind in processes of explaining unanticipated outcomes of behaviour can alter the operational interpretation and solution of a problem. Eventually, a change of balance can effectively substitute an alternative representation for the original; this could occur if the alternative representation is the more effective in formulating and coping with the

---

13. This view of mind is presented and applied in 'Cognitive Organization', Chapter 5 of *CECD*. A more extensive discussion of microviews appears in Chapter 7.

encountered problem. In terms of the domain of our explorations and our representations, there is no escape from the particularity of the GAC representation unless some other description is engaged. A description of the same circumstance, rooted in a different mode of experience, would surely have both enough commonality and difference to provide an alternative, applicable description. I identify the GAC absolute grid as one capturing important characteristics of the visual mode[14]; other descriptions based on the somatic or locomotive subsystems of mind could provide alternative descriptions which would *by their very nature* permit escape from the particularity of the former.

Why should explanation be involved? Peirce argues that 'doubt is the motor of thought' and that mental activity ceases when no unanswered questions remain.[15] Circumstances requiring explanation typically involve surprises; the immediate implication is that the result was neither intuitively obvious nor were there adequate processes of inference available beforehand to predict the outcome (at least none such were invoked).

We propose that a different set of functional descriptions, in another modal system, can provide explanation for a set of structures controlling ongoing activity. The initial purpose served by alternative representations is explanation. Symmetry, however, is a salient characteristic of body centred descriptions; this is the basis of their explanatory power when applied where other descriptions are inadequate. Going beyond explanation, when such an alternative description is applied to circumvent frustrations encountered in play, one will have the alternate structure applied with an emergent purpose. Through such a sequence of events, *the interaction of multiple representations permits a concrete form of abstraction to develop, an abstraction emergent from the application of alternative descriptions*. In the following scenario, I will trace the interaction of different modes of mind as an example of how this early form of functional abstraction, a possible precursor to any consciously articulated reflexive abstraction because it involves 'external interpretation' more than reflexive analysis, permits breaking out of the original description's concreteness with its limitations of particularity. To do so, I need to establish the basic kinds of alternative descriptions to be involved.

14. The GAC description is cast in terms of an external thing seen by the person referring to it, with no hint of an imaginary homunculus in view. Further, the absolute reference assigning numbers to specific cells preserves a top-down, left to right organization. Notice however, that even if a specific person's internal representation were different — based perhaps on a manipulative mode of thought and representation — the essential points of following arguments remain sound.

15. Peirce's position (presented lucidly in 'The Fixation of Belief' but ubiquitous in his writing) was the primary observation leading me to focus on on this theme. He uses the term *doubt* because his discussion is cast in terms of *belief*; mine, cast in terms of *goals*, finds its equivalent expression as *surprise*. Doubts require evidence for elimination (but see Peirce on this); surprises require explanations. Surprise is accessible to mechanical minds as the divergence between expectation and outcome under a specific framework of interpretation.

Alternative Descriptions in TicTacToe

I begin with the assumptions that the GAC formulation is primarily visual in character and that one should seek familiar schemes for representing things, relations, and actions that are from a different mode of experience. Descriptions based on activity lead to the somatic and locomotive body-part systems as the two obvious, primary candidates. I offer two suggestions for concretizing this search: let's consider first an 'imaginary body-projection' onto the tictactoe grid as the somatic candidate description; and second, an 'imaginary walk' through the tictactoe grid as the locomotive candidate description.[16] How would this work in practice?

Somatic Symmetries

Let's consider two essentially different types of symmetry for the tictactoe grid. *Flipping symmetry* will name the relation between a pair of forks (or more complex structures) when they are congruent after the grid is rotated around some axis lying in the plane of the grid. Examples of symmetrical forks might be {139} and {179}.[17] An example of an explanation for this *fork symmetry* based upon an alternative, somatic descrtiption would be the following:

> If I sat in the centre of the grid and lay down with my head in cell 1 and my feet in cell 9, then cell 3 would be at my left hand. The forks {139} and {179} are the same in the way that my right and left hands are the same, for cell 7 would be at my right hand.

Such an explanation focuses on symmetry with respect to the body axis. A similar argument can be made for *plan symmetry* in the common fork {137} achieved by two different plans [1 3 7] and [1 7 3].

> If I sit in the centre of the grid and lie down with my head in cell 1, the cell 3 is at my left hand and cell 7 at my right. If the plan is to move first at the head, next at the left hand, then at the right [1 3 7] then the other plan is the same to the same extent that it doesn't matter if I lie there with my face up or my face down.

It is harder to argue that such flipping forms of description are as natural for symmetries such as those of forks {139} and {137} because the axis of symmetry lies where no ego-owned markers are placed (along the cells {258}) and because other body parts have to be invoked as placeholders, as in the following:

If I sat in the centre of the grid, with my head going up between cells 1 and 3, my

---

16. The following descriptions are rather like imputing thought experiments to subjects but such with a decidely personal and everyday content; the 'dramatic style' seems natural enough for people. If it seems unnatural for machines, the reason is that we do not yet provide our machines with so rich and powerfully various a collection of interacting descriptions as humans are fortunate enough to inherit from the long history of life's evolution.

17. Referring only to the set of markers here, we need not distinguish between the forks achieved by various plans such as [1 9 3] or [3 1 9].

shoulders would be there at 1 and 3 and the other parts of the forks would be the same as are my right and left hands.

As this elaboration departs from the explanatory simplicity of the former, one should consider contrasting another model, and thus turn to explanations based on walking around.

Locomotive Symmetry

In contrast with the last explanation which placed a body axis along a line of empty cells, the locomotive symmetries involve moving from one ego-occupied cell to another. Consider now the type of locomotive description that could be used to explain the equivalence of these same forks {139} and {137}.[18]

Suppose I start at cell 1, walk to cell 9, then turn and walk to cell 3. Facing centre in place leaves me with occupied cells at my right and left hands. For the fork {137}, if I stood at cell 1, I would also have other occupied cells at my right and left hand. The forks are the same if nothing is changed by my jumping from one corner to the next and swinging around to the centre.

This Jump-and-Swing model of symmetry does more than explain a surprising win; the outcome is creative, as can be seen in the following scenario where it enables breaking out of the particularity of the GAC representation.

SCENARIO 1: From one corner to another

After describing different types of symmetries, and justifying their activitation to explain surprising serendipitous victories in play, we now ask whether they can have more than explanatory value. The conclusion is that the 'flipping symmetries' do not generate novelties through interactions in this model even though they are natural explanations of surprises. The rotational or jump-and-swing symmetries can do so, however, through the kind of tortuous but feasible path presented in the following scenario.

Generating a Second Descent Network

Let's suppose the IT plays with *minimal* look ahead. Remember also that IT knows nothing of opening advantage. IT has played successfully to victories even when the second and third step of its known plans were foiled, but never so when the first step was blocked. Supose now that REO begins a game with a move to cell one. All of the existing plans in IT's repertoire are useless. But IT knows that the GOAL {137} is the same as {139} by rotational symmetry, therefore it can try to generate the alternative plan for that symmetrical goal. The attempt to create and use the plan, based on 'jumping' from the pivot of cell 3 to a new pivot at cell 1, *will* fail on a later move, but IT *doesn't know that*.[19]

---

18. Under IT's learning mechanisms, the plan [1 9 3] will generate the goal {137} via the game [1974325] or [1932745]. These goals are essentially related. REO's move directly blocking IT's plan leads directly to the other determinate games.

---

19. IT does not look ahead, therefore IT doesn't notice that the use of cell 1 is relevant to plan [7 3 1]. Nor does moving second inhibit the attempt to escape the frustration of cell 1 being taken because IT does not understand opening advantage; but then, neither did Lawler's subject at age six years.

That game establishes the plan [7 3 1] in IT's repertoire. When IT once again has the first move, should it choose to begin a game in cell 7, it has a decent chance of winning either the game [7 5 3 1 9 . . .] or [7 5 3 9 1 . . .]. Such a victory will establish a new prototypical game, comparable in status to [1 9 3] from which a second descent network can be derived. This does *not* argue that such a second descent network will *actually* be developed in all its fullness (though it may). What it *does* show is one plausible scenario for how the incredibly particular descriptions of GACs can break away from one element of their fixity — commitment to opening in cell 1. The alternative description has served as a bridge to permit developing a second set of equally particular goals and plans.

Emerging Abstraction

If alternative representations can serve as an explanation for surprises developed through play, and if they can serve as a bridge to break away from the rigid formulation of the GAC representation, it is not impossible to believe they may begin to provide dynamic guidance as well — exactly of the sort found useful by adults in their play. When this occurs, the alternative description, useful initially as an explanation for the more particular system of primary experiences, will become the dominant system for play. Then the symmetry implicit in the body-centric imagery will become a salient characteristic of the player's thinking about tictactoe as the highly specific formulations of early experience recede into the background. Abstraction has taken place — because the descriptions of the body mode *are* implicitly less absolute in respect of space than are those supposed to operate with the GAC representation. But the abstraction is not by *features*, nor is it by the articulate analysis of reflexive abstraction, as described by Bourbaki. This is an EMERGENT ABSTRACTION via REDESCRIPTION, a new kind of functional abstraction. *Redescriptive abstraction is a primary example of the coadaptive development of cognitive structures*. As a kind of functional abstraction which does not yet require reflexive analysis of actions taken within the same mode of representation, but merely the interpretation of actions in one mode in terms of possible, familiar actions in another mode[20], it needs bear less of an inferential burden than would the more analytic reflexive abstraction described by Bourbaki.

Redescriptive Abstraction and Analogy

One might say that emergent abstraction via redescription is 'merely analogy'. I propose an antithetical view: emergent abstraction explains *why* analogy is so natural and so important in human cognition. Redescriptive abstraction is a primary operation of the multi-modal mind; it is *the way we must think to explain surprises to ourselves*. We judge analogy and metaphor important because redescriptive abstraction is subsumed under those names.

---

20. The point here is that the process is more like Peirce's abduction than any inductive process of learning. See *Deduction, Induction, and Hypothesis* for Peirce's introduction to this distinction or K.T.Fann's *Peirce's Theory of Abduction* for an analysis of Peirce's developing ideas on abduction.

Further, I speculate it is *the* essential general developmental mechanism. This process can be the bootstrap for ego-centric cognitive development because accomplished without reference to moves or actions of the other agent of play.

Escaping from Egocentricity

'. . .The internalization of socially rooted and historically developed activities is the distinguishing feature of human psychology, the basis of the qualitative leap from animal to human psychology. As yet, the barest outline of this process is known . . .'

L. S. Vygotsky

If the higher psychological processes to which Vygotsky refers are characteristic of productive intelligence in all forms, the issues of the progressive development of self-control and the internalization of exterior agents and context are profound transformations which need to be understood in both natural and artificial intelligence. The general objective of this section is to describe how it is possible for an egocentric system to transcend its limited focus. The central idea is that the system will adapt to an environmental change because of an insistent purpose; it will do so by interpreting the actions of its antagonist in terms of its own possibilities of play. Two essential milestones on the path of intelligent behaviour in interactive circumstances are first, simulation of the activity of an opponent, and second, the internalization of some control elements from the context of play.

In the human case, learning sometimes goes forward by homely binding, an instruction by people or things in what this or that means or how it works. Another kind of learning, which I call 'lonely discovery,' is the consequence of commitment to continuation of an interaction, despite the loss of the external partner. Such a desire, which can definitionally permit only vicarious satisfaction, is the motor of that internalization of 'the world and the other' which is the quintessence of higher psychological processes.[21] We use the case study experiences in respect of these issues to guide the development of two examples/scenarios of how a machine can confront such challenges. We will consider how a system can develop through interaction in such a way that when the environment becomes impoverished, the system can begin to function more richly, and therefore become generally more capable. The particular

---

21. The episode dealt with here is neither singular nor domain specific in character. The original observations on which this view is based were about the behaviour of a newly verbal infant. See *CECD* pp.113-115 in Chapter 4. This issue became prominent for me through its advocacy by Minsky and through its manifest importance in empirical observations on the learning of my children. The ideas can be cast in a Freudian framework for relative simplicity of explanation. The essential idea I advance for developing self-control can be read into Freud's description of the tripartite mind — Id, Ego, and Super-ego — which depends for development, first, on the introjection of authority figures by the child. After this introjection of an 'other', which we can take to be an adoption of goals of the Superego not compatible with existing goals of the Id, the Ego, by mediating interior conflicts between the Id and Super-ego, can develop control over both through *virtual experiences*; this permits the system of the self to become somewhat better able to deal with the disparity between the desires of the Id and the constraints of the external world.

problems through which I will approach these issues are the inception of multi-role play (one player as both protagonist and antagonist) and the inception of guarded (or mental) play. I do not want to impute to IT the motive of understanding the play of an opponent to whom it initially pays little attention. Therefore, we grant the system an initial purpose of continuing play even under such limitations as to amount to a crippling of the environment. From this initial purpose emerges another, that of the proper understanding of an antagonist's game. A major side effect of the solution I propose to this problem is creativity, in the specific sense of enabling the discovery of strategies of play not known beforehand nor learned by another's instruction. The ultimate achievement of such developmental mechanisms as I propose here is to learn new strategies through analysis of games played by others, i.e. learning by observation.

SCENARIO 2: The Beginning of Multi-role play:
The Human Case
After many sessions of her playing tictactoe with me, in one experiment I asked the subject to play against her brother so that I might better observe her play with another person. She surprised her brother by her significant progress at play (she beat him honestly and knew she would do so in specific games). When I was called away to answer a knock at the door, I asked the children not to play any more games together until I returned. Coming back, I found the game below on the chalk board. When I asked if she had let herself win, she explained that she had been 'making smart moves for me and the other guy.'

```
 A |  3  |  C
 ___|_____|___
   |  1  |  D
 ___|_____|___
 2 |     |  B
```

My formulation of this episode is as follows. She wanted to continue playing tictactoe. Her ability to do so was hindered by my specific prohibition: the normal environment was crippled. She adapted her earlier developed skills, partitioning them so that strategic play remained her prerogative while tactical play was assigned to her newly effective internal antagonist, 'the other guy'. Could such a process be made effective in a machine?

The Form of the Solution for Machines
If the deprivation of interaction in the social milieu is one motor of human cognitive development, within the world of machine intelligence the corresponding circumstance would be the crippling of some function of other programmed modules of the system. The desired consequence of this crippling should be one where continuing in the well worn path is an easily detectable, losing manoeuvre, thus necessitating changes in the functions of existing structures. Further, there should exist some alternative which is the marginally different application of an already existing structure capable of providing a functional solution to the problem which the 'social' vagary creates. This paper offers two examples of such challenges and possible outcomes in the reorganization of this system of game simulation functions.

The deprivation of interaction leads to the introjection of 'the other' within the 'self' through the assignment of one of alternative functions (strategic play) to the 'ego' (IT) and another (tactical play) to the 'alter-ego' (let's call this agent 'REO-sim'). What forces this reassignment is crippling the environment so that a decision needs to be taken on an issue which was immanent in but transactionally insignificant in the interactive context.[22] What makes this introjection possible is the successful application of established structures for a new function. Obviously, not every attempt to apply an old structure for a new function would be successful[23]; consequently, the character of structures which permits such successful re-application, their functional lability, needs to be established through some sort of experience, either of actual or imaginative interaction. In a system within which such imaginative experience is not yet possible, actual interchanges are needed.

The question raised by simulations was how extensive would be changes required to permit the system of programs to mimic the kind of behaviour Lawler's subject showed in this incident. For IT, the situation equivalent to having no opponent is: whenever IT returns its latest move, IT receives control again with *no* move made by REO. There are three possible responses to this situation:

1. IT could make its next planned move (without even noticing something novel had happened); the consequence of continuing to play with no responses from the antagonist is a sort of *rehearsal* of IT's plan.

2. IT could respond making moves for the antagonist but do so in an imperfectly discriminated manner (for example, using the moves of its own plan for both its own moves and those of REO-sim); when IT attempts to assign moves without making a strategy/tactic division of moves, the play appears random, but is best characterized as *confused tactical play* by both (that is, IT's first move for REO-sim blocks IT's own plan after which both agents play tactically.).

3. IT could partition its own capabilities so that IT alone made strategic moves and REO-sim made tactical moves; when IT's own internal structure is respected in the allocation of roles, play procedes in the normal fashion. This is the *articulation of complementary roles*.

---

22. Chapter 4 of *CECD* argues that in the human case 'whose-turn?' at play was one issue upon which judgments were made *at each move* to prohibit or permit the effecting of intentions in behaviour. Lawler's subject knew what she wanted to do, and when she knew also that the turn was not hers she suppressed her next intended move until it was her turn. Further, one of the ways the child cheated when she feared her plan might be frustrated was to make multiple moves in a single turn.

23. Because my simulations, in fact, share tactical code, the internalization of REO as REO-sim is perfect. Such need not have been the case. REO could have been any arbitrarily baroque system of decisions; IT's simulation of such an alternative REO would still be the same as described here. Allocating a part of itself to represent the other is *all* that IT can do. When it is successful, however, this functional re-application of existing structure is very powerful.

I have programmed IT to function in each of these three different manners under control of global switches. The question remains of how one should view the transition from the states of rehearsing, to confusion, to articulated multi-role play.[24]

For the transition from one mode of response to another I offer no general, theoretical justification. There are reasons. Very little change was required to the original code because of the modular separation of strategic and tactical play. This is an important observation if and only if the modularity of the code for tactical and strategic play is justified by psychological data or epistemological argument.

The assumption of the modularity of cognitive structures and IT's pervasive use of modularity is based on the empirical witness of Lawler's case study. If the human mind is organized as that study suggests, then it *should* be easy for the kinds of developments described here to occur. Further, if the transition is representable by no more than the *insertion of a control element*, choosing between formerly competing or serialized subfunctions; and if the transition is *driven by events in the environment upsetting ongoing proccesses which 'want' to continue*, the only 'theory' possible is one about the characteristics of structure which permit this adaptivity. My structural assertion in this context is that the *coadaptation of disparate cognitive structures is the key element of mind enabling the 'internalization' of external agents and objects.*[25]

SCENARIO 3: The Beginning of Guarded Play
The Human Case
When she was already quite adept at playing Tictactoe against an internalized opponent, Lawler's subject was confronted with a new challenge: given the first two moves of a game, to tell whether she could certainly win, might possibly win, or would certainly lose. When she was refused her request for materials on which to represent possible games graphically, she proceeded to play out mentally sequences of moves which led to determinate games. This is the quintessence of mental play.

In this example, as in the former, constraints upon interaction with the external world — in a framework committed to continuing the activity — led to the application of existing structures to the satisfaction of new ends[26]; the ends are new in the specific sense that knowledge and know-how developed for playing games against an opponent,

---

24. The path is straightforward. Here is how the program works. IT can tell when it receives control out of turn. The manifest failure of rehearsal need only require that IT do something different from the next step of its own plan, which could be nothing else but making some move for the non-existent antagonist. The manifest failure of IT's own plan application for both roles requires refined discrimination; again, a single decision to route control to either one or the other of the strategic and tactical functions based on turn taking is all that's required for the more precise articulation of roles.

25. The animism of the young child is not at all bizarre if his only means of understanding 'the other' is through self knowledge. Like Descartes, he knows he *has* a mind because he thinks; he *believes* in his own past because of memory; and he imputes *will* to things because he feels the meaning of wanting.

26. Here, guarded play began because of my experimental intervention. However, to the extent that children believe keeping their plans secret will help them win (they *surely* learn that by the age of seven), the development of mental play with the initial purpose of guarding plans is to be expected in general.

worked out with graphical tokens, were applied to answer speculative questions about the possible outcomes of games worked out in the mind. This functional lability of structure is the key to adaptive behaviour and thus to learning.

The Machine Case

In the inception of multi-role play, the prohibition of the antagonist role was the stimulus for the reorganization of functioning knowledge. In the machine case, this was achieved through a 'crippling' of the output function of the opponent, REO. The next extension asks what function should be crippled to impel the development of guarded play.

Tree generation within the module GEN is the primary function which creates all the possibilities of play; thus it is the candidate program from whose internalization mental play might emerge. GEN contains a mixture of interrelated LOOP macros and recursive invocations. Note, however, that these programs were created as experimental tools, as mechanisms to explore the learning of IT through experiencing particular games. Consequently, the mechanisms have no grounded epistemic status; their functions need be replicated but their mechanisms may be replaced freely by some alternative if that seems more natural.

Because IT does not contain any such tree-generation modules, rebuilding the GEN module structures within IT would require creating such structure from nothing. Because subfunction invocation with arguments is the primary mechanism within IT for transferring control, an invocation oriented solution is the preferred one: this is doing something already given within the module.

The essential insight IT needs for an invocation solution is that *if it can be called* with an argument by GEN, *it can call itself* successively with a series of arguments drawn from a list.[27]

The remaining issue is how the outcomes of these generated executions of games are handled; that is, the record keeping function is affected as well as the tree generation function. Two alternatives appear to be first, the (unjustified) rebuilding within IT of the list-manipulation aspects of record keeping, or second, the acceptance of an imperfect result in the following specific sense. If the aim of the game is to win, the desired outcome of play is a specific string of cell numbers which comprise a valid win for the first player. If such a single game is the result of the recursive internalization of the GEN module's tree-generation function, the result is an impoverished one (as compared to a

---

27. This is done in the simplest fashion, by tail recursion of IT with the cdr of the candidate moves-list until it is empty. The branching condition for entry into IT's handler is a data anomaly: a list of atoms is expected; when the previous game move is determined to be a *list* of atoms itself, 'something different' must be done. If IT's handler for this condition takes the first element of the end-list of the game and invokes itself with the game made of the prior state and the first member of that list it received, calling itself with the residue of that list will either route a path of execution in a second instantiation through normal IT processing or through the same condition handler, thus leading to further recursions and instantiations of IT. The lists created by GEN's tree generator will be replaced by the recursively generated structure of IT's multiple instantiations. (I do *not* claim people do this naturally.)

list of all possible outcomes) but nonetheless one that will serve an everyday function of winning a game.[28]

Conclusions

The immediate cause for internalizing some exterior function is a constriction of the surrounding context. Given the objective of continuing activity despite this constriction, a person or a programming module can proceed by simulating the crippled functions of the environment of with components of its own function. The functional lability of existing structures in response to a changed external circumstance is the key to internalization of exterior agents and context elements. In the very simple cases presented here, a machine learning system can internalize portions of the outer world as people do. There is no guarantee that any structure will work when applied in some non-intended function. On the other hand, setting up systems of programs to employ this technique in coping with an uncomprehended environment is surely worth considering for any mechanized learning system.

The test of the value of such a capability is creativity. If learning from one's own experience is a criterion of intelligence, is it not smarter to learn from another's experience? Such a capability is an emergent, with a few simple programming changes, of the facilities for multi-role and guarded play.

Learning Without Instruction

With the developments sketched so far, all the capabilities needed for learning from another by observation are in place. The most dramatic evidence for the accuracy of this claim in the human case comes from Lawler's subject's invention of a new strategy of play based upon her later analysis of a game played against herself at an earlier time.[29] In summary, reviewing a game played only to the point where she believed a draw would follow, Lawler's subject recognized that she had abandoned the game while a single further move would have led to her winning. She then worked through the moves she had made, both as protagonist and antagonist, and convinced herself that she had created a new strategy with which to win on condition that her opponent made any one of four responses to her opening corner selection. The kinds of abilities employed in her analysis were those of multi-role play, guarded play, and specific knowledge of three

---

28. This is implemented by choosing to return only a won game to the primary instantiation of IT with a throw. If only nil is returned, then no game can be won from the given initial moves. The objective implicit in GEN to fill the space of possible games is the experimenter's objective; the objective of program IT is to return the next move for any game presented to it.

---

29. The detail of this story and its analysis are presented in pp. 139-141 of *CECD*.

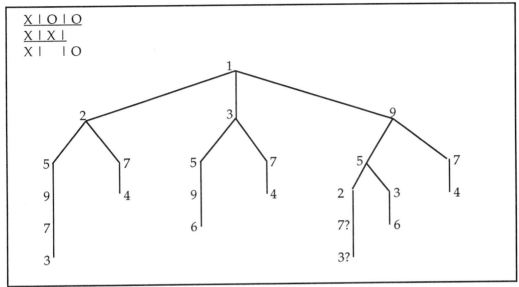

```
X | O | O
X | X |
X |   | O
```

The branch is pruned

sorts: of the particular game, about her own habits (starting in cell one), and procedures of play (she knew SHE would have made forced moves at need).[30]

SCENARIO 4: Analysis through synthesis

The Machine Case

What then needs to be added for IT to perform a similar feat of creative analysis? When presented with an externally generated game, nothing would be easier for IT to analyze *if* the order of moves were preserved. *Here* the challenge is different: the set of moves to be made is prescribed, but the order is to be determined. Lawler's subject's game is below; the tree of possible games following after. When a string is forced into a forbidden move (one not part of the *presented* pattern), the branch is pruned.[31]

Given as prerequisite a system that is capable of multi-role play and guarded play (the latter implies the former), the following changes need be made to existing code:

---

30. Lawler's subject's discovery or invention of a new strategy is obviously a creative application of her knowledge, but is it appropriate to claim that it represents learning from another? The sense in which the answer is 'yes' to this question is the following: Lawler's subject used *all* the relevant knowledge she had. If she encountered a game by some other person, she would have been incapable of interpreting it by any other means than this very analysis. The *claim* then is that this is what people do when they analyze the thought of another, that this is all they *can* do.

---

31. The process depends upon forcing as an operation of tactical play but it does not require a *concept* of forcing. Such a concept could however come as an *explanation* from mental trials such as this. Forcing is important initially less because it leads to a win, than because it is easier to think about a string than a tree.

FUNCTIONS IMPLEMENTED:

- Limiting Proposed Moves to those used:
  (by intersecting possible moves with 'visible' markers).
- Pruning Strings requiring forbidden moves:
  (this requirement is satisfied when a failure occurs, not by looking ahead).
- Exit from model based learning to *example based learning*:
  (this is a hook to an additional learning routine).
- Example Based Learning:
  (a routine fixing actual ego moves of the reconstructed game as a plan).
- Quitting when done:
  (a test for exhaustion of the 'visible' set of tokens).

If these seem like extensive changes, note that two of the five are control transfers on a single condition (EXIT and QUITING), one is a control transfer to top-level on a set membership condition (PRUNING), one is a set intersection of normally available possible moves with the given set of actual moves (LIMITING). The final change (EXAMPLE BASED LEARNING) extracts the ego-owned moves from the selected game in order (a subfunction common to all playing routines in the programs) and installs them as a list with other known plans. The basic mechanism is no more than is required to learn by instruction when shown an example — *but now the instructor is no longer needed.*

As a player becomes more adventurous with guarded play — willing to start in the centre and various corner cells, willing to move to side cells as well — the number of winnable games possible becomes quite large. This explosion of possible won games, the fact that there is too much to remember and all the games are superficially similar, introduces the need to impose a more abstract order on the experience. Answering that need demands feature based abstraction and conceptualization, the focus of work still ongoing.

Conclusions

Coadaptive development of cognitive structures is central to human learning. Human studies can provide valuable guidance for machine learning work to the extent that one both can analyze mature performance and can uncover anterior structures whose reorganization permits the emergence of that mature performance. Specifically, Lawler's case study permitted a characterization of the cognitive state of a young child (one quite congenial with the literature on young children) and more, a trace of the particular child's path of development to relatively more mature performances. This developmental path provided significant guidance for constructing programs that model the learning behaviour of the individual child. More generally, the constructed model illuminates in a computational form the elements and processes that enter into coadaptive development. The programs pass from learning by prototype modification to learning from experience by analysis without instruction.

Going beyond earlier conclusions in the human study, the discovery remarked here is the role of the multi-modal mind in creating the potential for abstraction emerging from redescription. This is an example of the *functionality* of coadaptation in cognitive development. The conjecture is advanced that the multi-modal structure is central to understanding the *possibility* of human cognitive development. Further, emerging abstraction through redescription can be appreciated as a primitive form of functional abstraction, of which reflexive abstraction is a more mature form. Redescriptive abstraction helps explain the importance of analogy and metaphor in human thinking and learning.

In this research, we have focussed only on the interaction between visual and kinesthetic systems. The other modes of mind, related to the linguistic system and the touch-salient manipulative system, add significant further dimensions of possible complexity to this non-uniformitarian model of mind. Such models, although basically simple, are complex enough to permit interesting development through plausible, internal interactions; that is, they permit the possibility of learning through thinking — a desirable outcome for *any* view of human minds, and one that may prove of some value with machines as well.

References

Caple, Balda, and Willis. Work reported in 'How did Vertebrates take to the air?' by Roger Lewin, *Science*, July 1, 1983. See also *American Naturalist*, 1983.

Fang, J. *Towards a Philosophy of Modern Mathematics*. Hauppauge, New York: Paideia series in modern mathematics, vol.1, 1970.

Fann, K. T. *Peirce's Theory of Abduction*. The Hague: Martinus Nijhoff.

Jacob, F. 'Evolution and Tinkering' in *Science*, June 10, 1977, and *The Possible and the Actual*. New York, Pantheon Books, 1982.

Lawler, R. *Computer Experience and Cognitive Development*. Chichester, England, and New York: Ellis Horwood, Ltd. and John Wiley Inc., 1985.

Lawler, R. and Selfridge, O. ' Learning Concrete Strategies through Interaction'. Proceedings of the Cognitive Science Society Annual   Conference, 1985.

Piaget, J. *The Child's Conception of Number*. New York: Norton and Co., 1952.

Piaget, J. *Biology and Knowledge*. Chicago: University of Chicago Press, 1971.

Piaget, J. *The Language and Thought of the Child*. New York: New American Library.

Peirce, C.S. 'The Fixation of Belief' in *Chance, Love and Logic*. M. Cohen, ed. New York: George Braziller, Inc., 1956.

Peirce, C.S. 'Deduction, Induction, and Hypothesis' in *Chance, Love and Logic*.

Satinoff, N. 'Neural Organization and the Evolution of Thermal Regulation in Mammals', *Science*, July 7, 1978.

Selfridge, M.G.R. and Selfridge, O.G. 'How Children Learn to Count: a computer model', 1985.

Vygotsky, L.S. *Mind in Society*. Eds. Michael Cole, Vera John-Steiner, Sylvia Scribner, and Ellen Souberman. Cambridge, Mass: Harvard University, 1978.

Acknowledgements

This paper began in a collaboration with Oliver Selfridge to extend work in 'How Children Learn to Count' (Selfridge and Selfridge) with ideas of *CECD*. With Oliver's genial prodding, I have carried forward that effort to confront the issue of abstraction from highly particular descriptions. Special thanks are due to Sheldon White, who first pointed out the similarity of my conclusions to those of Vygotsky. He has repeatedly emphasized the importance of ideas about the internationalization of external processes and urged me to develop them.

MULTI-SCHEMA MODELLING[32]

Learning from Frontier Experiences

Occasionally people can solve problems that on prior reflection they would have judged beyond their capacity. Such are frontier problems, and solving them provides frontier experiences. We propose to investigate learning from frontier experiences by studies in cognitive modelling and machine learning. A priori, the three primary types of frontier experiences are those derived from solutions depending on boundary conditions (accidental solutions), on the interaction of multiple agencies contributing simultaneously to a solution (interactive solutions), and on shifts of the problem representation (frame-shifting solutions). Our proposed research will try to distinguish between these three types of solutions and focus on learning through mechanisms involved in the latter two. In earlier work (Lawler and Selfridge, 1985; Lawler, 1987), we developed an alternative to this classical compositional model, one based on the elaboration and refinement of imitated actions.

Multi-Schema Modelling

We will use for guidance both compositional and imitated action models in constructing a system for multi-schema modelling (MSM). The principle to govern MSM is that significant learning can occur when a secondary scheme of representation provides internal explanations for the unanticipated success of a primary representation in a frontier experience (Lawler 1987); this secondary scheme can then be invoked to achieve a new level of performance on problems of the same class. Such a principle appears effective in human learning. Our research will explore the extent to which it can prove productive in cognitive modelling and machine learning also.

Related Work

If our attempt to understand and model ways in which knowledge, embodied externally in people and artifacts, becomes internalized, the work has affinity for Vygotsky's central concerns. To the extent that significant learning takes place from internalized reflection, the work is Piagetian at the core. With the modelling community, the work derives from the classical tradition of compositional modelling (through Selfridge), but moves through imitated action models in a direction similar to exhaustive state-space exploration more nearly in the CMU paradigm. In contrast with SOAR, whose single learning mechanism is chunking within a simple but monolithic memory organization, multi-schema modelling depends on variety in basic representations of knowledge and their interactions as a primary component of learning. Given that the primary motor of significant learning is a surprising success in problem solving, the work derives directly

---

32. 1987. Unpublished extract from a proposal text never submitted..

from Lawler's psychological studies. But it does so in a control framework inspired by Sussman's HACKER model (Sussman 1972) which depended on bug manifestations, a kind of surprise, to initiate learning. It also works within an epistemological framework that is indebted to Mitchell's establishing the power of interior explanations as a mechanism for generating learning.

Value

Learning through interaction is a primary means of internalizing knowledge that exists as part of the physical world or the culture. We need to develop comprehensible mechanistic models of such processes that are complex enough not to demean that very human intelligence they are meant to represent. If people learn from frontier experiences, we should strive to build fully comprehensible models with similar capability. Modelling learning with small and simple systems of multiple agents, among which are embodied complementary schemes of representation, is a sensible and achievable effort which will advance this grander goal. The importance to education of interacting multiple representations is beginning to gain recognition within the Mathematics Education community (Kaput, 1988; Lawler 1989). Functioning multi-schema models would clarify that discussion.

To the extent that groups of these simple models share schemes of representation, they could be taken to model families of knowledge structures developed in a common mode of sensory perception and motor activity. Lawler (1987) argued that such internal organizations of modally related knowledge provide a system which could permit the cycle of cognitive development we often observe in human behaviour. Such a notion of the modal specificity of experience-memories though still not widely popular, is now even being used to interpret particular deficit patterns in the behaviour of brain damaged patients (observation on current work of McCarthy and Warrington, see Rosenfeld, 1989). We expect the results of this research to be more of general scientific value than of immediate engineering application. But it would be strange indeed if better success at modeling and simulating humnan learning did not have very broad and significantly useful consequences in the long run. It is possible to imagine, for example, that interacting systems of learning models will be better able to improve user modelling in intelligent tutoring systems or might even lead to smarter software, but the possibility does not represent any claim we would wish to try to establish within the scope of this effort. Such results do, however, represent a long term objective of this line of research.

References

Kaput, J. (1988) *The Role of Reasoning with Intensive Quantities: Preliminary Analyses*. Educational Technology Centre, Harvard School of Education.

Lawler, R. W. (1981) *The Progressive Construction of Mind*. Cognitive Science, Vol 5, pp 1-30.

Lawler, R. W. (1985) *Cognitive Organization*. Chapter 5 in Computer Experience and Cognitive Development, R. W. Lawler, John Wiley.

Lawler, R. W. and Selfridge, O. G. (1985) *Strategy Learning Through Interaction.* In Proceedings of the 7th Annual Conference of the Cognitive Science Society.

Lawler, R. W. (1987) *Coadaptation and the Development of Cognitive Structures.* In Advances in Artificial intelligence, DuBoulay, Hoog, and Steels, (Eds.) North Holland. (Reprinted papers from the 1986 European Conference on Artificial Intelligence.)

Mitchell, T. M, P. Utgoff, and R. Banerji (1983) *Learning by Experimentation: Acquiring andf Refining Problem Solving Heuristics.* In Machine Learning, Michaelski, Mitchell, and Carbonell (eds). Tioga Press. Palo Alto.

Rosenfeld, A. (1989) p.26 in the March issue of Psychology Today.

Selfridge, O.G. and Selfridge, M. (1984) *How Children Learn to Count: A Computer Model.* Unpublished to date.

Sussman, G. (1972) *Skill Acquisition: A Computational Model.* Elsevier.

Vygotsky, L.S. (1978) *Mind in Society.* Eds M. Cole et al. Harvard Press, Cambridge, MA.

THE POSSIBLE SYNERGY BETWEEN INTELLIGENT TUTORING SYSTEMS AND COMPUTER-BASED MICROWORLDS[33]

Robert Lawler and Masoud Yazdani

Comparison of ITS and CBM

In AI research, there are currently two different approaches to the use of computation for education. These can be characterized by comparing an emphasis on the use of intelligent computer aided instruction with an emphasis on computer facilities for familiarizing students with important representations and models. The former were advanced in the literature by Intelligent Tutoring Systems (Sleeman and Brown (eds.), 1982 Academic Press) and Learning and Teaching with Computers (O'Shea and Self, 1983, Prentice-Hall); the latter by arguments of Mindstorms (Papert, 1980, Basic Books) and 'Designing Computer-Based Microworlds' (Lawler in New Horizons in Educational Computing, Yazdani (ed.) 1984, Ellis Horwood). Both these points of view were advocated by attendees at the conference. The dimensions in which their emphases can be contrasted most profitably are their Goals, their Strengths, and their Limitations.

Dimensions of Contrast

Intelligent Tutoring Systems have as a central objective communicating some content through computer facilities which may employ mechanized domain-specific expertise, error analysis, and user-knowledge modelling. Their user-oriented intelligence is controlled by mechanized instructional strategies which present problems and then test for understanding of the content. The more ambitious ITS aim to communicate strategies, generally conceived of as a collection of methods for problem solving, as well as domain specific content.

The strengths of ITS are their good definition and their completeness in the following senses. An ITS will have a well articulated curriculum embodied in its domain expertise and an explicit theory of instruction represented by its tutoring strategies. This completeness permits an ITS to package existing expertise and focus on the novelty, which is the use of mechanically embodied sets of rules as a tool for instruction. Because an ITS can be well defined for a given curriculum, the achievement of its goals can be unambiguously evaluated, in principle. The weaknesses set against these considerable strengths are inadequate complexity in models of what the user knows, how the user

---

33. 1986. Published as an introduction to a double special issue of Instructional Science, May 1986, (Lawler and Yazdani, eds.).

1987. Published as the introduction to *AI&Ed.*, vol. 1

learns new knowledge, and what could be an appropriate instructional theory for complex minds.

In contrast with ITS, computer-based microworlds have the differently focused aim of leading the students to powerful, authentic knowledge. This is partly a response to the observation of Piaget:

> If we desire to form individuals capable of inventive thought and of helping the society of tomorrow to achieve progress, then it is clear that an education which is an active discovery of reality is superior to one that consists merely in providing the young with ready-made wills to will with and ready-made truths to know with.[34]

Authentic knowledge means what is to be learned should not merely be 'added to the knowledge base' but rather assimilated into the person's pre-existing system of knowledges and even more, should be freely expressed from internal motives when appropriate. The emphasis leads to a focus less on significant domain knowledge than on the activity of learner because it must be HIS internal action that integrates new knowledge to old.

The essential strength of such exploratory learning environments is that they CAN provide individuals with simple, concrete models of important things, ideas, and their relationships.[35] For example, as compared to arithmetic drill, which may enhance the memory of specific sums, model based instructional systems can provide people with new ways of looking at the world. When it works, this is a very powerful result.[36] To the extent that such enhanced understanding provides the person more power over his own mind and life, the knowledge is its own reward.

The fundamental limitations of microworlds derive from their theoretical commitments. Establishing the impact of their use is very difficult because of the nature of the effects sought and the complexity ascribed to the human minds within which those effects take place. To the extent that their design embodies commitments to using the computer more as a medium than a preprogrammed tool, taking seriously the complexity of the learner, and trying to draw connections between new content and prior idiosyncratic experiences, implementing computer microworlds leads to major difficulties because:

- computation is a protean, imperfectly understood medium of communication,
- theories of how individuals learn through experience are inadequate, and[37]
- there exists no adequate model-based epistemology of instruction.

---

34. In *The Science of Education and the Psychology of the Child*. The Viking Press, 1971.

35. 'Concrete' in this sense refers not to physical manipulablity but to having a basis in personal experience. Even 'virtual' experiences with artificial worlds can be concrete. DiSessa's article illuminates this old distinction.

36. For an example of such an outcome, see 'Extending a Powerful Idea' in *C&C*, 1986.

---

37. Knowledge based systems, with rules stored separately from the processes which use them, have proven their utility because their very lack of organization permits the addition of new rules without reprogramming; if, on the other hand, the organization and reorganization of knowledge in the mind is THE central need in effective education, thinking of learning as 'adding another rule to the database' may be counterproductive.}

At a more pragmatic level, there are two main problems. The program doesn't know what the student is doing. The problem of giving guidance while permitting freedom of exploration has not been solved in any general way. Some of these problems can be addressed now.

New Directions

The core problem ITS now confront seems to be the complexity of actual users of the instructional systems. A short example will illustrate the point. In their famous work on children's arithmetic, Brown and Burton[38] label 'bugs' children's deviations from standard arithmetical procedures. In performing the sum below, the child exhibits a non-standard algorithm for performing an addition in the vertical form, but a description of the performance as a bug would misrepresent significantly the child's functioning knowledge and the sorts of inference employed:[39]

$$3\ 5$$
$$+\ 3\ 7$$
$$\overline{}$$
$$9\ 9$$

The child reasoned as follows:

'Seven and five are twelve, but two numbers won't fit underneath them. The biggest number we can put there is a nine. But that leaves us three left over, so let's carry three to the next place where we can add them with the numbers there. Three, six, nine. Ninety nine must be the answer.'

The child's logic is a deviation from the standard addition algorithm. Characterizing the performance as a 'bug', however, would miss the strong use of a conservation principle, the child's commitment to what she knows and understands well, and the inventiveness shown in her trying to cope with a problem beyond her capacity. These are primary values we want to support. One wants to support a child but not development of a 'wrong theory'. Beyond granting the complexity of the child's mind, we must recognize the complexity of the instructional situation.

The dilemma is ours: we want to support the child's commitment to his authentic point of view and its creative application; at the same time we want to modify that point of view. Can we circumvent this barrier? In the instructional situation, the teacher's great strength is getting around the inutility of materials which are not helping the individual child. In effect, the teacher is able to back up to a more global perspective and switch instructional contexts to another one, hopefully a more productive one. An intelligent human tutor might try, at such a juncture, to probe the child's representation schemes and processes of reasoning. Following such a model in a mechanized system would require developing a more comprehensive and well articulated epistemology of

38. 'A diagnostic model for procedural bugs in basic mathematical skills'. *Cognitive Science*, 2, 155-192.

39. From Chapter 2, *CECD* (Lawler, 1985).

instruction, for we must ask how to judge which representation could be more suitable for use by a specific student who does not yet understand a particular idea?

Consider an approach for circumventing our dilemma, as follows. Assume a system which is capable of casting its range of problems and knowledge in some set of different representations. Recognize that different representations of problems promote into salience different aspects of things and their relations.[40] If the student produces some response which the system judges a misstep according to domain knowledge, the diagnosis should procede by trying to determine how the child may be thinking about the problem. It is not enough to say the student has impoverished knowledge of a domain, even if he does not show knowledge as applicable within the surface representation being used by the system. If one hopes to develop an adequate instructional system one must ask if the student has enough local knowledge in some alternate representation which could be extended analogously and applied to enrich his capability within the surface representation being used by the system for the given problem. Shifting contexts to some alternative microworld, where the student could work or play with a different representation, and engage in exploratory familiarization with it, would permit his later, more effective return to the primary domain representation. With an extended repertoire of alternative knowledges available as the basis for analogical extensions, the student will be much better able to construct for himself an adequate specification of what's what and what follows for solving problems in the primary representation of the domain.

For example, in the problem above where 35 and 37 are summed to 99, the child's justifications show that for her the reality behind the things she was manipulating is one where counting is salient and grouping is not being considered. For her to understand carrying would require familiarity with the interrelations of groupings and values (such as one might develop through play with a money-based representation scheme), familiarity with groupings where a uniform multiplicative factor is salient (as one would encounter in playing with Dienes blocks with their unit blocks, rows of 10, and flats of 100), and finally experiences which would lead to unification of those separately mastered schemes.

There will surely occur cases where the student uses representations beyond the current scope of the system. What should the system do when it determines that it does not, and even more cannot, understand what the student is thinking? The system should have available an extensible repertoire of representations. No system should be called intelligent which is too rigid to learn. While people learn more from experience than from being told, for computers the opposite is more nearly true. Computers can learn from experts today; for use in education, an ideal instructional system should be able to learn new representations applying to its domain of primary expertise even from non-experts, as when the students are introducing some alternative way of thinking — however non-standard that way may be.

---

40. If addition is taken as an example, then a unit-based representation would emphasize counting; a coin-based representation would emphasize grouping; a vertical-form problem representation would emphasize the interaction of separable component sums.

One outcome of the AISB conference on AI and Education has been provoking realization of ways in which the agendas of researchers with disparate programs can support the achievment of their common aim, the use of new technology to enhance both the quantity and quality of knowledge in human minds. If ITS could be opened up to more complex understanding of what students bring to problem solving and if model based instructional systems could begin to make use of the sorts of techniques developed within the ITS community, a synergy could be possible that would permit the strengthening of both. Such an endeavour is now being advocated by Feurzeig under the banner of 'intelligent microworlds'. His paper in this volume appears to be a point of departure for such an effort. Even if we imagine some ideal instructional system which fuses the best of the ITS and Computer-based microworld paradigms, we must still admit that significant problems remain. But a second outcome of this conference, witnessed by the articles in this volume,[41] is the hope that advances to cope with those problems are within reach. Specifically, Feurzeig and the Lawlers show new approaches to rethinking curriculum in the light of what computational facilities make possible. The work of Carley and Drescher expand the objective of learning theories to broader coverage and greater technical depth. Ohllson's analysis of ITS and DiSessa's observations and arguments point the way to an epistemologically deepened program for curriculum materials design. There is much to be done, but the prospects are promising.

---

41. i.e. *AI&Ed*, Vol. 1

COMPUTER MICROWORLDS AND READING: AN ANALYSIS FOR THEIR SYSTEMATIC APPLICATION[42]

Robert W. Lawler and Gretchen P. Lawler

Abstract

Learning can be seen as a consequence of problem solving in particular cases. It occurs when one achieves a solution which is able to be used later. 'Anchoring with variation' is a common and important process, providing a framework through which one can discuss coping with something imperfectly understood in terms of what is already well known. Our purpose in the following discussion is to explore some possible implications of this process for reading education as a worked example of how educational technology presents us with an opportunity for reconceptualizing instruction.

English has the phonological potential for more than 60 thousand monosyllables. Our analysis asks how many monosyllabic words exist in fact and what organization can be imposed on them to make the phonological code more accessible. We've chosen to represent these monosyllables as an initial phonemic cluster plus residue. The most common 550 residues cover 73 percent of the existing 7000 monosyllables. If children can learn 550 different correspondences between sounds and spelling patterns, their knowledge of these words, coupled with the ability to modify interpretations of letter strings by anchoring with variation, will cover a major portion of the phonetic-orthographic correspondences of the English language. We believe this extensive, concrete foundation of word and sound knowledge will permit children to read well enough that instruction will become primarily a refining and perfection of such knowledge.

The primary design conclusion is that if we create computer-based microworlds using words with the most common residues as the names for their entities and their actions, we will be providing a set of systematically generated monosyllabic anchors which promises to be highly effective for children's interpretation of many words they will encounter in reading English. The potential revolutionary impact of such a pre-reading curriculum is worth exploring.

42. 1986. Published in *Instructional Science*, May 1986, (Lawler and Yazdani, eds.).
   Published as Chapter 5 of *AI&Ed.*, vol. 1 (1987)

DUAL PURPOSE LEARNING ENVIRONMENTS[43]

Robert W. Lawler and Alan Garfinkel

Introduction

Feurzeig[44] described his view of 'intelligent microworlds' as permitting the mode of interaction between the user and system to be switched (by the user) from exploratory to tutorial to evaluative. The view offered here derives from Feurzeig's suggestion but moves in a different direction, to focus more on the purposes of the parties involved — instructor and student — than on the performance mode of the system. Consider the following as an example of a system that will permit dual usage.

When engaging in explanation of grammar, a teacher wants to offer his students a lucid and well-articulated description of the principles which govern the forms of a language in use, along with succinct examples illustrating those principles. If an intelligent system supports such use, one can have instructional use of the system. Students often prefer a more exploratory approach to learning. One might say, for example, 'Let me try to do something novel to find out what I can do with this language' or 'Let me probe what the system can do, beyond requiring me to generate a sentence it will accept. Can I determine what the limitations of the system are? Can I improve the system's grammar in such a way that it will be more nearly perfect?' Pursuing such questions puts a student in a very active mode, one in which some students will learn much better than most other ways regardless of the domain or language focus.[45]

A system with such flexibility in use would be a dual purpose learning environment, one in which the instructor can have his way, provide his best guidance, but hopefully one in which the student can also act in a powerful and positive way to correct and augment the system itself and through doing so develop his own knowledge as much as he cares to.

Project Objectives

Observing that people in Europe have been more sensitive than Americans to the need for learning multiple languages and to second language instruction, we tried to take advantage of their expertise. A primary objective of this project was to port a European

---

43. 1991. Unpublished. A short version of this paper, under the name of Lawler alone, was published in
    International Journal of Computer Aided Language Learning, Vol. 4, no. 1.
       Published in *AISB Quaterly*, (summer, 1991; no. 77)
       Published in *Multilingual Multimedia*, (Intellect, 1993). M.Yazdani, editor.

44. Feurzeig, W.: 'Algebra Slaves and Agents in a Logo Based Mathematics Curriculum'. In: *AI&Ed.*, Vol. 1
    (1987)

45. One might ask whether a student can help a machine extend its command over a grammar which the
    student doesn't yet know. We believe so, and turn to the issue near the end of the paper

PC based instructional system, LINGER[46], for use on Macintosh computers in the USA. LINGER is an application package directed to instruction in several foreign languages. It's a Prolog-based intelligent tutoring system. The original version of LINGER was a research vehicle. We tried to scale up that system for wider use. Adapting LINGER for the Macintosh had two dimensions. First was the issue of the Macintosh port. We chose LPA Prolog as the implementation language, expecting little trouble in converting the source code. So we found the case. Some low level routines, primarily based on I/O calls had to be re-written. Interface improvements, especially when set up to take advantage of Macintosh features, required additional coding.

The second dimension of the project revolved around scaling up the size of the dictionaries and grammars used with LINGER. Although this sort of activity is commonly undervalued[47], it often reveals problems not apparent with small-scale prototypes.

The complete text of this article reports the successes and limitations of this effort and offers suggestions for further research to pursue.

---

46. The LINGER system was developed by Yazdani and others at Exeter University in England. We are grateful to these colleagues for making available their system, including prototype dictionaries and grammars, and for providing help and guidance throughout this project.

47. For example, Minsky [10] argues inattention to the question of scaling is a serious weakness in the currently popular AI connectionist movement, one which undercuts the claims and vitiates some components of that research program. See the Afterword to the Second Edition of *Perceptrons* (MIT Press, 1992).